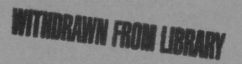

PURSUING HAPPINESS

PURSUING
HAPPINESS

**AMERICAN CONSUMERS IN
THE TWENTIETH CENTURY**

Stanley Lebergott

PRINCETON UNIVERSITY PRESS

• PRINCETON, NEW JERSEY •

Copyright © 1993 by Princeton University Press
Published by Princeton University Press, 41 William Street,
Princeton, New Jersey 08540
In the United Kingdom: Princeton University Press, Chichester, West Sussex

Library of Congress Cataloging-in-Publication Data
Lebergott, Stanley.
Pursuing happiness : American consumers in the twentieth century /
Stanley Lebergott.
p. cm.
Includes bibliographical references and index.
ISBN 0-691-04322-1 (cloth)
1. Consumption (Economics)—United States—History—20th century.
2. United States—Economic conditions—1918–1945. 3. United States—
Economic conditions—1945– . I. Title.
HC110.C6L393 1993
339.4′7′09730904—dc20   92-40491 CIP

This book has been composed in Palatino Typeface

Princeton University Press books are printed on acid-free paper
and meet the guidelines for permanence and durability of the
Committee on Production Guidelines for Book Longevity of
the Council on Library Resources

Printed in the United States of America

3 5 7 9 10 8 6 4 2

Some wish, some prevailing wish, is necessary to the animation

of everybody's Mind.

—JANE AUSTEN, *Letters*

If at the right season thou callest upon me too, little among the lesser

gods, thou shalt get thy wish, but crave not for great things. For I,

Tychon, have in my power to grant only such things as the people's god

may give to a labouring man.

—PERSES OF THEBES, *The Greek Anthology*

·CONTENTS·

· LIST OF TABLES & FIGURE ·

TABLES

FIGURE

· P R E F A C E ·

LIFE AND LIBERTY are "rights" in the Declaration of Independence. Happiness is not. For Jefferson, with terrible realism, only proposed its pursuit. (George Mason had referred to a "natural right . . . of pursuing and obtaining happiness." But, after all, any right to obtain happiness can only be enforced by a deity, not a Declaration.) Wordsworth did condemn mankind's vulgar "getting and spending." But he inherited much. And his sister did the housework.[1]

American consumers typically ignored such high-altitude criticism. The present study looks at how they spent their way toward happiness in the twentieth century, at major criticisms of that endeavor, and at such related matters as how economic well-being is assessed.

It is an unacknowledged excellence of modern economics that its foundations are pitched on the sands of human desire. It sees economies propelled by men and women buying a multitude of goods as they search for experience. (Critics denigrate the profusion of goods in capitalist markets. But the Soviet Union, even during its lean years, planned production of 2,500 confectionery items. And in 1958–61, Mao's Communist planners organized production of 1,500 varieties of tea, while thirty million men and women starved to death.[2])

Most economists accept these varied consumption choices because they must: such are the improbable facts of behavior. But Joseph Conrad offered a second reason:

[1] "I ironed till dinner time, sewed till near dark, then pulled a basket of peas, and afterward . . . picked gooseberries." Moorman, ed., *Journal of Dorothy Wordsworth* (1971), 33.

[2] For the plans, see chapter 4. For the famine, see Ashton, "Famine in China, 1958–61," 619.

I am content to sympathize with common mortals [who] . . . must endure . . . the gifts from Heaven: the curse of facts, and the blessing of illusions, the bitterness of our wisdom and the deceptive consolations of our folly.[3]

Of course, a reserve army of critics has scoffed at the "deceptive consolations" chosen by consumers. With metallic ridicule they package aesthetic objections, and pseudomoral ones, in economic phraseology. The bestseller that ended the 1920s, Stuart Chase's *The Tragedy of Waste* (1929), forcefully attacked consumer choices. Vance Packard's *The Wastemakers* began the 1960s attacking "consumerism" with no less vigor. Its vitality came from many forceful, if improbable, passages:

> Hedonism [is] actively promoted by campaigns to persuade the American people that they deserve . . . enriched living. . . . A supermarket operator . . . shook his head sadly as he pointed out to me all the "convenience" foods he was selling to bridge-playing wives. He muttered, "The husband works all day and then comes home to a dinky little pre-cooked pot pie." . . . Many modern women seem preoccupied with getting for themselves such things as wall-to-wall carpeting, completely automated kitchens, fur jackets, and their own convertibles.[4]

And a bestseller of the early 1990s intuited that Americans "overworked" in their obsessive search for a still higher material standard of living.[5]

A ground bass of academic ridicule has long been audible. Those responsible included zoologists and psychologists, professors of English and geology, plus well-known economists such as Thorstein Veblen, Joan Robinson, J. K. Galbraith, Tibor Scitovsky, and Ezra Mishan. One question that propelled the present volume was: "How much of all this is really personal taste masquerading as economic analysis?"

A second question asked: "For what has all the consumption increase gone?" Distinguished economists have, indeed, proposed a "golden rule"—that our economy should aim for ever-increasing

---

[3] Conrad, *Nostromo* (1904), preface.
[4] Packard, *The Waste-Makers* (1960), 166, 235.
[5] Cf. Chapter 9.

consumption. And many have wrung their hands whenever the U.S. "rate of growth" failed to increase (though the uses to which growth had been or would be put did not seem to raise equal concern).

What did "common mortals" consume during the past century of increasing American abundance? Personal consumption totals offer one answer. But it is a dusty one. For such totals lack the tang and meaning of specificity. Part II of this book, therefore, deals with specifics, from hospital care and lighting to housing and auto-mobiles. It looks, for example, at how housewives ended their 1900 tasks of carrying coal (7 tons a year) and water (9,000 gallons a year) and baking bread (half a ton a year) when they increased family food expenditures. To understand such choices requires specific numbers more than energetic adverbs.

Chapters 1 and 2 focus on consumers and their critics, and inquire why measured "happiness" does not keep in step with "economic welfare." The next two chapters look at how effectively advertising motivates consumers, and how consumption alters the environment. I then consider consumption inequality (as distinct from income inequality), to discern how much it may distort the meaning of long-term trends in spending by the average American. Chapters 6 and 7 consider how attitudes toward immortality, and children, shape consumer behavior, and why the usual measures of economic welfare mean less than they appear to. Chapter 8 examines how women changed their production of goods and services at home, and shaped the broad trends of national consumer spending. Chapter 9 considers whether Americans can be said to "overwork" to buy consumer goods, particularly when workers now spend as much time in recreation as on the job. Chapter 10 considers official proposals to ordain scientific, prudent levels for spending by consumers.

Part II reviews the forces that expanded spending in this century for food and housing, recreation and medical care, and so on. The specifics are improbable, fascinating, and serious. But then, as Archbishop Whately remarked, "Happiness is no laughing matter."

· PART ONE ·

ECONOMIC WELL-BEING

· C H A P T E R   1 ·

Consumers and Their Critics

ALL SOCIETIES pursue experience, not mere survival:

> Men are children of the Universe with foolish enterprises and irrational hopes. A tree sticks to its business of mere survival; and so does an oyster, with minor divergencies. [But] . . . the life-aim of survival is modified into the human aim of survival for diversified worth-while experience.[1]

Economic activity aims not for output, but for experience via consumption. So Smith and Mill declared, and Ruskin. So Fisher, Keynes, Nordhaus, and Tobin agreed.[2] Consumers buy bazaars full of goods, but only to create the diversified experience they ultimately seek.[3]

Of course, goods yield a wavering stream of satisfaction. Some movies prove to be boring; books, dull; automobiles, lemons. And yesterday's delightful purchase may be dumped in today's trash can. Consumers nonetheless keep searching. The reality principle may block enjoyment of some purchases, but the pleasure principle makes consumers persist, cheerfully or desperately. Their motto through it all remains that euphoric sentence from *Antony and Cleopatra*: "I hope well of tomorrow."

---

[1] Whitehead, *Modes of Thought* (1938), 42–43. Such experience consists of "states of consciousness," which Pigou declared yield welfare. Cf. Alfred Marshall, *Principles of Economics*, (1948), bk. 3, ch. 2.

[2] Smith, *Wealth of Nations*, (1963), book 4, chap. 8; Sherburne, *John Ruskin* (1972), 146–47; Keynes, *General Theory* (1936), 104; Nordhaus and Tobin, "Is Economic Growth Obsolete?" (1982), 363. Cf. also Becker, "On the New Theory of Consumer Behavior" (1976), 131–49.

[3] Primitive societies use goods to create experience as well. Sometimes more lavishly: "Not only are valuable goods thrown away and food stuffs consumed to excess but there is destruction for its own sake—[e.g.,] coppers thrown into the sea or broken." Mauss, *The Gift* (1954), 72.

Consumers may be constantly "in pursuit of happiness," to use Locke's immortal phrase.[4] But doubters find their choices regrettable, even repellent. Thus, a famous professor of zoology complained of the proliferation of "still more automobiles, color TV sets, speed boats, new gadgets, new models."[5] Male zoologists apparently were suitable car buyers. But not women. Or teenagers. Or families on welfare. (Since these latter groups did not own automobiles previously, it was largely they who accounted for "still more" automobiles.[6]) But what made them less worthy buyers than zoologists who specialize in fruit flies? What principle of zoology demonstrated color televisions to be objectionable, but not black and white ones?

How cogent are objections such as those by Veblen, Galbraith, Mishan, Scitovsky, Robinson, Nordhaus, and Tobin? They do extend a long tradition. In the 1900s Henry George declared a millionaire's life "abnormal" because he had a telephone in his bedroom.[7] In the 1760s, English law still required that "no man shall be served more than two courses at dinner or supper."[8] (France drew the legal line at three courses.[9]) A seventeenth-century writer on political economy complained that lesser men "dress like a gentleman . . . [thereby] corrupting our ancient discipline."[10] Another social critic attacked the bourgeois who sported "a more brilliant equipage than a duke or peer," and whose wives wore "more superb

[4] Locke, *An Essay concerning Human Understanding*, (1961), bk. 2, ch. 21.2

[5] Muller, *In Pursuit of Relevance* (1971), 88.

[6] More than 40 percent of American families "in poverty"—as defined by the Federal government—owned automobiles by 1970. See Lebergott, *American Economy* (1976), 7.

[7] "Indeed there is something abnormal about the lives of the owners of privilege at every turn, to wit: One multimillionaire has a telephone by his bedside, and before rising every morning he receives from his office all important telegrams . . . and gives preliminary orders and directions." Henry George, Jr., *Menace of Privilege* (1905), 79. George's chapter on "amusements, dissipations and marital relations" itemizes other regrettable expenditures.

[8] Blackstone, *British Constitution* (1979), bk. 4, ch. 13, p. 171. On "some great holidays," though not all, three courses might be served.

[9] In 1563 and the years following; cf. Mennell, *All Manners of Food* (1985), 30. France also imprisoned tailors who cut letters into the borders of ladies' gowns. England once forbade men to wear short doublets, or long coats. Quakers denounced the introduction of carpets for the wintry English floors. In 1770, the British Parliament forbade women to use wigs, false teeth, or scents. (They would entrap men into marriage.) Cf. Gummere, *The Quaker* (1968), 30, 23, 129.

[10] de Montchretien, *Traicte de l'oeconomie politique* (1889), 60.

clothes and more diamonds than a countess."[11] Ancient Rome limited the number of guests at a family dinner, and how much could be spent for boiled vegetables.[12] Sparta forbade cooks to use any spice but salt or vinegar. Russia promised death to smokers, and Turkey, to coffee drinkers.[13]

Students of American materialism have added their obiter dicta. Many decry money spent for services (though not goods). A leading Marxist economist scathingly described the unproductive, ever "growing, contingent of service workers"[14] (which, of course, included himself—and every other teacher, physician, social worker, musician, artist, writer, and government or hospital employee). A clinical psychologist cast no less scorn on other products. His verdict? The nation requires fewer cars—and more bicycles; fewer polyester suits—though not polyester dresses.[15]

More recently, a noted professor of English volunteered his list of "many things deplorable" in the United States. He, too, began with "the size of the service sector," thereby including the private university at which he taught,[16] and the theatres, art galleries, and restaurants to which his colleagues resorted. Not to mention their ministers, psychoanalysts, and ski instructors.

These professors shared a widespread distaste for service employees—teachers, bureaucrats, lawyers, bankers, physicians. But none bothered to specify any standard—zoological, psychological, economic, moral, aesthetic, philosophic, or political—by which to demonstrate that services were inferior to products.

Other scholars have contrasted uncomely expenditures with comely ones. Veblen began with his saturnine attack on American spending for domestic servants.[17] But the flood of academic criticism really dates from the 1950s, with Galbraith's classic observations on sheet steel. In his mordant phrasing, the American consumer

[11] The Abbe Mery, quoted in Paschal Larkin, *Property in the Eighteenth Century* (1930), 157.

[12] Athenaeus, *Deipnosophistae*, 1:274, 3: 233.

[13] Roscher, *Principles of Political Economy* (1878), 2:244–48. Braunsweig forbade more than three musicians to play for a wedding. Ibid., p. 245.

[14] Baran, *Political Economy of Growth* (1962), 91. Baran, of course, adhered to Marx's definition of productive industry, following Adam Smith and the physiocrats.

[15] Wachtel, *Poverty of Affluence* (1983), 253. Earlier systems of morality condemned worldly goals, not merely selected goods.

[16] Frank Kermode, *The New York Times*, July 3, 1983, p. 21.

[17] Mitchell, ed., *What Veblen Taught* (1936), 259–61 among others.

bought "big, ungainly, unfunctional" automobiles, sadly disfigured by "functionless bulges."[18]

Of these pejoratives, "ungainly" has little economic content. "Big" offers little more. Does aesthetics really demonstrate that the Bugatti is repellent because it is big? (Or the Rolls Royce? The Lincoln?) And even if philosophy can distinguish "gainly" eight-cylinder cars from ungainly ones, economics offers no theory on the subject, or measurement. At best, economists repeat casual aesthetic preferences.

Galbraith's quasiprofessional objection appeared in his third adjective: bulges are "unfunctional." Indeed, sheet steel would be economized if only functional bulges were allowed. But how does economics define a functional bulge? One shaped like the airplane nacelle that flies deep thinkers from speaking engagements in the United States to ski resorts in Switzerland?

What is functional for human consumers? Surely every (legal) consumer expenditure is.[19] For every one is made in the simple-minded pursuit of happiness. Does Western engineering declare that some expenditures are unfunctional? Or Western morality? Even if they did, Western economics cannot. True, some economists may see spending as functional if for rock concerts, but not Indian miniatures–or vice versa. Others approve baseball tickets, but not books—or vice versa. Still others accept beach buggies without bulbous fenders, and reject Chryslers with. And some economists are offended by "mauve and cerise" automobiles[20] (though perhaps not by simple cerise).

But what do such preferences have to do with "function"? What society is committed to mere physical survival? Even those with the grimmest prospects have devoted resources to art. So the cave paintings of Lascaux mutely testify, as well as the decorations on the ostrich shells in which Hottentots held their tiny stocks of water. In the medieval world, the bards of poverty-stricken Wales and the harpers of Ireland were no less "functional." In the twentieth century, a dour society bent on swift industrialization nonetheless fi-

---

[18] Galbraith, *Affluent Society* (1958), 194.

[19] Whether illegal expenditures also are functional is a moot point. In any event, they are included in neither the national income accounts nor our estimates.

[20] Galbraith, *Affluent Society*, 253. Both moralists and economists can agree that turpentine and inventory costs would have been saved if only Henry Ford's criterion had been followed: "They can have any color so long as it's black."

nanced Khatchaturian, Shostakovich, and socialist realism. And Mao's China supported the composers of the Yellow River Concerto. What society has sought mere survival, mere "engineering" functionalism?

Does Galbraith's distinction between functional and nonfunctional really lead to a useful conclusion? One remembers how Goneril proposed to reduce Lear's recklessly large retinue of knights. What need had he of one hundred? Of fifty? Nay, even of one? Lear's reply defined the scope of consumer expenditure in free societies: "Oh, reason not the need." That cry from the heart is more persuasive than the moral or aesthetic criteria that some thinkers excogitate. For consumption has always reflected "the sum of things hoped for"—not the "evidence of things seen."[21]

To vague concerns about offensive luxuries, Nordhaus and Tobin have added an analytic concern, about "regrettable" necessities. These, they say, "are not directly sources of utility themselves but regrettably necessary activities that may yield utility." Economists from the Midwest to Greece and Japan have followed their lead.[22] Consumer outlays such as the cost of commuting to work, they hold to be only "instrumental." They therefore banish from GNP all spending for

> regrettably necessary inputs to activities that may yield utility. [By] classifying defense costs—or police protection or public health expenditures—as regrettable and instrumental we certainly do not deny the possibility that given the unfavorable circumstances that prompt these expenditures consumers will ultimately be better off with them than without them. This may or may not be the case. The only judgment we make is that these expenditures yield no direct satisfaction."[23]

Their argument turns on the simple assertion that such goods "yield no direct satisfaction." But is indirectness so daunting? Must it automatically force exclusion? And if so, what sector of consumer

---

[21] As one Elizabethan wrote: we may "as well seek fish upon the mountains . . . [as readily] as peace during life in flesh. . . . The fair deceives; and only the untasted is pleasing." Lord Brooke, *The Prose Works of Fulke Greville* (1986), 151.

[22] Cf. work by Zolotas and Eisner as cited in Eisner, "Extended Accounts," 1627, 1633–34, 1670. See also Economic Council of Japan, NNW Measurement Committee, *Measuring the National Welfare of Japan* (1974).

[23] Nordhaus and Tobin, "Is Economic Growth Obsolete?" 367.

expenditure escapes? Food? Surely no one buys lard for the direct satisfaction it yields, or flour, or oregano. Clothing? Who revels in the acquisition of yard goods, buttons, or zippers? Transportation? Are trips to the grocery store, the doctor, the drug store, less "indirect" than trips to work (which Nordhaus and Tobin do exclude)?

Few categories provide direct joy, or thrills. Not driver education or coal oil, insurance costs or dish drains. All are driven by expectation. Expenditures typically provide consumers with a mere ticket of admission to future experience. Were "direct satisfaction" indeed *the* criterion, then GNP would omit almost everything consumers now buy.[24]

But suppose that "indirectness" were nonetheless damning. What would follow for measuring consumer expenditure? Quite the opposite of the Nordhaus-Tobin conclusion. For we can make one sure judgment about "regrettably necessary" expenditures: they are necessary. And the more necessary they are the more inevitably consumers will seek to make them. Should we then exclude from consumer expenditure the very items consumers desire most urgently?

The argument against "indirectness" fails because it starts from a faulty premise. Consumers do not "regret" necessary expenditures. If anything, they regret the state of the real world. They regret that friction exists. (If it did not, commuting costs would drop to zero.) They regret that disease exists. (If it did not, they would spend less for medicine.) They regret the neighbor's dog. (If it ran away, they would spend less on lawn repair, on cleaning.)

"Regret" is a word of seismic potency. It can be applied to a thousand facets of the real world. But how does it apply to expenditure? Consumers actually want to pay for commuting to work; their alternative is to walk. They wish to buy medicine; their alternative is to become sicker, or to die. They strongly desire to spend for antipollution devices—given the alternatives. Such expenditures help them to cope with menacing aspects of the real world, and the exasperating ones.[25] Consumers would find one thing worse than "having to"

[24] The argument also addresses defense and police costs, of course. But in a study of personal consumption expenditure. I do not address them.

[25] The same consideration applies to the Nordhaus-Tobin list of "public regrettables" (Nordhaus and Tobin, "Is Economic Growth Obsolete?" 386). They would exclude national defense, international affairs, veterans' benefits.

make such expenditures: being unable to make them. Consumer behavior, and welfare, can be understood no better by excluding "regrettable necessities" than by excluding "regrettable luxuries."

Meanwhile other economists chide consumers for spending too little (on certain goods). Thus it has been discovered that we Americans

> are known for our interest in nutrition and our lack of interest in the pleasures of food. . . . To quote . . . a scientific text on food selection and preparation: "In this country of lavish, almost shameful abundance, the great majority of Americans go through life without experiencing a single technically evaluated, good, representative dinner."[26]

(Is gluttony, a cardinal sin for centuries, now a minor virtue?)

The United States does indeed lack an official corps of tasters and chewers, to decide which dinners are "good, representative." But what of that vast, untidy party of amateurs who exhort and instruct in newspaper food columns? And what of the bestsellers in U.S. bookstores for decades—cookbooks? This record hardly demonstrates any "lack of interest in the pleasures of food."

How does a nation that lacks a Brillat-Savarin Academy of Cuisine decide which meals to serve? By ignoring its aesthetic responsibilities? Apparently. Scitovsky begins an eloquent chapter quoting "a distinguished Mexican poet-diplomat": "Pleasure is a concept [a sensation] absent from traditional Yankee cooking . . . it is a cuisine with no mysteries: simple, spiceless, nutritious food." It is hard, Scitovsky adds, "to document such an eloquent statement statistically."[27] But he nonetheless volunteers a gaggle of ratios to "confirm . . . that we Americans are less interested in the pleasures of food than are Western Europeans."

One is the high percentage of expenditures on red meat that Americans use for sausage or ground meat. Lower percentages for Europeans, however, call attention to their low incomes, and docile housewives, not to delicate sensibilities. European women may dutifully grind their hamburger at home. Americans do not. But how do such percentages demonstrate American "willingness to consume unimproved, in the shape of hamburgers, all the inferior cuts of meat, which others dress up with sauces and garnishes to offset

---

[26] Scitovsky, *Joyless* (1976), 183.
[27] This quotation and those immediately following come from ibid., pp. 186–88.

or hide their inferiority"? (Unless, among other improbabilities, a dubious brown sauce[28] proves an "interest in the pleasures of food" but catsup reveals disinterest.)

Still another percentage purportedly demonstrates additional American inadequacies. Belgians and Swedes, we are told, buy more rutabagas, turnips, and potatoes than Americans do. More precisely, of all spending on vegetables, the percentage that goes for canned and dried vegetables is lower in Western Europe than in the United States.[29] Yet that ratio surely reflects primarily greater willingness of European than American housewives to spend hours shopping for, cleaning, cutting up, and preparing fresh vegetables. How does that demonstrate greater European zest for the "pleasure component" of food?[30]

The panoply of percentages is, however, irrelevant. They would describe Americans as "less interested in the pleasures of food than Europeans" if Americans consumed twice as much food as Europeans, and spent all day doing so. For Scitovsky's ratios only show that Americans 1) had higher incomes and 2) consumed relatively greater amounts of foods considered inferior by some aestheticians.[31]

Americans have also been rebuked for not attending to "the physical environment of one's home and its furnishings [though] its importance for man's well being is well attested."[32] Statistical tables are offered as proof. (Oddly enough, they reveal that Americans spend three times as much on flowers and plants as Britons do, and

---

[28] DeBanville once declared that Parisian restaurants rely on "a brown sauce, which . . . must combine the most dangerous ingredients and the most frightful poisons. Everybody is terrified by this brown sauce." Theodore Zeldin, *France 1848– 1975* (1977), 742.

[29] Do "scientific texts on food selection" commend cabbages, brussel sprouts, and turnips kept through the winter as superior to imported canned peas, dried mushrooms, or even canned tomatoes?

[30] Scitovsky's entire discussion may, of course, relate only to an article of aesthetic faith—spices should be added by the cook rather than by the consumer. But that would hardly distinguish "the stimulus or pleasure component from the nutritive value of food."

[31] Cf. the four sets of ratios on page 187 of Scitovsky, *Joyless*. He also reports on "time spent at meals" (p. 190). But those figures omit the millions of hours spent in fast-food establishments, ice-cream parlors, or bars. That thirty billion hamburgers have been sold by a single chain may well chill the blood of a trained aesthetician. But is it really to be ignored when using "time spent at meals" to index "an interest in the pleasures of food"?

[32] Scitovsky, *Joyless*, 197.

as much as Western Europeans.[33] But these numbers are not mentioned.) American inadequacy is further derided by a ratio: the United States spends a smaller percentage of its national income on flowers than seven other nations. But what does that really mean? Americans could be embowered in nosegays, surround themselves with potted palms, and strew their highways with roses, yet still spend "a smaller percentage" on flowers than poorer nations.[34] Greater income would easily permit their doing so. Such revelations convey little to those who judge behavior by criteria other than ratio analysis.

Theologians and philosophers have long disapproved of much consumer behavior. But they disagreed as to which items were suspect. More recent social critics, economists included, have extended those lists. They object to catsup (but not brown gravy); to particolored cars (but not sober yellow); to stylish polar parkas (but not ones that only protect against freezing); to more automobile models (but not more book titles).

Consumer spending may serve Humanity no more frequently than most other human activities. But how forbidding society would be if one man's aesthetic/moral preferences decided what goods his fellow consumers might select. In open societies, human consumption choices share only one characteristic—they are made in pursuit of happiness. The importance and finality of consumers' freedom was italicized by William Penn. For he used it as a precedent to warrant equal freedom in religion: "Men have their liberty and choice in external matters; they are not compelled to . . . buy here and eat there, nor to sleep yonder. . . . That this liberty should be unquestioned, and that of the Mind destroyed [is, he said] the issue here."[35]

---

[33] Ibid., 198. Data for seven nations are shown.

[34] Scitovsky notes that the share of their national income the British spend on flowers is half that for the Italians (ibid., 197–98). But 72 percent of Britons have private gardens—and only 16 percent of Italians. Cf. Readers' Digest, *The European Common Market and Britain* (1963), table 22.

Scitovsky also finds that American figures "exaggerate": they include substantial expenditures on garden plants (because Americans have more single family homes). But are gardens not part of "the physical environment of one's home"? Indeed, the rising expenditure for single homes, rather than apartment rentals, suggests a greater preference for lawns, gardens, and home amenities.

[35] Penn, "The Great Case of Liberty of Conscience" (1726), 1:452.

· C H A P T E R   2 ·

Happiness and Economic Welfare

He knew that happiness was an unscientific term, such as a man of his
education should be ashamed to use, even in the silence of his thoughts.
—HENRY JAMES, "Pandora"

MUMMIFIED, and seated with his cane in the University of London,
Bentham has shaped attitudes for more than a century. Dozens of
nations now accept his goal—"the greatest good of the greatest
number"—and his democratic premise—"everybody is to count for
one, and nobody for more than one." Fortunately, few have puzzled
over Henry Sidgwick's inference: if human beings are indeed Benthamite "satisfaction-producing machines," could one person not
"be more capable of happiness than another"?[1] (One high-caste
Hindu lawyer, a Benthamite, admitted: "No doubt it is one difficulty
that according to my religion, a Brahman is entitled to exactly five-
and-twenty times as much happiness as anybody else."[2])

But doubters and Benthamites agree that societies all try to produce "satisfaction" in different ways. Inherited values restrict the
goods they specify. Available technologies limit the amount they can
produce. How, then, do they choose which products generate happiness, and in what mixture?

The anthropologists provide a point of departure. "Wild honey,"
declares Lévi-Strauss, "has an attraction for Indians . . . tanta-
mount to a passion. . . . Before setting off to gather honey, the
Ashluslay . . . bleed themselves above their eyes in order to increase their luck. . . . In Argentina too, the greatest diversion and
keenest pleasure enjoyed by the rural peon is that of honey-gathering.

---

[1] Sidgwick, *Elements of Politics* (1891), 583, 609.
[2] Stokes, ed., *Sir Henry Maine* (1892), 40.

For a spoonful of honey he is ready to work for an entire day . . . and often endanger his life."[3]

But what tribesman from Staten Island, or Dubuque, or Tiburon, ever bled himself for a pound of honey? Or worked all day for it? (Much less demanded that one-third of his salary be paid in honey, as did the Quadi of Egypt?[4]) The American economy includes few such obsessed consumers, not because intense rationality dominates their lives, but because U.S. markets offer so many substitutes. Supermarkets provide honey, plus an endless assortment of sugars, ice creams, jams and jellies, cakes, pastries, and cookies. Such variety—so abundant, so available—destroys the sweet, maddening monopoly that honey enjoys in primitive economies.

The United States offers near-substitutes for a thousand other goods. Those who seek the simple life can choose among seventy models of sleeping bags. Those who love modern music can select from fifty different John Coltrane records—and 70,000 other titles— in a single store.[5] Eight thousand items in the typical supermarket surely mute any consumer obsession with a single good.[6]

Marshall once described human wants as "countless in number and various in kind. As man rises in civilization," he added, "his wants rapidly become more subtle and more various."[7] Modern readers may query "more subtle." But who doubts they are "more various"? The expanding capitalist market offers more and more specialized products, and finds customers for all of them. Industrialized societies may be no more able than traditional ones to explain "Where is fancy bred?"—or happiness. But ordinary Americans choose among ten thousand items—from honey to *Consumer Reports*. The Ashluslay's daemonic lust for a single consumption item appears rarely, if at all. The industrialized society is not morally superior. But its members are no less moral, or happy, because their choices are wider.

What about changes in "happiness" or "welfare" over the years? Real consumption rose at a dizzy rate after 1900. What does that fact

---

[3] Lévi-Strauss, *From Honey to Ashes* (1973), 2:53.

[4] Mez, *Renaissance of Islam* (1937), 221.

[5] *Wall Street Journal*, June 7, 1986.

[6] Davidson, "Why Most New Consumer Brands Fail" (1976), 117–22.

[7] Alfred Marshall, *Principles of Economics*, III, II, I (1948).

reveal about economic welfare? "Very little," say those who point to surveys of "happiness." For the percentage of Americans who report themselves "very happy" was no greater in 1970 than in 1946. Nor did the percentage who were "pretty happy" increase.[8] The conclusion seems irresistible: "Our economic welfare is forever rising, but we are no happier as a result."[9]

But what warrants that inference? Even casual inspection of the "happiness" data reveals no contradiction. Real expenditure rose from 1939 to 1956, and the percentage of those who described themselves as "very happy" also rose—by one-third (39 percent to 53 percent). The "very happy" group then decreased, by 4 percent, during the depression of 1957–59, and by a further 6 percent to 1970—as the Vietnam War expanded and urban riots appeared. The percentage "very happy," therefore, was about as great in 1970 as in 1939.

Do such numbers demonstrate that economic growth fails to increase economic welfare? Or "happiness?" Perhaps they could if only one factor created "happiness." Or if economic factors dominated all other elements of "happiness."[10]

But who ever held such assumptions? Between 1946 and 1977, the Soviet Union increased its nuclear arsenal from 0 to 5,000 megatons, while the United States added 3,971 megatons.[11] What "rational man," what economic determinist, ever believed that people living with the hydrogen bomb *must* be happier than those living in a less ominous world—just because measured "real incomes" were rising? What theorist ever asserted, or implied, that the joy from more goods necessarily cancelled fear of collective suicide? Moreover, the "happiness" data quoted refer to a period when Americans increasingly worried about the welfare of Africans and Asians, and about poverty, civil rights, nuclear plant explosions, the environment. Rising real expenditure may advance "economic welfare." But who ever expected it to offset all the other forces that shape human "happiness"?

---

[8] See Easterlin, "Does Economic Growth Improve the Human Lot?" (1974), 109.

[9] Scitovsky, *Joyless*, 135. Cf. Hirsch, *Social Limits to Growth* (1976), 111–12.

[10] No lesser straw man would serve to justify using Easterlin's insightful study as relevant to such questions.

[11] Tonnage data from Charles Sorrels, in Pechman, ed., *Setting National Priorities* (1978), 269.

Did rising real consumer expenditures raise economic welfare in this century? There is no way to stand outside the universe, impartially comparing the units of happiness (or welfare) enjoyed by the generation born in 1900 with those of the generation born in 1920.[12] But judgments can be made in terms of today's consumer values.

One involves a short thought experiment. Suppose that automobiles and penicillin disappeared, and electric washing machines, refrigerators, disposable diapers, electricity and television. Suppose indeed that every economically significant good added since 1900 disappeared.[13] And suppose that the remaining items—salt pork, lard, houses without running water, etc.—were marked down to 1900 prices. Would today's Americans then judge that their economic welfare had improved? Or would they, if anything, conclude that they derive more "welfare" from their material goods than their great-grandparents did from theirs?

Consumers might, of course, have taken no pleasure in books once they saw television. But the array of available goods changes slowly. The high-button shoes of 1900 were still for sale in 1905. Vacuum tubes were stocked in the 1950s, even as transistorized appliances began to replace them. Twentieth-century consumers could therefore usually choose last year's budget items this year if they desired. Yet real consumer expenditure rose in seventy of the eighty-four years between 1900 and 1984, as consumers continually switched to new goods. Such repetition reveals consumers behaving as if the newer goods did indeed yield more "worthwhile experience."

There is an additional way to assess the American standard of living in this century. One can look more closely at the rises in spending for food, for housing, medical care, etc. Considering these specific changes may offer greater insight than drawing inferences from a formless estimate of "personal income in constant prices." That richer perspective appears in Part II.

---

[12] The theoretical issues are pursued systematically by Samuelson and Swamy, "Invariant Index Numbers" (1974): 566–93, and by Fisher and Shell, "Taste and Quality Change" (1968), 97–139.

[13] I use "economically significant" as shorthand for "requiring scarce resources for their production and distribution."

· CHAPTER 3 ·

Consumer Choice: Advertising

They ask themselves: what is usually done by persons of my station and
pecuniary circumstances? . . . It does not occur to them to have any
inclinations, except for what is customary . . . they like in crowds.

—JOHN STUART MILL

EDUCATED as they are in society, human beings necessarily absorb its
values. (Romulus and Remus, raised by nonverbal wolves, did not.)
Yet romantics since Rousseau have been outraged by that fact. Ap-
palled by human society, they contrive "the fiction of a timeless
untouched people."[1] Civilization, they imagine, imposes false
values, different from their own. It creates unnecessary needs, facti-
tous desires. All are imagined as absent in untouched nature.

But how does one adjudicate which needs are inherent and natural? Attempts to distinguish "essential" desires from "false" ones
have been unending, and futile. In the eighteenth century, Sir James
Steuart contrasted "physical" necessities with "political" ones.[2]
"Physical necessities" were pretty much those consumed by Robinson Crusoe. "Political necessities" were those added by custom and
"civilization."

But even brute "subsistence" was defined to include much more
than bread and water. Even Malthus included "political necessities"
in his list of coarse "means of subsistence."[3] Lasalle's "iron law of

---

[1] The phrase is from Rosaldo, *Ilongot Headhunting, 1883–1974* (1980), 25.

[2] Steuart, *Political Economy* (1805), 1:413.

[3] The "checks [that keep population] down to the level of the means of subsistence" include a would-be parent asking whether he "will . . . lower his rank in life,
and be obliged to give up in great measure his former habits? . . . Will he
be . . . unable to transmit to his children the same advantages, of education and

wages" was no less inclusive. Marx, too, included much more than "material wants such as food, clothing etc." He included "so-called necessary wants," which inevitably "depended on the habits and degree of comfort" in which workers were raised.[4] Modern Marxists go further. They even include as "socially necessary" whatever the average worker buys—TV's, automobiles, eye shadow, and new fashions.[5]

The drama still rings out from such fearsome words as "subsistence" and "immiseration." But the minimum consumption level for Marx and Lasalle, as well as Steuart and Smith, was never defined by life on an ice floe. For them, all the "means of subsistence" escalated with historical and social change.

A distinguished twentieth-century economist, indeed a titled one, declared that other economists had forgotten such insights. "Equilibrium theory as taught in regular textbooks in most of the universities of the Western world," he wrote, takes the "thoroughly misleading . . . [view] that men have 'wants' or 'needs' . . . given by man's nature, independently of the social environment and of the social institutions created for satisfying them."[6]

No such North American textbook can readily be located.[7] (The complaint may apply to Britain.) Though ostensibly he challenged the established view held by most economists, in fact Lord Kaldor simply reiterated it. "Genetic" views have indeed been popularized by some economists in recent years. These describe consumers as desperately trying to follow natural wholesome buying instincts, but being seduced by advertising and peer pressure. The most de-

---

improvement that he had himself possessed?" Malthus, *Essay on Population* (1963), ch. 2, p. 7.

[4] Marx, *Capital*, Moore and Aveling (1919), vol. 1, pt. 2, ch. 6. Marx described labor power as "determined by the value of necessaries of life habitually required by the average laborer," in the words of Morishima, *Marx's Economics* (1977), 53. The adverb "habitually" brings in the entire historic and social context. Indeed it is more explicit than Smith (*Wealth of Nations* [1963], vol. 1, ch. 8): "A man's wages . . . [must be somewhat more] than sufficient to maintain him; otherwise it would be impossible for him to bring up a family, and the race of such workmen would not last beyond the first generation." That rate is "evidently the lowest which is consistent with common humanity."

[5] "Socially necessary labor time is . . . the amount of labor embodied in the bundle that the worker . . . purchases with his wages." Roemer, *Free to Lose* (1988), 4.1.

[6] Kaldor, "Equilibrium Theory and Growth Theory" (1979), 273–74.

[7] Kaldor's bibliography cites only one volume that might qualify as a "regular textbook" presenting "equilibrium theory"—Samuelson's. It would be interesting to find even a hint of this straw-man position in the many editions of that book.

lightful pages of Galbraith or Baran, and the most acid, surely assume that advertising "hath such powers." (Cramp sees consumers not as "sovereign choosers [but as] closer to being helpless victims of an economic process whose motor is technical change."[8]) Perhaps consumers are all victims, but of whom?

"Many voices darken counsel." General Motors may advertise its cars seductively. But Toyota, Nissan, Ford, Chrysler, and Mercedes also advertise. And they, in turn, are challenged by multinational banks who promise consumers unearned increment for depositing money they could have spent on cars. Fashions in clothing and theatre compete with them.

The babel of greed does not stop there. Other corporations publish Veblen, Galbraith, Marcuse—who urge consumers to spend more for public goods, via taxes, and less for corporate products. Meanwhile Billy Graham, Jesse Jackson, Jerry Falwell, Malcolm X, Edward Kennedy, Ralph Nader, Norman Lear buy media space and time urging consumers to contribute money—to improve the human condition.

Faced by that barrage of advice, consumers do somehow choose. Even the largest corporations in the world then discover how hard it is to turn consumers to their corporate purposes. A host of well-advertised products annually fall into bankruptcy. Giant publishers remainder books. Major corporations test-market hundreds of new brands every year, and 70 percent of them fail.[9] They do not make it to national markets. Of 30,000 new products introduced in grocery stores after 1960, some 25,000 did not survive to 1980. Of 84,933 introduced between 1980 and 1990, 86 percent did not survive to 1990.[10]

---

[8] That economic process transmits "sales pressures by producers and social pressures from fellow consumers, as one new good after another spreads through society on the 'infectious disease' model." Cramp, "Pleasures, Prices, and Principles" (1991), 71.

How "technical change" drives ahead as an uncaused cause, forcing producers to junk old inventories and obsolete their equipment, is not clear. Perhaps consumers actually found cars more serviceable than horses, electricity than oil lamps, washing machines than washboards.

[9] Cf. p. 13, n. 6.

[10] *The New Product News of the Dancer Fitzgerald Sample Inc.* for December 1980 reports that 29,874 new products had been introduced from 1964 through 1980. They covered the range of items sold in typical grocery stores. A survey in *The Progressive Grocer* ([Apr. 1981]: 101) indicated that the typical grocery warehoused 8,085 items.

The failures of the American automobile industry since World War II are classic. Well-advertised, colossal examples included the Edsel, Tucker, Henry J., Hudson, Studebaker, Pinto, Monza, Corvair, De-Soto, and Willys—not to mention billion-dollar losses that stained the balance sheets of General Motors, Ford, and Chrysler in the 1980s and early 1990s.

Given that history of financial catastrophe, the ubiquitous faith in the mighty power of advertising appears quite endearing: faith by those who sell advertising, as well as by those who would root it out. Grant that Svengali-like producers all seek childlike consumers. But how successful are they? If advertising could make consumers spring from every rock, surely business would spend without stint up and down Madison Avenue. Yet American firms allocate less than 1 percent of all their spending to advertising. Even the giant auto companies allocate no more.[11])

Many others have roles in this melodrama. Consumers are influenced by newspaper columnists, by consumer-testing services, and by public-interest journalists as well (not to mention by articles by Kaldor, Scitovsky, Galbraith, and Hirsch). Most importantly, they live amidst neighbors and friends. Faced by a thousand clamoring advertisers, they consult actual experience—of others. National surveys reveal that they rely on the advice of friends and relatives three times out of four.[12] Who indeed could help them judge a new product better than those who share their values and attitudes?

The social environment has always shaped human values, and wants. How could it not? Does that "distortion" appear less fre-

---

Since they stocked at least 4,000 items in 1960, and another 3,000 were introduced between 1960 and 1963, as many as 29,000 could have failed.

By 1990, chain warehouses stocked 20,372 items (*Progressive Grocer* [Apr. 1991]). That increase of 12,000 items can be compared with 84,943 items introduced from 1980 to 1990 (*Gorman's New Product News* [Jan. 7, 1992] and unpublished information kindly provided by that publication). An 86 percent failure rate is implied by these numbers.

[11] U.S. Internal Revenue Service, *Statistics of Income, Source Book, Corporations, 1985* (1985), 008, 113. Half of that expenditure consisted in tax-deductible expenses, and therefore was really made by other taxpayers.

[12] A national sample survey reported that "advice from friends and relatives" was the source "used most often" (72 percent) for consumer information. Distant runners-up were "independent literature such as *Consumer Reports*" (35 percent) and "paid advertising" (33 percent). Cf. Sentry Insurance Company, *Consumerism at the Crossroads, A Survey*, conducted by Louis Harris and Associates (1976).

quently in socialist Hungary than in the United States? In Britain? Sweden? Japan? Were Russian consumers in the nineteenth century insulated from their neighbors and social order, or Greeks in the fifth century B.C.? It was not advertising that made communist Bulgaria a world leader in cigarette consumption, nor the Soviet Union in vodka. Consumers' choices were never guided by genes alone. In Becker's words, rationality does "not imply that each household's decisions are necessarily independent of those made by others . . . [for they] are linked ultimately by a common cultural inheritance and background."[13] Or, as Tobin put it: "Rationality does not exclude dependence of one consumer's preferences on the actual consumptions of others."[14]

[13] Becker, *Economic Theory* (1971), 26.
[14] Tobin, "Comment" (1984), 33.

· C H A P T E R 4 ·

Consumer Choice: Externalities, Varieties

Yesterday we rhapsodized about the celebrated soft mist that today is
transformed into a sulfur-anhydrite cloud.

—FRANCOIS NOURISSIER, *The French* (1968)

WHAT EXPENDITURE by consumers fails to affect their fellows, creating externalities? Some are positive, some negative, as with most social behavior. Over seven million Americans bought a video of Carreras, Domingo, and Pavarotti. They thereby brought the price down from, say, $250,000 (for a production run of one) to $25 (for a run of seven million). The price of electricity, automobiles, televisions, and calculators similarly fell when consumers expanded their markets.

But negatives fascinate critics more than such positive externalities. Automobile exhaust is today's prime example. Yet it has endless precedent. For a million days before Columbus ever reached America, cooks dirtied the environment every day. Primitive campfires reach back to at least 2000 B.C. And wood creates more deadly benzo (a) pyrenes and particulates per meal than gas does, or electricity from coal.

Meat consumers long left a trail of blood and guts, whether their abattoir was a water hole (in Kenya), a public street (in India), or a sequestered factory (in Iowa). Vegetarians leave their own trails, of corn shucks, rice husks, potato skins, orange rinds, pineapple spines. City dwellers on every continent carry groceries home in palm leaves, paper, or plastic bags, then litter their cities with discards. In the high pursuit of knowledge, universities generate an unending fall of discarded notices and flyers stuck on trees, walls, and walks.

For centuries the West possessed millions of acres in open land. The rich and wellborn then readily enjoyed the rents of "unspoiled nature." Population growth gradually began to menace those rents. Every baby, as Joan Robinson warned, threatened existing consumers:

> The most noticeable effect of a growth in numbers . . . when it occurs at a high standard of life, is the way human beings destroy amenities for each other through cluttering up the country with their bodies, their houses and their motor-cars.[1]

Rising incomes intensified the impact of "their bodies." And thinly peopled districts were transformed as more and more people reached them. As Marshall saw a century ago, "a closely peopled district is impoverished by everyone who adds a new building."[2]

Lakes and wilderness areas inaccessible to the public of 1890 became accessible by 1990. Cultured souls found the economic rents they had been enjoying free of charge were threatened. They began to view this with alarm. Few expressed their alarm more cogently than Joan Robinson and Hubert Henderson:

> The peace and beauty of the countryside will be increasingly threatened by the wide enjoyment of regular holidays, by the spread among town-dwellers of the taste for rural outings, by improved transport facilities, and by an increase in the numbers of those possessing motor-cars and motor-cycles.[3]

E. J. Mishan repeated their insight, in less-measured phrases:

> The English countryside is . . . being irreparably destroyed. . . . What a few may enjoy in freedom the crowd necessarily destroys for itself. . . . Aided by the ubiquitous automobile, and the estate agent and developer, [the airplane] has transmogrified every one of the once-famed . . . resorts of the Mediterranean into a neon lit jungle of cement blocks, reeking with gasoline fumes and crawling with transistorized traffic.[4]

---

[1] Robinson, *Economic Philosophy* (1962), 116.

[2] Alfred Marshall, *Principles of Economics,*, VI, XIII, 14.

[3] Great Britain, Royal Commission on Population, *Papers*, vol. 3, Report of the Economics Committee (1950), 50.

[4] Mishan, "Wages of Growth" (1973), 67, 79. The role of the simple unspoiled peasant in all this is unclear.

Did democracy per se ruin the oldest playgrounds of the leisure class? Did rising worker incomes? Only in part. The threat was not real until "greedy entrepreneurs" realized that mass markets could yield massive profits. It was, then, cheap cars and airplane tickets, plus rising wage rates to the mass of workers, that menaced the countryside. Once upon a time, well-to-do Americans such as Parkman, Roosevelt, Lafarge, and Adams toured the Western wilderness. (Not even the middle class could afford to.) The lovely Little Missouri was obviously created for their delight—as well as Yellowstone, and the Black Hills. They could, of course, have perpetuated their delight by buying those areas, and dedicating them as wilderness preserves. (Jefferson had set a precedent. He bought Virginia's scenic Natural Bridge to preserve it, then allowed all comers to view it.) Instead, the well bred supported a takeover by the federal government, but continued to squat on the public domain, rent-free. In a democracy, however, they could not block their fellow citizens from doing the same. They could only complain.

No issue would have arisen if (1) Henry Ford built cars only for the wealthy, and (2) worker incomes had not risen markedly. As late as 1870, the only two visitors to Yosemite in the entire year were two California teenagers.[5] But in due time, it was possible for 60 million families to travel to that once-primitive wilderness. (Some years it seemed as though nearly all tried to visit Yosemite or Yellowstone the third week in July.) Once the past became irretrievable, the wealthy sought other preserves, to which only the fortunate few could gain access. They discovered Kenya in the 1920s, and Yugoslavia and Afghanistan. They acquired tracts in Maine. They bought island homes in South Carolina and Greece.

Less-pecunious lovers of unspoiled nature found no such solace. Publicly owned parks and wilderness areas had become accessible to millions—including foreigners. Visitors to the national-park system increased by over 280 million from 1910 to 1988. And those millions enjoyed the public goods "after their fashion," destroying the grand isolation of nature.

As a minor offsetting externality, however, the number of automobiles rose rather than the number of horses. (Manure from urban

[5] Hammond, *Autobiography* (1935), 1:31.

horses in 1900 had sustained the daily production of 3 billion flies, and with them, typhoid and dysentery.[6])

Still more delicate externalities have been discovered, hidden and destructive. They are created, says Hirsch, by our "positional economy," with its "aspects of goods and services . . . that are (a) scarce in some absolute or socially imposed sense, or (b) subject to congestion or crowding through more extensive use."[7] The outcome is grievous: "Riches enjoyed by a minority cannot be enjoyed by a majority." The problem is not a mere lack of purchasing power. It is, Hirsch tells us, the sheer inability to produce "positional" goods. "The life depicted in the glossy magazines is clearly attractive. . . . The snag is that much of it is unavailable to very many of us at once, and its diffusion may then change its own content and characteristics."[8]

Three separate issues are implicit here—congestion (already considered), scarcity, and unavailability. That goods are "scarce" is the first lesson of economics. But what of "unavailability to very many of us at once"—the novel "positional" complaint?[9] Can one really believe that many items "depicted in the glossy magazines" were indeed unavailable—the $30,000 watches, the deluxe Lancias, the performances of *Aida* replete with elephants?[10] Tiffany's stock of

[6] Park visitors increased from 199,000 to 282,500,000. President's Research Committee on Social Trends, *Recent Social Trends* (1934), 920, and U.S. Bureau of the Census, *Statistical Abstract, 1991* (1991), 222.

In 1900 there were 1.4 million urban horses (see Table II.25). These averaged 25 pounds of manure each, with each ton of manure supporting 900,000 maggots (Hering and Greeley, *Collection and Disposal of Municipal Refuse* [1921], 569–572). Assuming that horses were on the street twelve hours a day, their stable manure alone would have yielded 6 billion flies a day. (A higher figure is implicit in Howard, *The House Fly, Disease Carrier* [1911], 40.) A contemporary empirical estimate is implicit in Herms, "How to Control the Common House Fly" (1910), 271. Dr. Herms sampled one four-day-old pile and collected 10,282 larvae from fifteen pounds of samples. His results would imply some 3 billion new flies daily from stable manure.

[7] Hirsch, *Social Limits to Growth* (1976), 27. "Positional goods" have also been defined as those "whose value depends relatively strongly on things owned by others." Cf. Frank, "The Demand for Unobservable and Other Nonpositional Goods," *American Economic Review* 75 (Mar. 1985): 101.

[8] The first sentence is from Heilbroner's summary of Hirsch's views; the others are from Hirsch. Both are quoted in the *New York Review of Books* (Mar. 3, 1977): 10–20.

[9] Novel only in phrasing. Cf. "We may . . . measure that which we wish to obtain . . . as an excess over what others can achieve." Von Wieser, *Social Economics* (1927), 26.

[10] The phrase—"Life depicted in the glossy magazines"—does not very clearly

expensive watches never fails. Hit plays run year after year. Best-sellers are printed until they have to be remaindered. Tickets to every Horowitz concert were available for half a century. Even querulous complaints about the lack of "good servants" reflect (1) an unwillingness to pay salaries that compensate for the modern world's denigration of domestic service, or (2) demands for service superior to what Frederick the Great commanded, or Idi Amin.

One anthropologist shrewdly described Hirsch's "positional" complaint: it focuses on "the part of having servants that cannot be replaced by appliances and convenience foods . . . the part derived from being the only one to have servants."[11] Now, to "be the only one" is an ancient preoccupation. (A French commentator once declared that "supreme luxury for a woman where I come from is to wear a hat that has no copy in the entire city of Paris."[12]) But is "position" (or "exclusivity") really what a decent economy should provide? Or is it—at most—a silly goal? And its quest—at best—a venial sin?

The Union of Soviet Socialist Republics planned the production of some 600 brands of wine,[13] and 2,500 different confectionery items.[14] China grows 1,500 varieties of tea.[15] All without the stimulus of advertising. By cutting back to ten or even fifty varieties, such poor nations could reduce the resources diverted to holding inventories, distribution, and labeling. They could instead produce more food, medical supplies, even poison gas.

These countries' proliferation of varieties was thus wildly irrational, if only costs mattered. Unfortunately, many moralists reject such varied consumer choices in the West by assuming that only costs matter. They applaud diversity in cultures, politics, and education. Yet they vigorously deplore the "cost" of variety in consumer

---

denote what is meant. I take it to encompass the items advertised in *Vogue*, the *New Yorker, Sports Illustrated*, the *Atlantic, Mademoiselle*. Most items so advertised—liquor, cigarettes, automobiles, skis, clothing, books, plane trips—are in fact produced in enormous volume.

[11] Cancian, "Consuming Relationships" (1979), 301–11.

[12] Duhamel, *Scenes de la vie future* (1931), 231.

[13] U.S. Congress, Joint Economic Committee, *Consumption in the U.S.S.R.* (1981), 35.

[14] Katsenelinboigen, *Studies in Soviet Economic Planning* (1978), 239.

[15] Van Slyke, *Yangtze* (1988), 102.

markets. Variety in religion has been accepted as an unshakeable right in the United States, which began this century with over 190 denominations.[16] Pluralism in U.S. politics is taken to be a constitutional right. Other nations either have no "loyal opposition," or one. America has a multitude of competing interest groups. (Indeed, a tiny minority, whose members could not even vote, forced an amendment to the U.S. Constitution.)

Is it surprising that consumers with such different beliefs and backgrounds seek different products in the market? Or is it more surprising that moralists draw back in horror from the pell-mell variety that results?

Social critics demand variety in some GNP categories even while they object to variety in others. Federal thinkers have urged fewer medicines (to save money), but 2,500 more grocery items (to save lives).[17] Petulant differences in taste masquerade as high analysis. As one economist approvingly summarized: Veblen taught us that "conspicuous consumption" and "pecuniary emulation . . . led to a vast waste of resources."[18] "Vast" is an impressive adjective, but somewhat vague. Fortunately, Veblen was specific: "Something like one half of actual output is consumed in wasteful superfluities."[19] What belonged in that half? He never specified. But the obvious suspects include books, newspapers, and magazines. In the thirteenth century, the Sorbonne's library had only 2,000 titles.[20] By 1836 it owned 800,000.[21] In Veblen's day, such libraries held over a million volumes. Yet his contemporary, President Eliot of Harvard, declared that a mere five-foot shelf of books could hold the best of human thought. Since most Americans had read no more than a few

[16] U.S. Bureau of the Census, *Religious Bodies, 1906* (1910), table 1.

[17] The attack on "me-too" drugs, begun in many private publications, appeared in successive reports by the Department of Health from the 1970s onward. This approach is based on an exotic accounting premise—that costs matter but benefits can be ignored. For patients, it is clear that one medication may produce disastrous side-effects while another creates no problem—though both are defined as the same by social critics and chemists.

More recently, the Public Health Service urged 2,500 items be added to the list of grocery products—items yet to be created, low in fat. U.S. Department of Health and Human Services, *Healthy People, 2000* (1991), 613.

[18] Fusfeld, *Age of the Economist* (1990), 102.

[19] Veblen, *Engineers and the Price System* (1921), 121.

[20] Franklin, *La Vie privée d'autrefois* (1888), 3:6.

[21] *Niles Register*, April 23, 1836, p. 132.

inches, more publications could only represent "superfluities." So, too, the 75 million separate issues of magazines and newspapers published since then[22]—and millions of new phonograph recordings, motion pictures, paintings, and musical compositions.

A hundred million new intellectual and cultural products have been marketed since Veblen's day, and their sales have been included in GNP. Many have been respectfully reviewed by writers on culture. (They have even become subjects of collegiate instruction along with Veblen's analysis. Certainly more students today are assigned readings in *Naked Lunch*, Marx's *Early Manuscripts*, or *The Well of Loneliness*, than in *Emma* or *The Divine Comedy*.) The number of cultural novelties added to GNP since 1921 is twenty times as great as the additional flavors, shapes, and kinds sold in supermarkets and pharmacies,[23] though seen as waste and superfluities by some onlookers. Many of these proved creative, desirable, or fresh to actual consumers. Grant that some "superfluities" should never have been published, or recorded. But what secular authority is entitled to specify which they are? And what principle would guide it except gut preference for, say, Sholokov rather than Akhmatova?

Those who volunteer to instruct us on the items appropriate for consumer markets call to mind Bishop Warburton's cheerful distinction: "Orthodoxy is my doxy. Heterodoxy is another man's doxy."

[22] Including about 28,000 separate issues of the 2,000 daily newspapers. About 6,000 weeklies were also published, plus 1,000 weekly periodicals and 4,000 monthlies. U.S. Bureau of the Census, *Historical Statistics* (1975), 2:810.

[23] Cf. Chapter 3, n. 10.

· C H A P T E R   5 ·

Consumption Inequality

Some sowing, some earning, with sweat of their brows,

The gain which the great ones in gluttony waste.

—Piers Plowman (1362)

How MANY twentieth-century issues have been debated more hotly than the inequality of income and wealth? The fortunate live in palaces, with a retinue of servants. Others therefore starve.

> Our institutions . . . prod us to get ahead economically. . . . They award prizes that allow the big winners to feed their pets better than the losers can feed their children.[1]

> With our present highly unequal distribution of income . . . the extreme luxury living of the few super-rich means lack of necessities for many other people.[2]

Does inequality in consumption distort the meaning of "consumption by the average American"?

The "problem" is not limited to the United States. For we hear from the Soviet Union of "periodic open-air dog shows . . . where shiny black cars with uniformed drivers disgorge noble animals. . . . The point is conspicuous consumption. Meat is precious in Russia. To *have* a big dog, or two, means that you can feed the equivalent of an extra member of the family."[3]

In Tawney's classic indictment:

[1] Okun, *Equality and Efficiency* (1975), 1.

[2] Sherman, *Radical Political Economy* (1972), 74.

[3] "And care for a show dog implies a spare pair of hands, at least part time." Train, "Reflections on the Revolution in Russia" (1988), 8–13.

Inequality leads to the mis-direction of production. . . . It diverts energy from the creation of wealth to the multiplication of luxuries. . . . A considerable part of the people of England are engaged . . . in making rich men's hotels, luxurious yachts and motor cars like that used by the Secretary of State for War, "with an interior inlaid in silver in quartered mahogany, and upholstered in fawn suede and morocco."[4]

Socialist prime ministers from MacDonald to Wilson continued to provide some public servants (such as the Secretary of State for War) with elegant motor cars. That well-known secretary (and public servant) Leonid Brezhnev was also well compensated, with his Rolls Royce, Mercedes, Cadillac, Lincoln Continental, Monte Carlo, Matra, and Lancia Beta.[5] Luxury cars, apartments, dachas, and access to imported luxuries have been welcome perquisites of other members of Russia's Politbureau.[6] Red Flag cars, larger apartments, and houses were similarly reserved for China's leaders.[7]

Do such allocations significantly "misdirect production," morality aside? To answer that question, two others must first be tackled. How great a share of total national expenditure is skimmed off by "the super-rich" in capitalist nations, or "government officials" in communist ones? What share do they take of the most essential products—e.g., food, medical care?

One first must define "the rich." We can begin with those who consume luxuries—excessively.[8] Veblen's coruscating attack on conspicuous consumption provides guidance. His scorn, it will be remembered, concentrated on families with legions of servants. The presence of such American lackeys demonstrated, with vulgar simplicity, that the husband was rich: his wife need not soil her hands with real work. A hundred novels and social commentaries described the rich: they were men with valets and footmen. It so happens that the U.S. Bureau of the Census actually counted servants

---

[4] Tawney, *Acquisitive Society* (1920), 37.

[5] Goldman, *U.S.S.R. in Crisis* (1983), 104.

[6] Voslensky, *Nomenklatura* (1984), ch. 5; Hedrick Smith, *The Russians* (1976), ch. 1.

[7] Chao, *Construction Industry in Communist China* (1968), 101, 106; Butterfield, *China* (1982), 70–77.

[8] Mere consumption of luxuries will not do. Some critics of U.S. capitalism have harsh words for motorized vehicles. But an even harsher critic, the head of the National Welfare Rights Organization in the 1960s, was killed in an accident to his cabin cruiser. One cannot merely consider those who own particular luxury items.

while Veblen was working out his ideas. It discovered 296 footmen, 2,436 valets, 22,000 nursemaids and ladies' maids—in a nation with twenty million households.[9] Less than one family in ten thousand had such servants. Veblen's magnificent diatribes, therefore, described an exceedingly tiny group, as did the stories that proliferated in the Pulitzer and Hearst papers. America actually had more monks than valets, though no one went on about its asceticism. The one in ten thousand "rich" whom Veblen, Hearst, and the McNamaras attacked were simply too few to absorb even 1 percent of America's consumption.

Suppose, however, the category is expanded. What about all families, say, who hired a coachman? To include them would include many with fairly modest incomes, e.g., Clarence Day's father (a minor Wall Street broker).[10] But even that larger group consumed less than one-tenth of one percent of U.S. output.

Yet it is not the income of the "rich" that is at issue for studying consumption. To know how much they fritter away, one must first deduct the income they divert to savings. That the rich save, and save largely, has long been recognized. In Hazlitt's words:

> Men like to collect money into large heaps in their life-time. They grasp it into their own hands, not to use it for their own good, but to hoard, to lock it up, to make an object, and idol wonder of it.[11]

How well does this characterize the American rich? According to a very skilled, and very populist, lawyer around 1910 top income recipients saved 41 percent of their income.[12] Applying that saving ratio to the percentage of families with coachmen or (valets or footmen) reveals that they accounted for well under 1 percent of total U.S. consumption.[13]

[9] U.S. Bureau of the Census, *Occupations, 1910* (1913), 430.

[10] Day, *Life with Father* (1935), 33.

[11] Hazlitt, "On Will Making" (1903), 115.

[12] Shearman, *Natural Taxation* (1911), 34. Shearman estimates that millionaires saved 83 percent of their incomes, and the top 1 percent saved 41 percent. He did not report the basis of his surmise. Possibly "the rich" arbitrarily saved one dollar for every dollar spent. Ever since beginning work as an office boy, Benn says, "I have seldom permitted myself to spend more than half of my earnings." Benn, *Confessions of a Capitalist* (1926), 80.

[13] In 1900 the income of the top 3 percent of the farm population averaged about $4,000. (Cf. Lebergott, *American Economy*, 322, 312–14.) This group constituted the bulk of the top 1 percent in that year (ibid., 321). The income for the top 1 percent,

Such diversion may have been morally important. (It was certainly politically vital: it helped pass the federal income tax.) But it reduced the "well-being" of the rest of the population by less than 1 percent—and distorted the efficiency of resource utilization even less.

Has inequality in consumption increased since then? Probably not. As the nation's leading Marxist economist once observed:

> Not even the most extravagant of the contemporary Croesuses can spend a large part of his income for personal purposes. . . . While for the stability of the capitalist economy an increase in his consumption would be altogether advantageous, this cannot be a guiding principle in the life of the individual capitalist. . . . For him, accumulation and thrift are still indispensable means to success and advancement, and lavish living beyond what happens to be the conventional level for people in his group can not be only destructive of his capital but also damaging to his credit-worthiness and standing in the community.[14]

Indeed, the top income groups saved 40–50 percent in both 1928–29 and 1972–74, almost half a century later. By 1983 the top 10 percent (i.e., $50,000 and over):

owned 60 percent of household net worth
received 33 percent of the income,
and took 20 percent of the nation's consumption.[15]

Confiscating their excess consumption would have increased the average American's consumption by 12 percent.[16] But the average family's real consumption had already risen more than 150 percent above its 1900 level by 1983. Hence "misdirection" toward the rich had reduced that substantial rise for the family by very little. That

---

then, could not have averaged above $10,000. Given 41 percent saved, their consumption of both necessities and luxuries would have averaged, say, $6,000, as compared with, say, $854 (95 percent of the $899 all-family average income). All of which implies that even the top 1 percent accounted for, at most, 7 percent of total U.S. consumption.

[14] Baran, *Political Economy of Growth*, 89–90.

[15] See Appendix B, "Savings," for estimating details.

[16] Their much larger share of wealth and savings eventually turned into (a) consumption by widows and children after the death of the husband, (b) consumption by children in later years, (c) consumption by the government from taxes levied on estates, (d) and charity.

fact may well explain "the puzzling . . . toleration of the masses for economic inequality."[17]

One may also ask: what share of essential goods do the rich consume? By 1988 the top 15 percent of American families consumed not 15 percent of the nation's food, but 22 percent.[18]

How about countries with national plans, and announced goals of equality? For thirty years India was guided by central economic plans—"a thirty-year control system," in the words of one of its planners.[19] Yet the richest half of the Indian population accounted for two-thirds of total food expenditure.[20] Mexico "has been controlled by the Party of Institutionalized Revolution" for fifty years.[21] Yet the bottom "30 percent of its population consumes 10 percent of the food produced."[22] Despite the Gettys and the Hunts and the Trumps, the poorest 30 percent of the population in the United States gets a greater share of the nation's food than the lowest 30 percent in Mexico. And the poorest 50 percent gets much the same "share" as Indian planners allocated.[23] (Of course, the poor in the United States get more calories than average for Mexico or India, more proteins, more vitamins, and higher-quality food.)

Justice Holmes once defined "the practical question . . . [as] who consumes the annual product, not who owns the instruments."[24] "Economically it does not matter whether you call Rockefeller or the United States owner of all the wheat in the United States if that wheat is annually consumed by the body of the people."[25] In Taw-

[17] The quotation is from Okun, *Equality and Efficiency*, 33.

[18] U.S. Bureau of Labor Statistics, *Consumer Expenditure Survey* (1988, unpublished), table 2. I compute the ratio for "food at home." Food "away from home" as consumed by the rich includes a disproportionate share for service in expensive restaurants.

[19] Krishna, "Economic Development of India" (1980), 176.

[20] Ibid.

[21] Pablo Gonzalez Casovana, "Economic Development of Mexico" (1980): 202.

[22] Ibid., 192.

[23] Computed from U.S. Bureau of Labor Statistics, *Consumer Expenditure Survey,* Bulletin 1992 (1978), table 1.

[24] Peabody, ed., *The Holmes-Einstein Letters* (1961), 34. In 1910, Holmes observed that "the luxuries of the few couldn't be more than one percent of the annual product" (p. 69). His definition of "the few" was undoubtedly less extensive than the equivalent of those with $25,000 and over in 1970. His reference to luxuries surely covered a smaller category than "all consumption."

[25] Oliver Wendell Holmes, Jr., "Economic Elements" (1920), 279ff.

ney's view, "What matters to a society is less what it owns than what and how it uses its possessions."[26] Income would therefore matter less than consumption. And Rawls, a philosopher of justice, prefers an expenditure tax to an income tax because it is levied "according to how much a person takes out of the common store of goods, and not according to how much he contributes (assuming here that income is fairly earned)."[27] But few of today's critics seem ready to accept such judgments.

Certainly our most startling millionaires—Michael Jackson, Bill Cosby, Kareem Abdul-Jabbar, Madonna, Colonel Sanders, Audrey Hepburn, Bobby Bonilla—could "feed their pets better than the losers feed their children. Millions of quite ordinary Americans, Frenchmen, Italians, and Canadians can do so as well. Americans tax the rich—even those without pets—to provide food for other people's children. For the past eighty years Congress annually decided how much to tax "the rich." It escalated their tax rates greatly during this century, and revenues from them. How much did Congress then allocate for other people's children? That allocation rose modestly, far more modestly than spending for defense, farm subsidies, irrigation, etc. The sequence of decisions presumably reflected the repeated elections and choices of the American electoral process, and the values of millions of voters. (Chapter 10 reviews how much individual charity added.)

In conclusion, the percentage of U.S. output totals consumed by "the rich" (via pets or otherwise) is the issue, not their income. And that share has remained steady enough to have had little impact on the 1900–1990 changes shown in Part II for consumption of food, housing, etc. by the average American.

[26] Tawney, *Equality* (1931), 103.

[27] Rawls, *Theory of Justice* (1973), 278. Kaldor's *An Expenditure Tax* (1955) and others have, of course, expressed such a view.

· C H A P T E R 6 ·

Immortality and the Budget Constraint

Were the happiness of the next world as closely apprehended as the

felicities of this, it were a martyrdom to live.

—SIR THOMAS BROWNE

IN THREE THOUSAND YEARS of history, Judaism, Christianity, and Islam shaped millions of lives. Each overthrew older ways, and older societies. Their massive impact on resource allocation has been little studied—not the resources they claimed for priests, ministers, rabbis, churches, crusades, and jihads, nor the allocations dictated by their contrasting views of eternity.

Of the three religions, the first failed to promise an afterlife—not even the threat of one. From the Ten Commandments onward, its exhortations dealt with moral behavior in this world. And it gained few converts. The other two religions emphasized future life and present behavior. Christianity's future world was filled with positive and negative elements. But its positive aspects, though intense, were vague when contrasted with vivid promises of hell and purgatory for most believers.[1] Islam, however, offered its adherents an eternity of tangible joy, extending the most intense pleasures of the present world.[2] (In the days of the Druids, Britons threw "them-

---

[1] "The majority of the entire human race . . . are damned because of mortal sins" according to "universal tradition, as testified by 73 church Fathers, Doctors and Saints, 74 theologians and 28 interpreters of the Holy Scriptures." Godts, *De paucitate salvandorum* (1899), 1. Matthew 7:14: "Straight is the way that leadeth to life, and few there are who found it."

[2] Other militant religions have also emphasized death as the portal to heavenly delight. The Mexicans facing Cortes demanded to know why he was so slow to

selves willingly on their friends' funeral pyres in order to share the new life with them."[3])

Of those three major systems of belief, the two offering immortality gathered millions of converts, and retained millions of children in the faith of their fathers. But it was the crusading faith in an eternity filled with earthly joys that created the most converts.

Now, the present value of an eternity of bliss is readily computed: it is infinite. It therefore implies an incredible return to active faith in this life. ("What profit it a man if he gain the whole world but lose his soul?") But the tide of faith in the West ebbed after Darwin. By the nineteenth century, many favored Fitzgerald's *Rubaiyat*: "Ah make the most of what we yet may spend, / Before we, too, into the Dust descend." The Western goal increasingly involved maximizing worldly pleasures, not an eternity of bliss. As of 1960, one American in four admitted he did not believe in life after death.[4] Still others shared that doubt, but would not voice it to strange interviewers.[5] Millions of Americans, then, consume as though they have only one life to live.

It follows that the more fundamental economic constraint on American consumers is time, not income—time in which to enjoy "diversified, worthwhile experience." The American economy offers many ways to loosen the "budget constraint." One way is its wide provision of consumer credit. Another involves free entry into the labor force.[6] Today's income, therefore, constitutes no absolute, binding constraint on family expenditure in the United States. But time still does.

Most Americans, assuming that they have only one life to enjoy, strive to maximize "worthwhile experience" during that life. One

---

deliver them "from our calamities by death? We would die, that we may pass to heaven, where our god Huhzilopochtli waits to give us the release and reward our fatigues and services have earned." Clavigero, *History of Mexico* (1979), 186.

[3] Pomponius Mela (1st century A.D.), quoted in Cunliffe, *The Celtic World* (1979), 298.

[4] National Opinion Research Center, *General Social Surveys 1972–1980* (1980), 90.

[5] Two Frenchmen in every three did not believe in an afterlife, according to a 1968 survey, though 85 percent of the population was Catholic. Zeldin, *France 1848–1945*, 982–83.

[6] Some argument on this point appears in Lebergott, "Labor Force and Marriage" (1965), 347–48.

Table 6.1
Expenditures in 1929
as Multiples of 1900
(1982 prices)

Category	Multiple
Gas and oil	1,814
Automobiles	47
Electricity	40
Telephone and telegraph	40
Musical instruments	12
Toilet articles	10
Barber shops	9
Household appliances	9
Women's clothing	9
Medical care	8
Stationery	8
Furniture	7
Flowers and seeds	5
All Consumer Expenditures	5
Religion	4
Domestic Service	4
Food	4
Funerals	3
Welfare	3

Source: Appendix A.

strategy seeks to lengthen life. Another seeks to lengthen each day's hours of experience. Both are evident in U.S. expenditure data (Table 6.1). The greatest spending increases from 1900 to 1929 did not go for necessities, or luxuries, or nonessentials. They were spent for items, in every category, that promised to extend lifetime hours of worthwhile experience.

To lengthen life, the most obvious tactic would appear to be to spend on medical care. Such spending did, indeed, gain largely. But from 1900 to 1929, it rose no more than spending for stationery, or for furniture. It gained so modestly, however, because medical care then could only extend lifetime hours modestly.

Consider the prevailing causes of death (Table 6.2). The major reductions—influenza, pneumonia, tuberculosis, gastritis, typhoid—were not achieved by medical intervention, but by improving sewage systems and water supply, and by spending more for housing: fewer persons per room cut contagion and deaths from tuberculosis and pneumonia. The dramatic declines in scarlet fever, measles, and other notifiable causes required only a relatively small expenditure for vaccinations.[7]

But after 1929, and certainly after 1946, medical expenditures soared. The reason was only partly the miracle drugs discovered after the late 1930s—sulfanilamide, penicillin, etc. New surgical techniques extended life. Novel tests and x-rays proliferated. The Joint Committee on Internal Revenue Taxation further stimulated an exponential rise for medical expenditure, for it defined medical insurance as taxable income if paid from wages earned by workers, but not if paid by their employers. As labor income rose in the postwar years, unions pressured employers to provide health insurance. Their considerable success led to a proliferation of third-party medical payments. These, in turn, helped escalate hospital and other medical expenditures.

Death rates did not respond to this spate of spending in any obvious way. The host of tests and x-rays did, however, help reduce the days of anxiety. Medical expenditure thereby increased the days available for "worthwhile experience."

Beyond the days were the hours. Four items lead Table 6.1 because they extended the hours for worthwhile experience so fully. Artificial lighting obviously did so. The gambit is an old one. Herodotus describes how an oracle predicted death for an Egyptian king in six years. "Perceiving his doom was fixed, [he] had lamps . . . lighted every day at eventime, . . . and enjoyed himself turning

---

[7] Medical expenditure could not moderate consumers' desires for cigarettes and speedy travel; hence the rising death rates from cancer and auto accidents.

The medical profession was not even convinced that cigarette smoking was a primary cause of the rise in deaths from cancer. For one thing, as a famous biometrician argued many years later, cigarettes were even more serious as a cause of heart disease—thus removing some victims under a quite different rubric. It is at least suggestive that the U.S. National Office of Vital Statistics in 1930 "recorded [an] increase in cancer of accessible cities." As a cause it could note only one: "Improvement in diagnosis accounts from some of the apparent increase." U.S. Bureau of the Census, Mortality Statistics, 1930 (1934), 32.

Table 6.2

Infectious Disease Cases and Deaths, 1912–89

	1900	1912	1940	1950	1960	1970	1980	1989
Eight specified infections—cases (N)								
Measles	295,539	291,222	319,000	441,700	47,400	13,500	*	*
Diptheria	132,516	15,571	5,796	918	435	3	*	*
Typhoid	77,984	9,765	2,484	816	346	510	*	*
Poliomyelitis	5,234	9,765	33,300	3,190	33	9	*	*
Whooping cough	16,416	18,230	10,747	14,800	4,200	1,700	*	*
Mumps	n.a.	n.a.	n.a.	n.a.	105,000	8,600	*	*
Rubella	n.a.	n.a.	n.a.	n.a.	56,600	3,900	*	*
AIDS	—	—	—	—	*	*	*	25,107
TOTAL[a]	511,000	510,000	481,000	461,000	214,000	28,000	0	25,000
Death rates (per 100,000)								
Seven specified infections	595	395	130	59	47	35	26	44
Influenza and pneumonia	202	138	70	31	37	31	24	30
Tuberculosis	194	145	46	23	6	33	1	2
Gastritis	143	80	10	5	4	1	1	1
Typhoid	31	16	1	n.a.	n.a.	n.a.	n.a.	n.a.
Measles	13	7	1	n.a.	n.a.	n.a.	n.a.	n.a.
Whooping cough	9	10	2	*	*	*	*	*
AIDS	—	—	—	—	—	—	—	11
Cancer	64	77	120	140	149	163	184	200
Cardiovascular/renal	345	376	486	511	523	496	436	376

Sources: U.S. Bureau of the Census, *Statistical Abstract, 1991*, tables 2, 116; idem, *Historical Statistics*, 8, 58, 77; U.S. Public Health Service, *HIV/AIDS Surveillance* (Aug. 1991).

[a] Rounded to the nearest thousand.

*Less than 1.

the nights into days and so living twelve years in the space of six."[8]

Candlelight for a giant ball cost half as much as a lavish dinner, lavishly served, when London celebrated the victory of Waterloo.[9] In the late seventeenth century, Cibber had to cancel a performance of a play because "there was not company enough to pay for the candles."[10] High cost thus long restricted artificial lighting (as did the danger of fire within doors). As late as 1830, shops with only one or two craftsmen used no more than half a candle a day to light their work.[11] But cheap kerosene became available after the Civil War.

Electric light, a hundred times more brilliant, took over in the twentieth century.[12] It extended the hours of sensation and recreation. It made plays and movies visible after sunset. It opened libraries, restaurants, bowling alleys, baseball parks, and clubs in the hours of darkness. The change in home lighting is indicative (see Table 6.3).

Consumers used a third expenditure strategy to increase their hours of desired experience: reduce travel time. The telephone did just that. How many consumers could walk as many miles as their daily phone calls reached? The automobile further expanded consumer time by contracting space. Travelers once relied on horses or public transportation, with their 2½-mile-per-hour rate and frequent delays.[13] Automobiles then sped along two, five, and eventually forty times faster. Spending on them rose 47-fold.

But mere ownership did not extend the consumer's day. It was the 1,814 multiple for gas and oil that did so. Such spending cut the hours needed for chores (grocery shopping, trips to the doctor or shoemaker), as well as the time required to get to a movie or an amusement park. The automobile proved even more serviceable when the goal was not simply "the nearest" market (as in the Middle Ages) but a preferred one. Gas and oil could bring these miracles.

---

[8] Herodotus, *Histories* (1927), bk. 2, ch. 133.

[9] Cf. Bourke, *The History of White's* (1893), 184–86.

[10] Cibber, *An Apology for His Life* (1938), 300.

[11] [McLane Report], *Documents Relative to Manufactures* (1833), 670, 439. Rates of home consumption were presumably lower still.

[12] Bell, *Art of Illumination* (1912), 82–229. A candle provided 1 candlepower; a kerosene lamp, 15; a gas burner with a welsbach mantle, 60.

[13] Public transportation, of course, also includes airplane travel. But its net contribution to the saving of hours is so spectacular as to explain its increase over the years.

Table 6.3
U.S. Homes by Lighting Source, 1900–1990

	Electricity	Coal, oil and/or kerosene	Gas
1900	3%	88%	9%
1910	15	67	18
1920	35	42	23
1930	68	*	32
1940	79	*	21
1950	94	0	6
1960	99	0	*
1970	99	0	*
1980	99	0	*
1990	99	0	*

Source: For 1900–1960: Lebergott, *American Economy,* 279. The figures for 1910 and 1920 shown there were revised, using the ratio of households to stoves and heaters connected to mains (U.S. Bureau of the Census, *Manufactures, 1919,* 10:724. For 1970–90, figures are assumed at 1960 levels.

*1 percent or less.

Spending on such items rose seventeenfold by 1929, and more thereafter.

Other spending changes shortened hours. They are noted in Part II. But three of the most important may be signalled here. (1) Spending rose far more for processed than for raw foods. Housewives thereby cut their weekly food preparation by about nine hours, turning it over to factories. They acquired nine hours for desired experiences. (2) Expenditures for finished clothing also rose, as housewives turned over to factories their task of making family clothing. (3) A multitude of appliances, from washing machines to vacuum cleaners, shortened housework as well.

· CHAPTER 7 ·

Per Capita Consumption and the
Angel of the Lord

Let us honor if we can

The vertical man

Though we value none

But the horizontal one.

—W. H. AUDEN

THAT DEATH should increase human welfare has probably occurred
to no one but specialists in the causes and cures of poverty.[1] Indeed,
it might never have occurred to them but for a heady combination of
Latin and long division.

Such specialists, and most economists, agree that a nation's welfare is to be measured by per capita income (or consumption)—i.e.,
the nation's total income or consumption divided by its population.[2]
Thus Barbara Ward asked, "How are we to define the 'poor' nations?" Her answer was: "Perhaps the most satisfactory method of
defining poverty is . . . in terms of per capita income."[3] But long

[1] This chapter is a revised version of the material in Lebergott, *Wealth and Want*
(1976).

[2] Cf. the influential study by Myrdal, *Economic Theory and Underdeveloped Regions*
(1957). His proof of deleterious "backwash effects" rests on the widening gap
between national per capita incomes. "Neither economists nor other observers
would as a rule regard sheer increase in the numbers of people enjoying the same
standard of living as a gain in welfare." Nordhaus and Tobin, "Is Growth Obsolete?"
(1973), 514. Pollack and Wales, "Welfare Comparisons and Equivalence Scales" (1979),
220, note that "it is very difficult to make welfare comparisons between families with
very different demographic profiles."

[3] Ward, *Rich Nations and Poor Nations* (1962), 37.

division tells us that dividing $1,000 by two gives a higher per capita income figure than dividing by three. To rely on per capita income for measuring the welfare of nations and groups is thus to assume that death increases welfare. For when a baby dies, the nation's "per capita income" rises, and so does expenditure. When a baby is born, "per capita income" falls abruptly, as does per capita expenditure. If the baby then dies, both return to their previous level. Death, in sum, reduces "poverty" and increases "per capita welfare."[4] The miserably low U.N. "per capita" income figures for underdeveloped countries reflect this treatment of life and death.

Do experts in arcane analysis really believe a family, or a nation, becomes "better off" when one of its children dies? That curious conclusion does not rest on a competent chain of logic. Neither Latin nor long division warrants the belief that "per capita income" tells us much about welfare differences between cultures, or even very long time periods. To find out how the "long-division" view of human welfare arose, we must consider the two major cultural perspectives on children.

"Be fruitful and multiply" is an exhortation held in high respect by the world's major religions, and accepted by the most diverse cultures. Bishop Jeremy Taylor wrote,

> We have a title to be provided for as we are God's creatures . . . and therefore it is a huge folly and infidelity to be troubled and full of care because we have many children. Every child we feed is a new revenue, a new title to God's care and providence; so that many children are a great wealth.[5]

[4] The widely held position that links income and welfare was accurately and succinctly summarized in Samuelson, *Economics* (1961), 801, by a graph of rising per capita income, labeled "Advanced Nations Expect Rising Per Capita Welfare." Other typical statements: "The growth of GNP per capita is . . . probably the best single indicator of growth in living standards, since it takes into account the rise in population." (Fusfeld, *Economics* [1972], 102); "Per capita figures . . . indicate how well each individual fares" (Brandis, *Principles of Economics* [1972], 130).

[5] Taylor continues, "If it be said they are chargeable, it is not more than all wealth and great revenues are. For what difference is it? Titius keeps ten ploughs, Cornelia hath ten children; he hath land enough to employ and feed all his hinds; she, blessings and promises, and provisions and the truth of God, to maintain all her

"Every child we feed is a new revenue"—surely that phrase means that the mere existence of a child expands the well-being of its parents. That long-established religious view implies that total "welfare" increases when children are born, and certainly does not decrease as the "per capita income" calculation insists.

The positive value of children is not doubted by most members of the United Nations.[6] Nor has the political desirability of children gone unnoticed. Thus one of India's political leaders urged its untouchables to reject birth control: they "are a minority in the villages, without land, without homes, in bondage to caste Hindus. To advance they must be in the majority."[7]

Rachel de Queiroz, one of Brazil's "most respected citizens," declared:

> From a national and human point of view . . . international pressures . . . put on us to limit the birth of Brazilians is not only impertinent but also suspect. . . . Would Red China have the force and power to confront a coalition of almost the whole world, if it were not for the tremendous capital represented by her immense population? . . . Let our people grow. . . . And do not preach national suicide for fear of lack of food.[8]

And the leader of one of the world's major religions regularly reaffirms his church's traditional opposition to "forbidding the poor to be born."[9] Secular leaders, too, believe that "the national interest" benefits when more children are born. In Sir William Petty's quaint

---

children. His hinds and horses eat up all his corn, and her children are sufficiently maintained with her little." Taylor, *Rules and Exercises* (1862), ch. 11, sect. 6.

[6] China is an obvious exception. Couples having more than one child may be punished with "stiff fines" equal to as much as a year's salary. See *The New York Times*, Feb. 4, 1990.

[7] Mrs. Satyavani Muthu, quoted in *The New York Times*, Sept. 22, 1974.

[8] Quoted by Daly, "The Population Question in Northeast Brazil" (1970), 557. Domingos Susmao de Lima writes: "While recognizing the financial anguish in which the proletariat vegetates . . . I believe it immoral to advise a creature of that type to practice birth control" (ibid., 566).

[9] "It is inadmissable that those who have control of the wealth and resources of mankind should try to resolve the problems of hunger by forbidding the poor to be born" (Pope Paul, quoted in *The New York Times*, Nov. 10, 1974). Cf. the encyclical *Humanae vitae* (1968), which condemns "every action which . . . renders procreation impossible" (reviewed in John Marshall, "Population Policies" [1971]).

phrasing: "Fewness of people is real poverty; and a Nation wherein are Eight Millions of people, is more than twice as rich as the same scope of land wherein are but Four."[10]

Measuring changes in welfare by GNP per capita can only lead to grotesque conclusions for traditional societies that hold such religious and social views of population. Suppose the Angel of Death destroyed thousands of their babies. Their GNP per capita would rise. Poverty would decline. And "welfare" would improve. If an earthquake destroyed thousands of their old people, GNP per capita would also announce tidings of joy. And similarly if disease carried off thousands of women. Indeed, death tends to increase GNP per capita in most nations—except deaths of middle-aged people who produce goods valued into the GNP.[11]

Political advantage may accrue to some from such grotesqueries, and masochistic advantage to others. But few users of "per capita income" measures seek to misapprehend the values of such societies. Why allow figures on GNP per capita to distort our understanding of welfare in the traditional societies that comprehend the greatest portion of the earth?

What of the industrialized nations? There, the decision to have children is not dictated by ancient cultural or religious imperatives. Nor is it enforced by pronatalist military leaders and governments.[12]

---

[10] Quoted in Georgescu-Roegen, *Entropy Law and the Economic Process* (1971), 301. The case for positive impacts of population increase on economic growth is presented in Simon, *Economics of Population Growth* (1977).

Compare: "The airlift of children from South Vietnam . . . has left in its wake bitter argument over whether taking children from their homeland is an appropriate or necessary way to deal with a crisis. Those who have always opposed foreign adoption because they see it depleting nations of their children are angrier than ever" (*The New York Times*, Apr. 9, 1975). The expressed concern involves "depleting" a nation's population resources.

[11] Even deaths among middle-aged males would immediately increase expenditure per capita—though GNP per capita would decline in the following period. Deaths of housewives, children, or older persons increase GNP per capita because their output is not included in the GNP. The subject here is the conceptual problems of measuring and understanding per capita expenditure. (Thus the dynamic impact of the Black Death is quite another topic.)

[12] Perhaps the obvious exception emphasizes the point: Romania ended legalized abortion in 1966, and initiated premiums for births. The pronatalist position taken by the Third Republic, Fascist Italy, and Nazi Germany clearly contrasts with present European policies, except for France.

Only rarely do its members emphasize the political advantages of having children.[13]

The decision to have children is made by the family itself, as widespread birth control in those nations strongly suggests. Over 85 percent of all U.S. couples practice birth control; over 80 percent of American Catholic couples do so.[14] Moreover, a reliable survey of parents indicates that 85 percent of all births are wanted.[15] Must we not conclude that parents of the nearly 4 million babies born in the United States each year expect to derive "welfare" from their children?[16] And derive as least as much as it will cost to raise them? (Even "unwanted" children are treated by parents as though they were worth the stream of costs they impose—and more.) "Some more souls, some more joy" is a proverb from one of the oldest industrialized nations—Holland.[17]

Consider a hypothetical choice: "Would you give one of your children up for adoption in return for a check that repaid the cost of raising that child?" Surely few U.S. parents would take the money. It is a fair inference that children increase well-being, by not less than the cost of raising them.

[13] And then only in response to perceived threats, rather than directly commended. Thus the Reverend Jesse Jackson stated: "We are clamoring for birth control in this nation when population has in fact declined since the 1950s. . . . Birth control as a national policy will simply marshal sophisticated methods to remove (and control when not removed) the weak, the poor—quite likely the black and other minorities whose relative increase in population threatens the white caste in this nation." Eugene Callender, president of the New York Urban Coalition, has stated that "minority groups in the country view any push toward national birth-rate controls or population constriction as a move towards genocide." Commission on Population Growth and the American Future, *Statements at Public Hearings* (1972), 7:165, 228.

[14] Westoff and Ryder, "Family Limitation in the United States" (1971), 2:1311.

[15] Westoff and Ryder, (ibid., 1312) report that 30 percent of white women and 52 percent of nonwhite women stated that their last pregnancy was "unwanted." The group included married women "ever-pregnant under 45 who intended no more children." Allowing for prior births, these figures are consistent with the statement that about 15 percent of all births in the period 1966–70 were unwanted. (See Ryder and Westoff, "Wanted and Unwanted Fertility" (1972), 13, 474.)

[16] I assume only a majority response to the hypothetical question. There might be exceptions. Thus *The New York Times* in 1853 argued that "he who insures his life or health must be indeed a victim of his own folly or others' knavery." Its premise was that a poor mother would murder her child for insurance benefits—as had reputedly occurred in the United Kingdom. Cf. Hoffman, *History of the Prudential Insurance Company of America* (1900), 10.

[17] Cf. Koopmans, "Objectives, Constraints and Outcomes in Optimal Growth Models" (1967), 13.

Suppose we leave the grand level of national aggregates and national per capita figures. After all, only individuals can experience welfare. Consider three states in the life of a working couple. Assume they produced a constant level of output, and spent their entire income at each stage.

In Stage 1, married but childless, they buy doilies and dresses, insurance, tickets to rock concerts. In Stage 2 they adopt a child. They then spend for milk, toys, and pediatric care rather than rock concerts. GNP totals do not change between Stage 1 and 2.[18] The resource aggregate required to produce their demands remains roughly identical. Their income per capita remains invariant through it all, as does the nation's.

But suppose this couple then begets a child of their own (Stage 3) instead of adopting one (as in Stage 2). Their "welfare" drops immediately; their contribution to GNP per capita declines by one-third:

	Income (output produced)	Expenditure (output consumed)	Per capita GNP
Stage 1	$X	$X	X
Stage 2	X	X	X
Stage 3	X	X	$^2/_3$X

Can it really be true that parents reduce their welfare if they have a child of their own—but not if they adopt one? Does that wild conclusion pop out of the principles of national economic accounting? Or welfare economics? Can economic theory really assert that adopting a child must create more "economic welfare" than having a child of one's own?

The contradictions between adopting and begetting a child mark the source of the confusion. To make per capita income changes measure "economic welfare," we must assume no change of tastes. But every great demographic event in human existence—birth, marriage, death—reflects a massive change in tastes. A couple reveals certain tastes in their consumption behavior when a child is born. They almost inevitably decide that their newborn child must be fed, kept suitably warm, etc.[19] They therefore stop spending in accord

---

[18] For the rare case in which children of other nations are adopted—e.g., Vietnam in 1975—the conclusion does not hold.

[19] Human beings conform to this "law" at least as well as they do, say, to economists' favorite "law of demand."

with their prior preferences. They move on to a completely new indifference curve. How on earth can the mere substitution of pediatric charges for football tickets demonstrate that their welfare has declined?

We may inquire even more closely. If per capita economic welfare declines when a child is born, whose welfare declines—the parents' or the child's? Surely the parents' economic welfare did not decline. Their income did not change. Nor did market prices. If the parents' welfare declined, it could only do so if they preferred the budget of goods they consumed before the child was born. But if so, why did they have a child (85 percent of births being "wanted")? And why, having had one, don't they simply continue in their old expenditure ways? No one concludes that welfare falls when consumers shift from big cars to small ones, or from movies to television. We assume they made that shift to increase their "welfare." The per capita calculation, however, implicitly takes an expenditure shift to indicate that parents were coerced into consuming an inferior set of goods. Is this a reasonable view?

Behavior testifies to the contrary.[20] Many women are scheduled to enter maternity wards, but few wait in foster-home offices. Most Americans prefer to rear children they beget rather than ones they could adopt. (The outré example of Baby M is a case in point.) Moreover, many adoptions, if not most, take place only when parents discover they cannot have children of their own. Such behavior suggests that own-children are not viewed as inferior to adopted ones. If the adoption of a child does not change welfare, the birth of a child certainly does not produce a decline.

But we have further behavioral information. Given the prevalence of birth control, one must assume that most births are in fact desired by parents. Do parents, then, have children to decrease their utility? Or should we assume, more reasonably, that they expect to derive satisfactions from children?[21] Market behavior actually indicates that they reap substantial satisfaction—and in terms relevant to GNP analysis.

[20] Market behavior, of course, empirically demonstrates a prior change in tastes. One might argue that the couple's tastes had shifted toward a different set of goods before they were actually married, before their child was actually born.

[21] GNP figures relate only to goods and services from which consumers expect satisfactions. The catalogue of disappointing movies, cars that turn out to be lemons, etc., is long and ever-changing. No harsher rule can be applied to expected satisfactions from children.

A three-person family spends at least 20 percent more than a two-person family.[22] Foster parents in 1985 were paid $4,550 annually for every child they raised.[23] Since own-children are preferred to foster children, the utilities from own-children must at least equal that sum. Since foster children tend to be raised by families with below-average incomes, own-children must provide at least as much utility to their parents as the $4,550 figure for which people were willing to take care of a foster child. What follows? The birth of a child must raise parents' utility. It will not reduce it, as the per capita income calculation implies.

There remains only one way for social policy to attribute any meaning to per capita income or consumption. If parents' welfare is not reduced by the birth of a child, perhaps the child's is. Yet it is hard to imagine that the staid users of income or expenditure data really wish to assume that newborn children are worse off because they were born. True, that belief was not unknown to ancient and melancholy philosophers: "The best of all things for earthly men is not to be born, and not to see the beams of the bright sun" (Theognis, fifth century B.C.). But what a very odd premise on which to build a measure of "economic welfare." After all, "income" or "consumption" relate only to ephemeral things of this world. They do nothing but attribute value to such things. Can Theognis's weary view be relevant for assessing aid to dependent children, foreign aid, etc.?

Consider incomes in different nations—plutocratic in the United States, miserably low in Pakistan and Jordan. The latter nations, with their larger families, tend to have lower per capita incomes, lesser command over goods that "come within reach of the measuring rod of money." Such "goods" do not, in most societies, include children.

[22] In 1972–73, about 24 percent of mean family income (for whites in the North), according to Jerome Bentley et al., in Mathtech, *The Cost of Children: A Household Expenditure Approach* (1981), 141, 143. An estimate of 42 percent appears in Seneca and Taussig, "Family Equivalence Scales" (1971), 259. The *Monthly Labor Review* (Nov. 1960) estimates a 27 percent to 32 percent difference between expenditures for married couples with no children and those with one child. Estimates are derived from 1950 expenditure data and the WPA maintenance budget, as well as 1935–36, 1941, and 1944 survey data. Cf. also Commission on Population Growth and America's Future, *Demographic and Social Aspects* (1972), 2:337.

[23] U.S. Congress, Committee on Ways and Means, *Background Material* (1986), 525, 528.

Children are not monetized.[24] But neither are they delivered to unsuspecting parents by storks, to be raised by elves. Most parents choose to have children (rather than abortions). They then divert income to raising their children (rather than spending still more on themselves). So doing, they cross an invisible line between "economic" welfare and other sources of welfare—to increase their total welfare. Yet the per capita income calculus tacitly, resolutely, declares that they are decreasing their welfare. But what is the goal of those who compare per capita incomes, of nations or of families? Surely to use income as an index of welfare. It is time for them to cease relying on so biased a measure.

What may I say in brief conclusion? The apparently greater precision of GNP per capita than total GNP for indexing economic welfare rests on its tacit premise that births reduce economic welfare, while deaths increase it. That improbable assumption may be fine for publicists who seek to emphasize the "gap" between per capita income in one country and another, or between ethnic groups. But economists would do well to consider the fastidious counsel of one founder of modern economics: "It is also a question outside my subject whether it is better to have a great multitude of Inhabitants, poor and badly provided, than a smaller number, much more at their ease; a million who consume the produce of 6 acres per head or 4 million who live on the produce of an acre and a half."[25]

[24] Slavery and the sale of children was abolished in Abu Dhabi in 1980, in Saudi Arabia in 1962. I assume the trade has ceased. The advent of women bearing children for others in the 1980s fixed a market price. If babies are worth $10,000 in the market, then that figure can be imputed into national income.

[25] Cantillon, *Essai sur la nature du commerce en general* (1931), 85.

· C H A P T E R 8 ·

Women's Work: Home to Market

In marketing . . . the mother of a family is . . . trying to make the money
go as far as possible, and . . . [then] so distributing [her purchases]
among the various claimants . . . as to make them tell to the utmost.

—PHILIP WICKSTEED, *The Common Sense of Political Economy*

AMERICANS SPEND over 70 percent of their days in and around their homes—though they work elsewhere, drive, shop, go to the movies.[1] In 1900 they spent even more time at home, mostly working. But by 1990 they increasingly bought the goods and services they had produced in 1900. "Consumerism" appeared when housewives began to buy goods they had once produced. The chief producer under the old regime became the chief buyer under the new. As noted below, Fourier, Bellamy, Lenin, and Charlotte Gilman wrote much about changing housework. But while they wrote, the American housewife acted, cutting her work day, as shown in Table 8.1.

Even in the industrializing world of Debs and Rockefeller, Mark Hanna and Emma Goldman, consumption items had been mostly produced at home. The family still created the nation's food. Obviously this was so for rural families, which then made up half the nation. But even in towns of under 10,000 people, every second family raised most of the vegetables, fruit and chickens it ate. So did

[1] The Survey Research Center of the University of Michigan itemized time spent in 86 different activities during the 1,440 minutes of each day in the period 1984–85. By deducting the time spent in "normal work," travel, shopping, etc., plus half the time spent "visiting with others," one can estimate that 73 percent of the day remained for time at home, in house/yard work, etc. Cf. Juster and Stafford, *Time, Goods, and Well-Being* (1985), 171–73.

Table 8.1
Housework, 1900–1975, by Weekly Hours

	Meals and meal clean-up	Laundry	Cleaning
1900	(44)	7	7
1910	42	n.a.	n.a.
1914	40	n.a.	n.a.
1925–27			
Rural	27	6	9
Urban	22	5	9
1965	15	n.a.	n.a.
1975	10	1	7

Source: See pp. 59, 60, 106, 112.

a third of those in midsized cities (populations between 10,000 and 50,000).[2] The transition away from home production became the primary force behind increased consumer spending.

In 1900, cooking, baking, food preserving, and canning were nearly all done at home. Most clothing was made, washed, and repaired at home. Not to mention house cleaning, child care, and medicating the sick. Since families took less than two days of vacation a year, virtually all recreation was likewise produced at home. All that work was done by dedicated, versatile workers who kept no scheduled hours.

The earliest effort to shift home tasks to the market reaches back two thousand years. In the first century B.C., a poet described how water power could replace the housewife's hand quern for milling barley and wheat:

> Cease from grinding, O ye toilers;
> Women, slumber still,
> Even if the crowing roosters call the morning star;
> For Demeter has appointed
> Nymphs to turn your mill,
> And upon the water-
> Wheel alighting here they are.

[2] Mitchell, ed., *Income in the United States* (1922), 230.

See, how quickly they twirl the axle whose revolving rays
Spin the heavy hollow rollers quarried overseas.[3]

Twenty centuries later, however, most American Indian women,
and many pioneers, still used querns. They devoted 20 to 25 hours a
week to grinding grain for the family's food, and 6 to 10 hours to
spinning yarn and making cloth.

Between 1750 and 1900, such tasks were largely taken over by the
market. The consequent reduction in women's work was not no-
ticed by Charlotte Gilman or others who labeled the "status of domestic industry" in 1900 as "prehistoric." The prior century and a
half of change may have seemed unimportant to writers who still
had maids to do such work. In any event, rising consumer expenditures after 1900 continued to shift work from home to market.

Out of the Enlightenment and the turbulent Industrial Revolution
came schemes to reorganize home production. The new planners,
unlike those who invented the mill and the spinning jenny, did not
try to cut down the amount of work. They sought to reorganize it.
Robert Owen, the historic leader of English socialism, described his
ideal community in 1812. Each family of four was to be allocated a
single room, a large one. It would also have access to a public kitchen
and mess room. (One room was enough: children over age three
would live in public dormitories.) Women were to work "in rotation
in the public kitchen, mess-rooms and dormitories." They would, of
course, also (a) keep their own "dwellings in the best order," (b)
"raise vegetables for the public kitchen," (c) make clothing "for the
inmates," and (d) work—though for no more than four to five hours
a day—in the various manufactures.[4] (Was that why Marx labeled
Owen a "Utopian"?)

Fourier was equally suffused with goodwill (though he gave most
of his attention to the sexual activities of the citizens, to where
ceremonial chimes should be placed, and to construction details).[5]
Housework differed under his system only because children and old

---

[3] Antipater of Thessalonica; translation from Higham and Bowra, eds., *The Oxford
Book of Greek Verse in Translation* (1938), 632.

[4] Robert Owen, *New View of Society* (1927), 162–63, 267, 98, 276.

[5] The "most important part of this Phalanstery"—i.e., the buildings of the new
order—was a "heated and ventilated street gallery," from one building to another on
the second floor. It was to be modeled after the gallery of the Louvre. See Charles
Gide's Introduction to Fourier, *Selections* (1901), 145–47.

people were sequestered apart, in five-story apartment buildings, and because food somehow became available in "public dining halls."[6]

Later that century, the head of the Socialist International, August Bebel, proposed a socialist future. Private kitchens were to be abolished. Only the institutional kitchen remained—a "large kitchen, equipped with electricity for lighting and heating." That, he declared flatly, "is the ideal one." No smoke. No heat. No disagreeable odors.

> The kitchen resembles a workshop furnished with all kinds of technical and mechanical tasks. Here we see potato and fruit paring machines, apparatus for removing kernels, meat choppers, mills for grinding coffee and spice, ice choppers, corkscrews, bread cutters . . . the same is true of the equipment for housecleaning and for washing the dishes. . . . The abolition of the private kitchen will come as a liberation to countless women. The private kitchen is as antiquated an institution as the workshop of the small mechanic.[7]

Lenin saw still further. Like Robert Owen, he proposed that women should work in factories. He sought more than efficiency and more goods. To "achieve the complete emancipation of women . . . we must have social economy, and the participation of women in general productive labor." Women were to be freed from the tyranny of "petty housework, which crushes, strangles, stultifies and degrades, [chaining them] to the kitchen and nursery."[8] Emancipation by factory work, the conveyor belt, machine tending? Would men then do housework, or at least share in it? Hardly. Even when Lenin was an exile in Siberia, he and his wife hired a maid to do the housework.[9] "Public dining rooms, creches, kindergartens—these are examples of the [developments] . . .

---

[6] See Benevolo, *Origins of Modern Town Planning* (1985), 60–61. And because instead of 300 fires to warm 300 families there would be only 3. Heating for the apartments would be rare, since the residents "seldom returned to their quarters [from the common dining room, balls and assemblies] before the hour of returning, when he contents himself with a little [charcoal] brasier while undressing." Fourier, *Selections*, 152.

[7] Bebel, *Women and Socialism* (1910), 462.

[8] *Women and Communism, Selections from the Writings of Marx, Engels, Lenin, and Stalin* (1973), 52.

[9] Pomper, *Lenin, Trotsky, and Stalin* (1990), 57.

which can in fact emancipate women."[10] It turned out that workers emancipated by Lenin worked 83 hours a week, as did many housewives. Their emancipation under the Soviets consisted of 6 fewer hours of sleep, 20 fewer hours in the kitchen—plus 46 more hours of work in the factory.[11]

These ideas had American precedents. "Efficient meal preparation procedures" were common under the lash of slavery. Long before Fourier, American planters had noted that a dinner for ten families could be cooked in 2½ hours. But if ten slave housewives each cooked their own, then 10 hours were required. Hence planters required that midday slave dinners be prepared by communal cooks.[12]

After the Civil War, an American physician foresaw workers living in "lofty" buildings, each with "its tenement on a flat or single floor." No one could cook in their apartments. Instead, "a kitchen on a large scale, buying everything wholesale, and furnishing food at actual costs, [would] supply wholesome food, the families selecting from a great variety of dishes."[13] He did not discover the mass cafeteria; Owen or Fourier had done that. But he did award it a monopoly.

Two decades later, one of the most famous American books of the late nineteenth century was published—Edward Bellamy's *Looking Backward*. "Women of the merely well-to-do and poorer classes," Bellamy wrote, "lived and died martyrs to household cares." His solution? An "industrial army." Every woman aged 21 to 45, and every man, would be "mustered into the industrial service" of the

---

[10] Ibid., 56. The translation used has "shoots" instead of "developments."

[11] Data from Soviet time-budget surveys for 1923–24 in twelve industrial centers appear in Zuzanek, *Work* (1980), 178. Workers also spent 10 fewer hours in child care and 9 fewer hours tending vegetable gardens.

Employed women spent no more time in child care on their days off. That fact suggests that women factory workers with young children did not necessarily give ten fewer hours to child care.

By the 1960s, urban employed women in the U.S.S.R. worked about 75 hours weekly (compared to 63 for housewives) and spent 11 fewer hours in cooking, preparing food, and marketing.) Cf. Zuzanek, *Work*, 268, 289.

[12] *De Bow's Review* (1836), 2: 334. Fourier described how one of his groups of 300 families could sell wheat to three other groups. Thus "the work of grinding and baking will not extend to 900 householders but only 3." Fourier, *Selections*, 150.

[13] *One Hundred Years' Progress of the United States* (1870), 523.

state. Each draftee would then choose an occupation "in accord with his natural aptitude." (Some Americans were evident and natural-born grocery clerks. Others were first basemen, or natural ditch-diggers.) Suppose twenty million people discovered a "natural aptitude" for being a poet, or chief executive officer? The implicit answer that captivated Altgeld, Darrow, and other Bellamy admirers was simple. The "Administration" (Cleveland? McKinley?) would make all occupations "equally attractive to persons having natural tastes for them." How? By intuition. Or by testing to ascertain their "natural tastes." The Administration would then "make the hours of labor in different trades differ according to their arduousness."[14]

To the question, "Who does your housework, then?" Bellamy answered crisply: "There is none to do. Our washing is all done at public laundries at excessively cheap rates, and our cooking at public kitchens."[15]

Bellamy's references to "martyrs" and "public kitchens" were taken up by Charlotte Gilman. She proposed to end "the sacrifice of the wife . . . to that primal altar, the cookstove." How? By "professional service"—described succinctly as "cooked meals brought to the home, and labor by the hour."[16]

Who were these new servants to be? What classes were waiting to provide family service? Ready to serve meals, wash pots, and take out garbage? Gilman said only that they would be "skilled experts. . . . one properly constituted kitchen can provide food for five hundred people," saving the expense of "a kitchen and laundry to every house."[17] But others dreamed with great specificity. Writers

[14] Bellamy, *Looking Backward, 2000–1887* (1967), 132–34. Whether the president, or a council of psychological advisers, determined their "arduousness" is not specified.

[15] Ibid., 168. Presumably many readers recognized the "public kitchens" of Owen and Fourier. To charge "excessively cheap rates," the laundries must have paid its workers less than the usual rate for domestic servants. Perhaps these wage-earners paid the community for the privilege of cleaning its dish towels and diapers.

[16] Gilman, *The Living, An Autobiography* (1975), 321.

[17] Cf. Gilman, "The Waste of Private Housekeeping" (1913), 92–93.

"Melusina Fay Pierce [complained] that Bellamy and Charlotte Perkins Gilman had stolen her ideas." In 1869 she had "organized the original Cambridge Cooperative Housekeeping Society, composed largely of the wives of Harvard faculty." Cooking, Pierce's historian notes, "was to be supervised by the gourmet authority Professor [Pierre] Blot . . . [and meals] delivered . . . to the several blocks covered by the association." She adds that "Gilman's emphatic rejection of genuinely

from Cambridge to Chicago came upon the solution: apartment buildings with central kitchens.[18] Somewhere in the lower depths, those unspecified beings would cook humanity's food.[19] The meals were then to be hoisted up the dumbwaiter shaft to individual apartments. (Would those fed at that first sitting then prepare meals for the first cooks? Or would a still more lowly class do the job? No one ever asked.)

Entrepreneurs did put up apartment buildings with basement kitchens. But the meals were too cold after a trip on the dumbwaiter. Or the cuisine was indifferent. Or perhaps the entire approach met the needs of an affluent minority, not the average woman. (One remembers Art Young's great cartoon from this period. A weary, slatternly woman looks up from sweeping a dingy room to address her filthy, ragged husband at the door: "Here I've been slaving over a hot stove all day, and you in a nice cool sewer.") In any event, no new class stepped smartly forward to sacrifice itself on the "primal altar." The outcome was inevitable in America. For women, as men, found better alternatives in the labor market.[20]

Far away in Pittsburgh, Henry Heinz heard the complaints. Gustavus Swift heard them in Chicago. And Joseph Campbell heard them in New Jersey. They began cooking the catsup, the hams, and the soups once prepared on family altars. Ten thousand years of home cooking, sacrificial and skilled, began to end. Specialists (chiefly women) now began to produce parts of meals in factories. Naturally, Messrs. Heinz, Swift, and Campbell charged for their efforts. So did their thousands of employees.

---

cooperative . . . associated housekeeping stemmed from a childhood experience in a cooperative household." Dudden, *Serving Women* (1983), 184–88, 311.

[18] Hayden, *The Grand Domestic Revolution* (1981), 72–76.

[19] Its members were termed "experts." Gilman believed that "the true line of advance [was] housework done by experts instead of amateurs." Cowan, *More Work for Mother* (1980), 108–9.

Would that new job title uplift the souls of scullery maids, houseboys and footmen? Or even today's employees at McDonalds?

[20] Ever-widening human horizons may also have been involved. Eunice Beecher remembered when "cookstoves . . . were first brought into common use [in the 1830s] and how positive the good housekeepers were that nothing could be prepared with these strange contrivances. But only a few days were needed to work a complete conversion." Her pleasure in the advance from fireplace cooking to cookstove contrasts with the younger Caroline Corbin. Writing at the same time, Corbin described "the black beast of her despair. It is the kitchen stove. There it stands, sullen, immovable, inexorable." Dudden, *Serving Women*, 293, 131.

Family production, however, involved more than the kitchen. Thus Bebel sought to teach the family communal ways, hoping to transform housework:

> As the kitchen, so our entire domestic life will be revolutionized . . . central heating and electric lighting plants will do away with all the trouble connected with stoves and lamps. Warm and cold water supply will enable all to enjoy daily baths. Central laundries and drying rooms will assume the washing and drying of clothes. . . . Garbage and all kinds of offal will be carried out of the houses by wastepipes like the water that has been used. In the United States, and in some European cities . . . we already find wonderfully equipped houses in which well-to-do families . . . enjoy [central heating, hot water, electric light, baths, elevators, vacuum cleaners, gas].[21]

A socialist orientation seems not to have brought such materialistic advances to Eastern Europe. By 1975, for example, one-third of the Soviet Union's urban families still shared kitchens and bathrooms with others.[22] The state's priorities were in outer space and distant Africa. The United States never officially sought such sharing. And few American families chose it—however poor they were.

Twentieth-century advances in U.S. household operation were not achieved by central planning any more than by capitalist altruism. They came as housewife after housewife quietly diverted part of rising family incomes to new products. The share of family food spending outside the home rose tenfold.[23] Housewives spent four times as much for kitchen appliances (in constant prices) in 1929 as in 1900. To do so, they drew chiefly on their husband's income. (The percentage of wives in the labor force, 6 percent in 1900, was only 13 percent by 1929.[24]) By 1990, husbands still provided 80 percent of family income. Hence they paid most food-factory profits and wages. Perhaps they did so graciously, perhaps not. If husbands empathized with their wives, they increased their own utility. In any

---

[21] Bebel, *Women and Socialism*, 462–64.

[22] Andrusz, *Housing and Urban Development in the U.S.S.R.* (1984), 179; Andreev, *Housing* (1978), preface, pp. 14, 15.

[23] *Monthly Labor Review* (Mar. 1990): 23.

[24] Compared to 50 percent by 1979. Cf. Lebergott, *The Americans* (1984), 368. Meanwhile, the percentage of urban housewives providing money income to the household by cooking for boarders and lodgers fell from 23 percent in 1900 to 4 percent by 1960. Cf. Lebergott, *American Economy*, 252.

event, housewives changed the world of entrepreneurs, and of workers—to their mutual advantage.

Few American housewives made public statements of their delight in kitchen appliances and canned goods. (Certainly fewer did than men who criticized it all as arrant materialism.) But by 1950, over 95 percent of U.S. families had the facilities of Bebel's "wonderfully equipped houses": central heating, hot water, gas, electric light, baths, and vacuum cleaners. The 1900 housewife had to load her stove with tons of wood or coal each year, fill her lamps with coal oil or kerosene. But electricity ended the "trouble connected with stoves and lamps." Central heating also reduced the housewife's tasks. She no longer had to wash the carbonized kerosene, oil, coal, or wood from clothes, curtains, and walls, nor sweep floors and vacuum rugs as persistently. Automated and mechanical equipment reduced her labor further. How that was accomplished is considered in Part II.

How much did this "outward movement of duties previously performed in the home" cut housewives' work? Their weekly hours for household and family chores fell from 70 in 1900 to 30 by 1981. (Since they increasingly entered the formal labor market, their total work week fell less, from 70 to 48.) Because the massive increase in labor force participation occurred after 1950, the additional income from working wives helps explain the extreme rise in consumption after that date.

That women's work week decreased, despite anecdotes and adjectives to the contrary, is indicated by the following. In 1900, a 72-hour average work week was reported by employers of a sample of Boston area domestic servants. Few employers would have overestimated the length of the work day they made their servants work. What about the average housewife? She had more children to care for than did upper-class ladies with servants. She also spent 10 hours or so tending the gardens, feeding chickens and pigs. A 70-hour average is unlikely to be too low for her. For 1981, a national sample survey by the University of Michigan's Survey Research Center reports 30 hours of housework by the average woman.[25]

---

[25] For 1900: Commonwealth of Massachusetts, *Labor Bulletin*, (1901), 70.

That farm housewives spent about 10 hours weekly on farm chores is indicated by studies summarized in Vanek, "Keeping Busy" (1973), 80–81. Most urban housewives did the same in 1900; as of 1909, half of the families in villages and cities with populations under 10,000, and one-third of those in cities with populations between

For the details in Table 8.1 (above), I began with the 44-hour kitchen work week estimated for both 1910 (by Charlotte Gilman) and 1914 (from a small sample survey).[26] Studies initiated by Hildegarde Kneeland indicate that by 1925–27, the figure had fallen by at least one-third.[27] More precise survey data for 1965 and 1975 report further substantial declines.[28]

By 1975, housewives worked 32 fewer hours each week than in 1910 preparing meals and cleaning up. That figure clearly marks consumer gain. (Whether the quality of meals rose is another matter. Few gourmets describe factory cooking as superior to home cooking.[29])

How much did the American household pay for time saved in meal preparation? As of 1989, about 35 cents per hour.[30] Surely most women considered the saving in their time and sacrifice worth far more than 35 cents an hour. The charge for reducing time spent at that "primal altar, the cookstove," was modest indeed.[31]

10,000 and 50,000, kept poultry and tended vegetable gardens (Mitchell, ed., *Income in the United States* [1922], 2:230).

For 1981: Juster and Stafford, *Times, Goods, and Well-Being*, 317. Their detailed breakdown of time by task in 1975 (p. 171) gives a similar total.

[26] Gilman's 1910 figure is quoted in Lebergott, *American Economy*, 106. The 1914 estimate is in Leeds, *Household Budget* (1914), 39, 43, 48.

[27] Ogburn and Tibbitts, "The Family" (1929), 669.

[28] The 1965 data are in Szalai, ed., *Use of Time* (1972), 691. Juster and Stafford, *Time, Goods, and Well-Being*, 171, report just under ten hours for all women in 1975.

The decline emphasized in Joann Vanek's reading of various surveys apparently took place largely after World War II. See her discussion in Voydanoff, *Work and Family* (1984), 97. Her lower estimates for earlier dates rely on reports for upper-income, upper-status families. Cf. Vanek's "Keeping Busy," 59.

[29] For more recent decades, this generalization may be challenged. Betsy Morris writes: "Whatever the reasons for cooking, many women don't do it as well as their predecessors. . . . When Pillsbury recently removed the directions from its can of corn ('put the corn in a pan on a heated burner'), it received so many calls from puzzled consumers that it reinstated them." Cf. *Wall Street Journal*, July 25, 1985, p. 23.

[30] Value added in food manufacturing rose from 19 percent of value of product in 1899 to 36 percent in 1989. Hence 17 percent (36 percent − 19 percent) of value of product at the later date went for additional processing of raw food. The U.S. Bureau of Economic Analysis estimate for off-premise food purchases in 1989 was $373 billion. Hence additional processing of food to be consumed at home amounted to 17 percent of $373 billion, or $63 billion. Divided among 92.8 million households (as of March 1989), that increased processing came to $13.04 a week. Dividing that figure by hours saved (42 − 10) gives 41 cents an hour. Allowing for depreciation of capital equipment otherwise required in the home—e.g., soup kettles, canning equipment, etc.—would reduce that figure to less than 35 cents.

[31] Food manufacturers' net profit accounted for $1 a week.

By 1932, Viva Boothe concluded that "modern industrial pro-
cesses have robbed the home of almost every vestige of its former
economic function." The remaining work, she noted, "consists
largely of services. In the homes of the well to do labor saving
devices have reduced even the service . . . contribution to a minimum."[32] And women were well along in changing even that.

Grant that millions of housewives gained. Was there some offsetting social cost? As with many other changes, scholarly critics
seemed to go one way as housewives chose another. Robert and
Helen Lynd reached the head of their profession on the basis of their
analyses, including their ominous warning that American culture
"has been hypnotized by the gorged stream of new things to buy."
Among those new things, "electrical equipment for the home" was
specified, including "refrigerators and all but automatic ways to
live."[33] Housewives nonetheless abandoned the good old scrub
board for the automatic washing machine and dryer (below, pp. 112–
16). Not the least factor in reducing laundry time from seven hours a
week to one was the shift from washing 40,000 diapers (for four
children) on scrubboards to washing 1,500 with a washing machine
in 1990.[34]

Specialists in American Studies discovered another cost: "Canned
foods were pleasant amenities, but made life seem curiously in-
substantial . . . tinned meat, condensed milk and other 'modern
conveniences' . . . insulated people from primary experience."[35]
Housewives did indeed relinquish hours of "primary experience" in
cleaning, cutting up, and cooking vegetables, and putting up
pickles, preserves, meat, and fruit. They also insulated themselves
more and more from the "primary experience" of death by typhoid
or botulism. (Canned products proved safer, if sometimes less
tasty.) Few contemporaries had ever voiced feelings of "curious in-
substantiality."[36] And decades later, who complained—housewives
or specialists in American Studies?

[32] Boothe, "Gainfully Employed Women in the Family" (1932), 77.

[33] Lynd and Lynd, *Middletown in Transition* (1937), 46.

[34] Page 112 below estimates 40,000 diapers for four children in 1900. By 1990 there
were only two children in the average family, and 85 percent of diaper changes used
disposable diapers. (For the 85 percent, cf. Arthur D. Little, Inc., *Disposable versus
Reusable Diapers* (March 16, 1990) II-20.)

[35] Lears, "From Salvation to Self-Realization" (1983), 7.

[36] Except perhaps to the alienists of the time.

· C H A P T E R   9 ·

Work, Overwork, and Consumer Spending

SOME AMERICANS sing for their supper. Marian Anderson did, and so does Sherrill Milnes. But most Americans pay for their bread and beer, or caviar and champagne, by other work. They then spend over 90 percent of their incomes for consumption. On what terms did they make that exchange? Figure 9.1 reports how much an hour of work bought in 1900, 1929, 1960, and 1990 (cf. Appendix B). The advance was considerable by almost any standard.

Two factors shaped that escalation in what some have called "the immiseration" of workers under American capitalism. First, hours of work fell, almost 50 percent, for those in the labor force and for women working at home. Second, national productivity soared.

It was, of course, the combined result that chiefly mattered to workers. Focusing merely on hours worked would not yield very useful conclusions. For short work years mean little per se: they are most common when unemployment is widespread. If a nation has a great deal of unemployment, its "work year" can be very short indeed. Few societies force unemployed people to work. (Queen Elizabeth I did not imprison men who failed to work, only those who begged without a license.[1])

Are primitive societies a bright exception to the ancient and worldwide process of exchanging work for food?[2] Does "our cul-

---

[1] Some were hauled into court for counterfeiting one. Cf. Cockburn, ed., *Calendar of Assize Records* (1979), 2586.

[2] For "hunters and gatherers all the people's material wants can usually be easily satisfied." "Hunters have affluent economies, their absolute poverty notwithstanding," according to Sahlins, *Stone Age Economics* (1972), 3, 37. Three of his references to systematic field studies indicating they have "a kind of material plenty" are cited in Schor, *Overworked American*, 178. These include Mountford, ed., *Records* (1960), 2:145–95; Lee and de Vore, *Man the Hunter* (1968), ch. 4; Pospisil, *Kapauku Papuan Economy* (1963); plus an 1825 missionary's account (with no data).

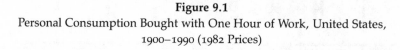

Figure 9.1

Personal Consumption Bought with One Hour of Work, United States, 1900–1990 (1982 Prices)

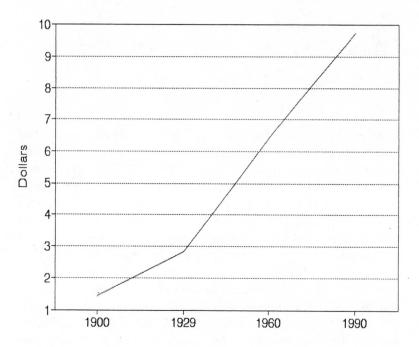

ture" gratuitously ignore the virtue in their simple life when Americans work as many hours as they do for all the goods they consume? One economist has concluded that

> Faith in progress is deep within our culture. We have been taught to believe that our lives are better than those who came before us. The ideology of modern economics suggests that material progress has yielded enhanced satisfaction and well-being. But much of our confidence about our well-being comes from the assumption that our lives are easier than those of earlier generations or other cultures. . . . The lives of so-called primitive peoples are commonly thought to be harsh. . . . In fact, primitives do little work. By contemporary standards we'd have to judge them extremely lazy. If the Kapauku of Papua

work one day, they do no labor on the next. !Kung Bushmen put in only two and a half days per week and six hours per day.[3]

College students searched for a simple life in the sixties by moving to Vermont and Maine. Should they have tried Papua instead, or the African Bush? The question really has nothing to do with modern economics, or its "ideology." It is instead: Would American workers work all day for some nuts and half a pound of raw meat, as adult Bushmen do?

Anthropologists provide no very entrancing vision of what "little work" means among "so-called primitive peoples." Their studies show adult !Kung Bushmen took 12 1/4 hours to gather their daily diet (of 300 nuts, half a pound of meat, and half a pound of vegetables).[4] (The studies allow no time for cooking or cleaning up. Either they ignore women's work or Bushmen ate their meat raw.)

There is, however, a further consideration. The natural simplicity of the Bushmen's aboriginal society "allows for a relatively carefree childhood and adolescence and a relatively unstrenuous old age." To achieve that result, "about 40 percent of the population [i.e., children and the old people] . . . contributed little to the food supplies."[5] Did those carefree youths go hungry? Or the unstrenuous aged starve? If not, someone else gathered their food. Adult Bushmen, therefore, spent about eighteen hours a day, seven days a week, gathering and hunting for food—twelve hours for themselves plus six for their relatives.[6]

Americans could choose equal simplicity, and live on 300 nuts a day, half a pound of raw meat, and some vegetables. But they would need to work only 2 hours a week to do so, given superior U.S.

[3] Schor, *Overworked American*, 10.

[4] Data computed from Lee and de Vore, *Man the Hunter*, 33, 39–40. Lee and de Vore report that it took one man-hour to gather vegetables yielding 240 edible calories, and that the Bushmen consumed 1,260 calories a day from vegetables (of which 87 percent came from 300 nuts). Dividing 1,260 calories by 240 indicates that 5.25 hours were needed to gather nuts and other vegetables. Since one hour of hunting brought in 100 edible calories, Bushmen had to spend 6.9 hours hunting for the 690 calories they consumed in meat each day.

[5] Ibid., 36.

[6] Figuring 12 1/2 hours per person for their own food, divided by (100 percent − 40 percent) for the proportion that gathered and hunted, implies that adults worked 20 hours a day collecting food. If youths and the aged did some work, but also ate less than adults, the adult workday might only be, say, 18 hours.

production methods and division of labor, not the 126 hours the Bushmen must.[7]

The Kapauku Papuans enjoyed the sunny Pacific described by Hearn, Gaugin, and Margaret Mead. Their usual diet included insects, fish, and potatoes. Fishing was "a major responsibility of women." Women also gathered insects for food. On average they caught 2.2 pounds of fish in eight hours.[8] Papuans also worked two hours a day to grow the sweet potatoes a family of four consumed each day.[9] If women spent time cooking potatoes and fish, caring for children and chickens, or making cloth, clothing, fishhooks and digging sticks, their workday far exceeded nine hours.

Americans exchange work for goods on much better terms. They grow 48 times as many sweet potatoes per workday as Papuans.[10] They catch 118 times as much fish as Papuans,[11] and 144 times as

[7] A pound of peanut butter provides far more calories and protein than 300 ngongo nuts (U.S. Department of Agriculture *Composition of Foods*, Handbook no. 8 [1963], 100, compared with nutrient data in Lee and de Vore, *Man the Hunter*, 33, 39). In 1987, peanut butter cost 46 cents a pound, and pork, 83 cents, farm value (U.S. Bureau of the Census, *Statistical Abstract, 1991*, 488). Farm laborers' wages then averaged $4.57 an hour (U.S. Department of Agriculture, *Agricultural Statistics, 1988*, 384). Two hours' work therefore bought over seven pounds of peanut butter and three pounds of pork.

[8] Pospisil, *Kapauku Papuan Economy*, 227, 254: "The average catch of a good fisherwoman [when net fishing for tadpoles] . . . will rarely exceed ¾ of a kilogram." In crayfishing, "a lucky woman may well end up with well over one and a half kilograms a day." If fishing with forked sticks, "an industrious fisherwomen may thus catch as much as half a kilogram of insects and crayfish a day."

An average for all fisherwomen of one kilogram a day would thus be not ungenerous. I take Pospisil's (164) reference to a workday of eight hours for fishing as well.

[9] Pospisil (ibid., 423, 444) reports 138,730 kilograms of sweet potatoes produced during 35,212 hours. Of these, 53,000 were fed to pigs, sold, or unaccounted for. Thus 85,000 kg is "calculated consumption by the 181 Botukebo residents" (pp. 164, 218), or 4.3 pounds of potatoes a day. (Adult male Irishmen consumed 12 pounds of potatoes daily just before the Great Famine. See Mokyr, *Why Ireland Starved* [1983], 7).

[10] U.S. Department of Agriculture, *Gains in Productivity of Farm Labor*, Technical Bulletin 1020 (1950). 70. Unpublished data for 1982–86 from George Douvelis and Rachel Evans (U.S.D.A.-E.R.S.) indicate 26.7 man-hours per 100 bushels. A U.S. bushel of sweet potatoes is 55 pounds.

[11] U.S. Bureau of the Census, *Statistical Abstract, 1991*, 684, indicates 40,187 pounds caught per worker in fishing in 1988. The *Survey of Current Business* (Jan. 1992): 68 indicates an average of 1,230 hours a year worked by people in agricultural services, forestry and fishing. Dividing by Pospisil's eight-hour day gives 154 days

much as Australia's aborigines[12]. Such considerable differences reflect the gap between primitive economies and more complex (capitalist?) ones. Machines and fertilizer shortened U.S. work hours. So did the immense division of labor involved in making all the other goods the nation produces. That is why Papuans worked ten hours a day for their food, while Americans could earn the same diet in ten minutes.

> In the Sandwich islands of Hawaii, men work only four hours a day. And Australian aborigines have similar schedules. The key to understanding why these "stone age peoples" fail to act like us—increasing their work effort to get more things—is that they have limited desires. In the race between wanting and having they have kept their wanting low—and, in this way, ensure their kind of satisfaction.[13]

C. S. Stewart (the nineteenth-century source for the Sandwich Islands), however, offered an altogether different explanation—not renunciation but confiscation. Stewart described extreme taxation and takings from peasants, not their firm belief in Zen Buddhism or Epictetus: "Two-thirds of the proceeds of anything a native brings to the market, unless by stealth, must be given to his chief, and not infrequently the whole is unhesitatingly taken from him."[14] Such confiscation explains the "stone age" trade-off between work and consumer goods far better than Hawaiian values hypothesized a century later.

How did work in the West exchange for consumer goods in earlier generations? Part II of this book compares the United States today with an earlier era, that of our parents and grandparents. But per-

---

per worker, yielding 260 pounds per day—118 times as much as the Papuans (or 75 times as much as a "lucky" Papuan).

12 A median catch of 1.8 pounds per hour is estimated from reports on pp. 150–91 of Mountford, *Records*.

13 Schor, *Overworked American*, 10, 178, citing C. S. Stewart from Sahlins, *Stone Age Economics* (1972), 56.

14 Stewart, *A Residence in the Sandwich Islands* (1839), 117. He adds: "Any increase in stock, or growth of plantation beyond that necessary to meet the usual taxes, is liable to be swept off at any hour, and that, perhaps, without any direct authority from king or chief, but merely at the caprice of someone in their service." Stewart adds that the bulk of the infants "perish by the hands of their parents before attaining the first or second year of their age" (P. 191–92). How much this single report by a missionary (or other brief reports) help describe the values of "stone age" peoples is another matter.

haps it is useful first to refer to a recent, fairly exotic view of levels in a still earlier era. It presumes that English peasants in the Middle Ages worked only 208 days a year (or even 120), but nonetheless achieved an adequate consumption level:

> Our ancestors may not have been rich, but they had an abundance of leisure. . . . Working hours under capitalism, at their peak, increased by more than 50 percent over what they had been in medieval times.[15]

It is, of course, true that the unemployed always worked few hours. Labor had an "abundance of [such] leisure" even before capitalism. But how did workers then keep from starving? Unemployment insurance did not exist, or food stamps, or savings, or more than trivial charitable help. Even those employed presumably earned only a minimum. (Charitable monastic orders were surely more generous than feudal lords. But they provided very modest subsistence for their lay workers. St. Benedict specified one pound of bread a day, while Bernard of Cluny only added a jug of wine at noon and a glass in the evening.[16])

Surmises as to how few days "farm laborers" worked in medieval times do not describe people, for whom we have scant data, but archetypes. Real farm laborers without farm work had to labor at other tasks—to keep from starving. They dug ditches, carried sacks of wheat on their backs, thatched roofs, cleaned out privies, groomed horses, wove textiles, cleared land. Medieval agricultural economies probably produced no more than 10 percent as much food for each hour's work as the United States did in 1990. Productivity in the Middle Ages was so low that England produced only one-tenth as much of its primary food (wheat) per acre even in 1660 as it did in, say, 1860.[17] Such economies could hardly have provided what today's American workers would remotely consider an adequate standard of consumption, or even a "modest" one.

American men devote as much time to television and other recre-

---

[15] Schor, *Overworked American*, 44ff.

[16] These were rates for the famuli, not the monks. Knowles, *Monastic Orders in England* (1949), 462. Constable, *Cluniac Studies* (1980), 333.

[17] For 1250–1400: Allen, "Growth of Labor Productivity" (1988), 117. For 1620: Turner, "Agricultural Productivity in England," (1982), 504. For 1860: Mingay, ed., *Agrarian History of England and Wales* (1989), 138, 1051.

ation as to their jobs.[18] One wonders about calling them "over-worked." If they are "overworked," so have men been in nearly every society since the Garden of Eden. And what of millions of women in Asia and Africa who still work 60 to 70 hours a week, in their homes and on peasant plots? Many millions of men and women, even in Europe, work 40 to 60 hours a week on farms or in nonfarm activities. But Americans today work half as many hours in factory, farm, and store as they did when this century began.[19]

In 1900, nearly half of all American farm workers labored 67 hours a week—10.5 hours every weekday, plus 4 hours on Sundays feeding animals, milking, and so forth. By 1990, the farm average had fallen to two-thirds the 1900 level.

Nonfarm workers in 1900 put in a sixty-hour work week (ten hours a day, six days a week). Forty hours have been standard since 1938, when the U.S. Congress legislated time-and-a-half pay for hours worked beyond forty. By 1990, the average reached 39.3 hours, two-thirds that in 1900.

Domestic servants, and probably most housewives, worked twelve-hour days, seventy-two hours a week in 1900.[20] By 1990, domestic servants put in a third fewer hours, and housewives, a quarter fewer.[21]

By 1990, an hour's work earned six times as much as in 1900. Given that enormous increase in real goods and services, Americans cut their work week substantially.[22]

Few nations have shorter work weeks than the United States.[23]

[18] American women, adding home work and time on the job, do about the same. See Part II, "Recreation," p. 139.

[19] These and other hours data below without source specified are from Appendix B.

[20] Commonwealth of Massachusetts, *Labor Bulletin,* 70. Hours on farms may well have been longer.

[21] U.S. Bureau of Labor Statistics, *Employment and Earnings, 1990* (1991), 20, reports 45.5 hours for servants "on full-time schedules." For housewives not in the labor force in 1965, the Institute of Survey Research reported 44 hours worked, and for all married women, 52 hours. By 1990, increased labor-force participation, and increased reliance on restaurants, prepared foods, etc., might have raised the average to 54.

For 1965: Juster and Stafford, *Time, Goods, and Well-Being,* 148.

[22] Few failed to substitute less work for more goods. In 1980, Current Population Survey counted only 5 percent of those employed as having two jobs.

[23] Hours data are lacking for agriculture, the primary industry in most of the world. Work hours as reported to the International Labour Office for nonfarm

And in none of 130 nations studied by Sumners, Heston, and Kravis does the average worker consume more.[24]

The terms on which U.S. workers exchanged work hours for goods and services thus advanced markedly this century. Less work went hand-in-hand with more consumption. Economic analysis cannot adjudicate whether Americans in 1990 "underworked" and overconsumed. But a simpler judgment is possible. By 1990, workers put in fewer hours a week in the United States than almost any other nation. And they exchanged their labor hours for goods and services at a better rate than workers did in almost any other nation.[25]

---

workers are probably at least as high as for farm workers. International Labour Office, *Yearbook of Labour Statistics 1991* (1992), 723ff., shows only Belgium with a shorter nonfarm work week than the United States. A similar conclusion is likely for the work year of all its workers.

[24] See the 1985 estimates in Summers and Heston, "New Set of International Comparisons," table 3. Kuwait's distinctly higher per capita GNP in 1985 does not, however, demonstrate that consumption per worker exceeded that for the United States, given the special role of the ruling group. I assume that none of the half-dozen centrally planned economies would have higher per capita consumption if one could allow for services and other conceptual differences.

[25] "Almost," because the validity of expenditure estimates and hours data in many other nations is more questionable than data for the United States.

· CHAPTER 10 ·

More Goods: The Twentieth Century

If, as Demetrius says, you want to make Pythocles rich, you must not
increase his money but decrease his greed.

—Poggius Bracciolini, in Phyllis Gordon, *Two Renaissance Book Hunters*

FEW ARTICLES in the economist's creed outrage noneconomists more
than the pure, imperturbable belief that human wants are insatiable.
Yet that belief has long been shared by other disciplines. America's
most distinguished psychologist (and philosopher) observed, with
incomparable zest, that

> Man's preeminence over the brutes lies . . . solely in the number and
> in the fantastic and unnecessary character of his wants, physical,
> moral, aesthetic and intellectual. Had his whole life not been a quest
> for the superfluous, he would never have established himself as inex-
> pugnably as he has done.[1]

One of the founders of sociology, his works still read in college
classrooms, saw that

> our needs are unlimited . . . so far as they depend on the individual
> alone. . . . [How can anyone] determine the quantity of well-being,
> comfort or luxury legitimately to be craved by a human being? Nothing
> in man's organic or psychological constitution sets a limit to such ten-
> dencies. . . . It is not human nature which can assign the limits neces-
> sary to our needs. . . . The more one has the more one wants, since
> satisfactions received only stimulate instead of filling needs.[2]

[1] James, *The Will to Believe* (1979), 104.
[2] Durkheim, *Suicide* (1952), 247–49.

Social scientists thus echoed centuries of comment by moralists. William Penn had declared it "truly a reproach to a man that he knows not when he hath enough; when to leave off; when to be satisfied."[3] Or Jeremy Taylor: "Your desires will enlarge beyond the present possession, so long as all the things of this world are unsatisfying; if therefore you suffer them to extend beyond the measures of necessity or moderated conveniency, they will still swell."[4] Or Machiavelli: "Nature has created men so that they desire everything, but are unable to attain it."[5] Or Samuel Johnson: "We desire, we pursue, we obtain, we are satiated; we desire something else, and begin a new pursuit."[6]

Yet when economists repeat (in Marshall's words) that "human wants and desires are countless," they infuriate noneconomists—and some economists.[7] As one prophet of the 1960s fumed,

> Founders of the "dismal science" believed that we could never achieve abundance. [But] abundance has arrived. We can produce more than $460 billion in additional goods and services with our existing capacity.[8]

That mountain of goods, he assured us, could never find buyers. The "spectre of saturated markets" therefore confronted the nation.

[3] Penn, "No Cross, No Crown, a Discourse" (1726), 1: 341, ch. 13. "The desire of goods . . . is grounded only upon opinion."

[4] Taylor, *Rules and Exercises*, 45.

[5] "Desire thus always being greater than the faculty of acquiring, discontent with what they have and dissatisfaction with themselves results from it." Machiavelli, *Discourses*, (1975), ch. 37.

[6] Bate, *Samuel Johnson* (1977), 330.

[7] "Neoclassical theory takes for granted that needs have always been infinite. Therefore their analysis must ignore the fact that capitalist production is at the root of insatiable consumers." Matthaei, *Economic History of Women in America* (1982), 363.

De Sismondi, from whom Marx quoted so often, saw production outrunning demand: "Workers, thanks to their advancing productivity, can earn as much from six hours work as they once gained for twelve. What guarantee is there that the[ir] taste for the pleasures of life . . . will increase precisely as a result of the increase in labor [productivity]?" Since "each successive object of luxury provides a less lively pleasure, still will one be ready to procure it by a great sacrifice?" Will "the laborer . . . agree to expose himself to the intense sunshine of midday, to the ice of winter" . . . for the pleasure of wearing an embroidered silk shirt . . . and a silk mantle, while driving his car?" After all, "by depriving himself of such bagatelles he can get up later, fatigue himself less, . . . without a care for the corresponding output of the manufacturer." De Sismondi, *Nouveaux principes d'economie politique* (1827), 2:395–96.

[8] Theobald, *Free Men and Free Markets* (1962), 20.

Many writers therefore rejected the bland "assertion that American[s] would spend . . . income[s] accruing to them at all levels of business activity. . . . We have no such assurance, and never have had."[9] Yet despite such magisterial judgments, real consumption (per capita) actually rose in the quarter-century after that warning—by fifty percent. And gave no sign of halting.

Has anyone—government agency or learned committee—determined "the" judicious level for expenditure, beyond which lies excess, superfluity, and waste? "Moderate" lists have frequently been specified, presumably for moderate people. But they have all gone with the wind. In 1920, the U.S. Bureau of Labor Statistics specified what the average worker's family required "for health and decency." Its catalogue was fascinating. It certainly sought that eminently Victorian goal, "decency." For it included a lemon squeezer, and a butter knife; and it declared that every "workingman's family" required a domestic servant, every week.[10] (Did those servants, in turn, require their own servants?) That family also needed to consume twenty-three pounds of canned peaches, and two pounds of canned pineapple. (Had Hawaii then been a state, would "health and decency" have argued for more pineapple?)

In 1947, the U.S. Department of Labor chose another learned budget committee, to determine the goods needed for "efficiency" and "the maintenance of self-respect and the respect of others."[11] Fortunately, partisan politicians never questioned the irony of the Nixon Administration specifying, throughout its career, what Americans needed for "the maintenance of self-respect and the respect of others."

In 1980, the Bureau of Labor Statistics directly asked American families: "What would be the smallest income . . . your family would need to make ends meet?" It rediscovered Durkheim: the more one has, the more one wants. Families with incomes below $5,000 felt that $7,822 a year would suffice.[12] Families with incomes from $5,000 to $10,000 felt $10,139 was needed. Those who averaged $44,837 knew that almost three times that sum was absolutely neces-

[9] Bernstein, *Price of Prosperity* (1962), 10.

[10] Bureau of Applied Economics, *Standards of Living* (1920), 1.

[11] U.S. Bureau of Labor Statistics, *Workers' Budgets in the United States*, Bulletin 927 (1948).

[12] U.S. Bureau of Labor Statistics, *Consumer Expenditure Survey: Interview Survey, 1984*, Bulletin 2267, (1986), 8.

sary. Which group had discovered the true, the necessary, income minimum? Going to the people apparently gave answers quite as ambiguous as the science of learned committees.

Surely the American standard of material living in 1900 was adequate when compared to almost any other nation. It far exceeded that of common history. Yet it continued to rise. Even in the pit of the Great Depression (1932), real expenditure per capita exceeded that in 1900—by 17 percent. In 1943, though the United States was supplying armies on three continents and civilian goods were rationed, workers' real expenditure ran 35 percent above 1932. They gained a further 128 percent by the "Reagan depression" year of 1982.[13]

Such increases far exceeded the amount needed to bring every poor person up to average consumption in 1900. Indeed, as already noted, Thorstein Veblen held that "something like one-half of the actual output is consumed in wasteful superfluities" as early as 1921.[14] Real output (per capita) subsequently rose more than 250 percent. GNP in 1990 must therefore have consisted chiefly of Veblenian "superfluities."

Why did so great a further increase take place? Mere reference to materialism or capitalism is not sufficient. For one thing, the consumption (per capita) of some products fell. And those which gained did so at amazingly different rates. To understand the aggregate rise in consumption, one must go further. Part II of this book, therefore, considers the varied impulses and desires that increased each major expenditure group, making it possible to point the finger of scorn at some, and to understand the motivations of others.

---

[13] Appendix Table A. Objections to the price deflator used for 1940–45 are reviewed by Higgs, "Wartime Prosperity" (1992), 49ff. As Higgs notes (p. 50), real per capita consumption per civilian rose.

[14] Veblen, *Engineers and the Price System*, 12.

·PART TWO·

MAJOR TRENDS, 1900-1990

It is a fine and a great thing to know how to earn money,

but a finer and greater

one, to know how to spend it with moderation,

and where it is seemly.

—PAOLO DA CERTALDO, fourteenth century

ONE OF Rome's great open-air markets has been described as a "fantasia of human commodities, wearable, edible, combustible, aesthetic, hygienic, and vehicular, the gamut of man's utensils, and all the push and pleasure of life that went into their changing hands."[1]

Such consumption fantasias can be summed into one series for total expenditure. But doing so reveals little about why consumption rose or fell, or about what desires were at work, what needs were served. The series includes a range of delights as wide as those provided by Al Capp's famous Schmoo—equally delicious baked, fried, or roasted; could amuse infants or jack up flat tires; etc.

Why did American consumption take the path it did in the twentieth century? No single explanatory factor emerges from the cacophony of consumer desires. Breakfast at 7 A.M. is sought because of one set of desires; gasoline is bought at 8 A.M. thanks to a second; a compact disc at 10 A.M. because of another; a dozen roses at 5 P.M. because of another. Ten more items are bought by midnight in response to still others. Only by considering separate categories can one trace why the grand total for "consumer expenditure" changed as it did between 1900 and 1990.

Part II of this book addresses that inquiry. It traces, in turn, the sequence of expansion shown in Table II.1.

[1] Clark, *Rome and a Villa* (1952), 136.

Table II.1

U.S. Consumer Spending, 1900–1990, Per Capita

(1987 dollars)

	1900	1990	Percent gain
Food	1,178	1,814	54%
Tobacco	69	129	87
Alcohol	169	249	47
Clothing	272	920	238
Shoes	79	113	43
Housing	256	1,898	641
Fuel	40	96	140
Domestic service	37	212	473
Household operation	467	1,621	247
Appliances	5	108	2,060
Water	20	87	335
Electricity	0	265	
Health expenditures	172	1,928	1,021
Medicines	8	195	2,338
Medical personnel	143	724	406
Hospitals	19	871	4,484
Transport	143	1,621	1,034
Automobiles	3	680	2,166
Public transport	138	133	−4
Recreation	83	1,026	1,136
Religion & welfare	131	298	128

Source: Appendix A.

· F O O D ·

[A world] where we all . . . with great gusto and dispatch,

stow a portion of victuals finally and irretrievably

into the bag which contains us.

—R. L. Stevenson, *Virginibus puerisque*

By 1900, Americans typically spent more on food than citizens of almost any other nation. Few ate as enormously as Diamond Jim Brady, as lavishly as Mrs. Potter Palmer. But they consumed more food than the English, the Dutch, the French, or the Swedes. And often fresher food, a better diet.

It therefore seemed unlikely that Americans would spend still more as the century wore on. After all, "the capacity of the human stomach was limited." Indeed, from 1900 to 1990, the amount of food the typical American ate per year fell by about 350 pounds. Caloric and protein intake changed little (see Tables II.4, II.2).[2]

Nonetheless, per capita spending for food rose by over three-quarters between 1900 and 1990.[3] How much of that was necessary? Two engineers have contrasted actual consumption with the cost of an adequate diet (Table II.3). From their calculations, one can account for the entire dollar difference: more food away from home, and more meat, bakery products, and delicacies.

Good health did not require buying food away from home, for lunch pails long provided adequate meals to workers and students. Moreover, restaurant meals cost twice as much as home-prepared food (given the usual 100 percent mark-up for purchasing, inventorying, and preparing food). Americans nonetheless increased their share of total food expenditures on purchased food from perhaps 5 percent in 1900 to 30 percent by 1987.[4] The decline in home

[2] Only a small caloric and nutrient change occurred from 1897–1901 to 1909, according to Barger and Landsberg, *American Agriculture* (1942), 151.

[3] In real terms, 83 percent in per capita.

[4] In 1900 there were 107,000 waiters (U.S. Bureau of the Census, *Occupations, 1900*

Table II.2

Changes in U.S. Consumption
of Nutrients between 1910 and 1989

Nutrient	Change
Calories	+2%
Fats	+34
Proteins	+1
Calcium	+7
Vitamin A	+36
Thiamine	+31
Asorbic acid	+12

Source: U.S. Department of Agriculture, Statistical Bulletin 702; and idem, *Food Consumption, Prices, Expenditures,* Statistical Bulletin 825.

Note: This table omits the increase for nutrients in vitamin and mineral products consumed by 43 percent of children and 36 percent of adults (as of 1986).

cooking was surely one reason. But workers and their families also used rising income to indulge their taste for different food, in different surroundings, with no cooking and washing up.

The second reason why food spending exceeded the "health minimum" was meat. "According to Vauban, Bossuet and Lagrange—three names illustrious in war, religion, and science—that country must be considered the most prosperous in which the inhabitants are able to have the largest ratio of meat for their food."[5] There was little question to which country this writer referred.

[1904], 7). I assume waiters were 45 percent of all employment in "eating and drinking places," as in 1940 (U.S. Bureau of the Census, *Occupational Characteristics, 1940* [1943], table 1a). In 1900, male heads of families who were waiters earned about $475 yearly (U.S. Commissioner of Labor, *Eighteenth Annual Report* [1903], 264). Assuming that the lower earnings of waitresses offset the higher ones of cooks and proprietors, I take $500 as average income to the 200,000 people engaged in the trade. An equal $100 million for raw food, plus rent and light, would give about $250 million—or 5 percent of my food total (off- and on-premise).

[5] Mulhall, *Progress of the World* (1880), 13. A century later, of course, other experts were denouncing meat consumption.

Table II.3

U.S. Family Food Expenditure, 1972–73

	Necessary for health	Actual
Food away from home	$0	$440
Bakery products	0	104
Poultry	0	54
Fruits	0	79
Sugar and sweets	0	35
Beverages	0	88
Seasonings and prepared foods	0	96
Meat	7	325
Subtotal	$7	$1,221
Milk products	$156	$160
Vegetables	122	89
Cereals	348	35
Fats	80	31
Fish and seafood	42	32
Subtotal	$748	$347
Total	$755	$1,568

Sources: Necessary for health: Lewis and Peng, "The Three-Consideration Diet Revisited" (1977), table 6; their National Academy of Sciences-National Research Council daily allowances were multiplied by average prices in Atlanta. Actual: U.S. Bureau of Labor Statistics, *Consumer Expenditure Survey,* Bulletin 1992, table 1. Minor items omitted.

As an astonished traveler wrote of the United States (in 1756), "Even in the humblest or poorest houses no meals are served without a meat course."[6] European migrants were delighted to discover that in the United States, "every day is like Christmas day for meat."[7] (In France, meat consumption averaged a quarter of the U.S. level.[8]) Eating meat rather than vegetables did require far more

[6] Mittelberger, *Journey to Pennsylvania,* reprint (1960), 49.

[7] Quoted in Potter, *To the Golden Door* (1960), 130.

[8] Toutain, *La Consommation alimentaire en France* (1971), 1947 for France, and Lebergott, *The Americans* 70. The Russian level, even by the end of the nineteenth

land for feed crops, and nine times more energy.[9] Yet Americans increased the meat in their diet, not potatoes and bread.

Their preference was not exceptional.[10] Anthropologists, looking at experience back to the Pleistocene, have noted that "people world-wide eat meat . . . when they . . . have enough food or enough wealth," "eating cereals and tubers only when they must."[11] And a leading English Marxist has found it reasonable "to take meat consumption as a criterion of standard of living" of the working class.[12] For centuries, cheap meat constituted one of America's attractions. When the incomes of other nations rose after World War II, their meat consumption likewise soared: by 50 to 80 grams (per capita) in Austria, France, West Germany, Greece, Italy, the Netherlands, Spain, Switzerland, the United Kingdom, and Canada; by 30 to 40 grams in Japan, Taiwan, and Yugoslavia. Successive meat riots in Poland, and persistent imports of food grains by the Soviet Union (to fatten cattle), suggest that citizens in centrally planned economies evidenced an equally powerful desire for meat. The similarity of preferences, and expenditure behavior, in Western and Eastern economies emphasizes the wide gap that separates (a) a host of publicists who urge growing more grain, to feed still more people, from (b) the millions who want more meat, in both socialist and capitalist nations. (Imaginative emphases on the rising consumption of fish mask the simple fact that fish consumption rose less than 5 pounds over 90 years, while poultry consumption rose 30 pounds in three decades.[13])

---

century, and including lard and poultry, was one-tenth that in the United States. Hemardinquer, ed., *Pour une histoire d'alimentation* (1970), 73–74, 196.

[9] In 1936, a consumer interest group began publishing *Consumer Reports*. Its second issue published an article by "a physician" urging Americans to consume more meat. But in a few decades other advisers volunteered an urgently negative view. See among others, Lappe, *Diet for a Small Planet* (1975). The energy figures are from Steinhart and Steinhart, "Energy Use in the U.S. Food System," (1974), 307–16.

[10] Two thousand years ago, the "administrators of the great provinces [of China] were termed 'meat eaters.'" Quoted in Braudel, *Capitalism and Material Life* (1967), 68.

[11] Cohen, *Food Crisis in Prehistory* (1977), 146.

[12] Hobsbawn, "The British Standard of Living" (1964), 111.

[13] Czechoslovakia increased meat prices by 30 percent "a few days after the Polish debacle of June 1976" (in which Poland tried to limit the soaring demand for meat by price rises). W. Brus, "Political System and Economic Efficiency" (1980), 48.

"The unremitting praise of virtually everything piscan . . . over the past thirty years . . . [meant] T-bone and porterhouse have given way to . . . salmon, swordfish and tuna. Overall fish consumption is up 50% since 1960." *Time* (June 29,

The change to meat inevitably brought a corresponding decline in its substitutes. Diets in the West had long consisted largely of grain and vegetables. As affluence spread, the United States broke with that tradition. Americans moved away from inherited European farm diets—heavy in grain and potatoes. They cut their per capita flour, meal, and potato consumption by 224 pounds from 1910 to 1989.

The third great excess expenditure was for bakery products. Bread had been central to the human diet for a thousand years. It remained central. (How many humans had petitioned: "Give us this day our daily bread"?) The housewife in 1900 still baked over half a ton of bread a year (the equivalent of 1,400 loaves).[14] She spent well over an hour every week baking bread, plus a second hour for cakes, cookies, etc.[15] Year after year, housewives shifted more such work to the factory. (That shift can hardly be attributed to the charms of Wonder Bread. Or the price rise from a nickel to a dollar a loaf.)

The fourth excess was spending for sugar and sweets—directly or in bakery products. Sugar had been formidably attractive even in primitive cultures (see Chapter 3). It remained one of the delights of civilization. The prospect of cheap sugar was a major inducement for Europe to introduce slavery into the Caribbean ("the sugar islands"). More recently, physicians warned that sugar consumption should be cut. It harmed human health more consistently than any other item regularly in the diet. But even infants still manifested an overwhelming preference for sugar. And socialist sugar producers in Cuba accepted such medical advice no more willingly than capitalist producers in East Germany or Utah.

1992): 70. Fish consumption did increase by 4 pounds—while poultry increased 30 pounds and red meat fell by 15 to 16 pounds per capita. Cf. U.S. Department of Agriculture, *Food Consumption, Prices, and Expenditures, 1968–89*, Statistical Bulletin 825 (1991), 29.

[14] Or their equivalent in rolls, etc. Lebergott, *American Economy*, 294. One hundred pounds of flour made 150 pounds of bread according to data from Commonwealth of Massachusetts, *Labor Bulletin*, 78–79. In 1910, U.S. army bakers were expected to make 160 pounds of bread. (U.S. Subsistence Department, *Manual for Army Bakers, 1910* [1910], 44,49). In more recent years, civilian bread production averaged 154 pounds of bread from 100 pounds of flour (U.S. Department of Agriculture, *Price Spreads*, Miscellaneous Publication 576 (1947), 137–39).

[15] Rowe, "Time Necessary to Do Work," (1917), 571. The Massachusetts study cited in note 14 reported that 39 minutes were needed to bake two loaves (2.6 lbs.). Given the size of the average oven, 27 pounds would have required several bakings, and well over one hour.

A fifth major change came with the disappearance of inferior foods. When the century began, 95 percent of all American families used lard. By 1980, only 9 percent did. The proportion using salt pork fell from 83 percent to 4 percent; corn meal, from 90 percent to 22 percent; molasses, from 69 percent to 2 percent.[16] (In time, Europe followed the American move away from such "inferior" foods.[17]) The significant rise in consumption of preferred foods, and fall in inferior goods, can be summarized easily as shown in Table II.4.

Table II.4
Change in U.S. Food Consumption
between 1900 and 1989
(pounds per capita)

Food	Change
Sugar and syrup	+84
Meat	
Red meat	−35
Poultry	+46
Flour and cereal	−144
Potatoes	−105
Dairy products (fat content)	−199
Fish	+3

Source: See Table II.2.

Finally, spending rose and housework declined as vegetable preparation changed. No doubt good fresh vegetables were far superior to canned, or even frozen ones. But the ecstasies of quality required home chores. Potatoes had to be washed, trimmed, scraped, and cooked. So did beets, carrots, and corn. In 1900, housewives also put

[16] Lebergott, *American Economy*, 294.

[17] In a mere twenty years, per capita wheat intake fell by about one-third in Austria, Denmark, Finland, France, West Germany, Ireland, the Netherlands, Norway, Sweden, Switzerland, and the United Kingdom. Potato consumption fell as much as 50 percent in West Germany and Denmark. Food and Agriculture Organization, *Production Yearbook, 1971* (1971), table 136, p. 135. I compare data for 1948–50 with the figures for 1969–70. Comparable data for later years have not been published by the F.A.O., but the figures on meat production and imports indicate a continuation of the trend.

them up in jars for winter use, washing, scalding, cooking, and pouring paraffin seals. Such chores were increasingly handed over to factory workers in the twentieth century (see Table II.5).[18]

Table II.5
Vegetables and Fruits:
Fresh Consumption as a Percentage of
Total, United States, 1910–89

Year	Vegetables	Fruits
1910	93%	98%
1930	87	86
1950	79	71
1970	70	67
1980	72	64
1989	79	64

Sources: For 1910–50: U.S. Department of Agriculture, *Food Consumption, Prices, and Expenditures,* Agricultural Economics Report 138, table 6.

For 1970–89: Idem, *Food Consumption, Prices, and Expenditures, 1968–89,* Statistical Bulletin 825, table 2. For vegetables, however, continuity with earlier data required inclusion of garden vegetables. I therefore used idem, *Food Consumption, Prices, and Expenditures,* Statistical Bulletin 702, table 2, for 1970 and 1980, and then extrapolated by the 1980–89 change in Bulletin 825.

[18] Since the U.S.D.A. figures refer to pounds of vegetables consumed, it is likely that the share of spending for processed vegetables and fruits rose even more. For example, asparagus, among the more expensive vegetables, was canned in volume long before potatoes were canned or frozen.

· TOBACCO ·

A cigarette is the perfect type of a perfect pleasure. It is exquisite, and
it leaves one unsatisfied. What more can one want?

—OSCAR WILDE *The Story of Dorian Gray*

Over the centuries, humans have smoked a considerable variety of
materials. But tobacco was a luxury in the West prior to the nineteenth century. (As late as the 1890s, the English upper classes ban-
ished smokers to rooms specially built for the purpose.[19]) New machinery, however, began to provide lower-cost cigarettes in the
1880s. As prices fell, markets widened. Ministers of finance in a
dozen nations then discovered a wonderful new fiscal resource.
France and Russia set up state distribution monopolies, thus guar-
anteeing a maximum tax yield from smoking. Later, Soviet Russia
and the Communist nations began state production, deriving the
full monopoly profit possible from state production for a highly
inelastic demand. The U.S. government, however, did not propa-
gate the smoking habit.[20] It left that to the market, and to forces
described by Freud and the newer psychology.

Table II.6 indicates how cigarette consumption escalated in the
United States. The greatest percentage rise occurred between 1910
and 1920. Over 95 percent of the men sent overseas in the American
Expeditionary Forces used tobacco.[21]

[19] Before 1895, Lord Armstrong, one of the wealthiest men in the United Kingdom, and builder of warships for the nations of the world, "had no smoking room;
and it was curious to see a row of Japanese or other foreign naval officers, in charge of
some war vessel building at the famous Elswick works, sitting in a row on the low
wall outside [their] front door, puffing away for all they were worth." Quoted in
Girouard, *Victorian Country House* (1979).

[20] If anything it reduced it. Beginning with Henry Wallace, the parity program
increased the price of tobacco land. That in turn tended to keep up the price of
tobacco, and keep down its consumption.

[21] U.S. War Department, *Annual Report, 1918*, vol. 1 (1919), 304.

Table II.6
Cigarettes Consumed per Capita,
United States, 1880–1989

Year	N
1880	11
1890	40
1900	51
1910	106
1920	454
1929	998
1940	1,435
1950	2,596
1960	2,827
1970	2,843
1980	3,091
1989	2,900

Sources: U.S. Bureau of the Census, *His-torical Statistics*, 689–90; and idem, *Statistical Abstract, 1991*, 755.

Table II.7 locates the United States in the international smoking league. Advertising and private profits versus state ownership play an obscure role, as indicated by the small difference between averages for Sweden and East Germany, for Romania and Australia. Income and tobacco consumption by country correlate hardly at all.[22] Long-continued national habits are evident in the extreme figure for Bulgaria. The United States, with its combination of high incomes, relatively low prices, advertising, and Surgeon General's reports, proves to be one of the higher users of tobacco, though not in the peak group.[23]

[22] $R^2 = 0.16$. Consumption data for 1977 are correlated with per capita real product figures for 1977 from Summers, Kravis, and Heston, "International Comparison of Real Product and Its Composition" (1980), 63–66.

[23] A more precise comparison would, of course, require allowance for the importation of manufactured tobacco products. Given the importance of smuggling in nations with heavy cigarette taxation it would be difficult to make such an adjusted estimate for most nations on this list.

Table II.7
Tobacco Consumption per Capita,
by Nation, 1990
(pounds per year)

Nation	Consumption (pounds)
Bulgaria	22.4
Netherlands	11.7
Portugal	14.6
Turkey	7.7
Belgium-Lux.	7.1
Denmark	7.0
Switzerland	7.0
UNITED STATES	6.1
Yugoslovia	5.1
West Germany	4.9
Spain	4.9
United Kingdom	4.3
Hungary	4.2
Italy	4.2
Greece	3.9
Czechoslovakia	3.2
Romania	3.2
Poland	3.0
France	2.8
Sweden	2.7
East Germany	2.4
Norway	2.3
U.S.S.R.	1.8
Japan	1.4
Argentina	1.3
India	1.1
Pakistan	1.0
Canada	0.9
Australia	0.6

Source: Production data (from the Food and Agriculture Organization, *Production Yearbook, 1990,* table 82) plus imports net of exports (from F.A.O., *Trade Yearbook, 1977,* table 98) divided by population (from F.A.O., *Production Yearbook, 1990,* table 3).

· ALCOHOL ·

Most of the money apparently spent for liquor is really spent to carry on
the system of the State, thereby relieving unpatriotic (and extremely
ungrateful) teetotallers of their just quota.

—GEORGE SAINTSBURY, *On a Cellar Book*

Holy writ assures us that strong liquors go back to Noah. Since then,
moral judgments on drinking have altered expenditure even more
decisively than income or price changes. For example, the modest
installation of a Massachusetts minister one Sunday in 1729 required
302 gallons of cider, wine, brandy, and rum.[24] But attitudes changed
and Prohibition arrived. By 1928, Al Smith's desire to end Prohibition helped defeat his bid for the presidency. Yet only fifty years
later, the U.S. Department of Justice was helping to sue a college
that refused to retain an alcoholic worker.[25]

By 1900, U.S. consumption ran well below that in Britain (and
probably Europe as well; see Table II.8). American drinking patterns
were originally set by the Europeans who dominated migration to
the United States. London employers had long made a practice of
paying wages in taverns, much of which the workers then diverted
to "treating" their mates.[26] As a best-selling British novelist described his youth:

> Glasgow on a Saturday afternoon in the first January of this century
> was a sight completely incredible today. Once we had emerged from
> the respectable surroundings of Kelvinside the streets became a phan-
> tasmagoria of drunkenness. Many men and even a few women were
> lying blind drunk in the gutters; others were staggering about singing;

---

[24] Cist, *Cincinnati Miscellany* (1845), 1:200.
[25] *Wall Street Journal*, August 29, 1978.
[26] M. Dorothy George, *London Life in the Eighteenth Century* (1964), 292–300.

Table II.8

Weekly Alcohol Consumption per Adult Male,
United States and United Kingdom, 1900

	United States	United Kingdom
Shots of hard liquor (1 oz.)	11	10
Glasses of beer (12 oz.)	12	24
Glasses of wine (6 oz.)	0.6	34

Source: See Appendix A.

Note: About 33 gallons per capita were consumed in the United Kingdom, compared to 32 gallons in France, 31 in Germany, and 15 in the United States. See Jeans, ed., *American Industrial Conditions and Competition* (1902), 61.

some were fighting. I suppose the same scene might have been witnessed in the Old Town of Edinburgh at this date.[27]

Treating never really developed in the United States, despite British tradition and immigration. American workers had seen the devastation in workers' lives caused by liquor. And American employers had seen the lower productivity and higher accident rates linked to hard drinking. They, too, sought to cut liquor consumption.[28] For decades membership of the Women's Christian Temperance Union grew as wives and mothers tried to end the human sacrifice. Yet U.S. alcohol consumption changed little from 1900 to 1920.

Prohibition started its long term decline in alcohol consumption (see Table II.9). In 1900, U.S. adult drinkers consumed about 23 drinks a week—11 of hard liquor, 12 glasses of beer, plus about half a glass of wine for a chaser. Alcohol consumption declined spectacularly by 1990. Marijuana usage eventually spread concurrently among the young. Cocaine, heroin, and crack were enjoyed by a small group (less than 5 percent of adults). None of this, however,

[27] Mackenzie, *My Life and Times, Octave 3* (1964), 41.

[28] That "Ideal Communities" built by employers forbade saloons created a worker grievance. Cf. Jeans, ed., *American Industrial Conditions and Competition* (1902), 61, 572, for a description of Vandergrift in Pennsylvania. Jeans notes that "at many of the principal works beer is not allowed on the premises under any conditions." Doing so eliminated "the worship of Saint Monday, and the irregularity of the employment of machinery and plant which that worship involves."

reduced the 54 percent who consumed some alcohol.[29] But the resurgence of a Women's Christian Temperance Union seemed remote.

Table II.9

U.S. Alcohol Consumption,
1900 and 1989
(gallons per adult drinker)

Type of alcohol	1900	1989	Change (%)
Spirits	4.7	2.1	−55
Beer	58.8	33.7	−43
Wine	1.4	3.0	+114

Source: Gallons per capita from U.S. Bureau of the Census, *Statistical Abstract, 1900*, 354, and idem, *Statistical Abstract, 1990*, 125.

Note: In 1887, about half of the adult population (48 percent) drank alcohol (see Appendix B below). In 1988, about 56 percent of those aged 18 and over drank (U.S. Bureau of the Census, *Statistical Abstract, 1991*, 12, and idem, *Historical Statistics*, 2:15).

The estimate for 1900 here differs somewhat from that in Rohrabaugh, *Alcoholic Republic* (1979), table A1.2, because he uses population aged 15 and older rather than aged 21 and older, as I do. (See his "Estimated U.S. Alcoholic Beverage Consumption" (1976); 359. He chooses age 15 on the basis of studies by Jellinek for the 1930s. For 1900, I prefer the U.S. Treasury percentage for 1886 (in Appendix B below).

[29] Percentages are from U.S. Bureau of the Census, *Statistical Abstract, 1991*, 121. 1989 data are from U.S. Department of Agriculture, Statistical Bulletin 825, 21.

· CLOTHING ·

Young women of such birth . . . naturally regarded frippery as the

ambition of a huckster's daughter. Then [too] well-bred

Economy . . . made show in dress the first item to be deducted when

any margin was required for expenses more distinctive of rank.

—GEORGE ELIOT, *Middlemarch*

Critics of American life have punctuated their remarks on "gim-mickry," "vague inanities," and "pseudo-innovations" by forceful attacks on "fashion goods" and "clothing fads."[30] Where do their fretful objections lead? As Sir John Hicks noted, "Everything that Professor Galbraith [has] said about pseudo-innovation" applies to dress design. Are "we therefore committed to . . . putting the female population into warm and comfortable uniforms?"[31]

Clothing fads are not new. Nor are objections to such worldly indulgence. Under Edward IV, common laborers, as well as servants and artificers, were forbidden to wear cloth worth more than two shillings a yard.[32] And indeed, resources would be conserved if everyone worked in cheap comfortable uniforms. They did so during Mao's "blue ant" period in China. But a demand for fashion goods nonetheless appeared in China—despite the lack of advertising, concentration camps, and forceful policy guidance from the rulers. By the 1980s, official government fashion models turned and pirouetted, displaying the newest styles. Such "inefficiency" and "waste" even in a centrally planned economy can hardly be attri-

---

[30] Mishan, "Wages of Growth," 86. Cf. also Robert Lekachman: "Corporate marketing and advertising strategies engender public demand for all sorts of dubious toys, trinkets, beauty aids, guides to health, and clothing fads." *New Leader*, June 14, 1982.

[31] Galbraith, "Technology in the Developed Economy" (1968), 49. Galbraith asserts that the consumer discovers his "needs" in neoclassical economics, but "persuasion" by "the technostructure" creates "needs" in today's real world.

[32] Fortescue, *De laudibus legum Angliae* (1942), 190.

buted to anything but consumer desires for sheer variety and "use-less" fashion.

How does U.S. experience accord with this record? The U.S. "technostructure" expanded during the twentieth century, we are told. Did fashion shows and advertising increase spending for clothing? Apparently not. For the share allocated to such vanity actually declined in the twentieth century (see Table II.10).

Table II.10
Share of Personal Expenditures
Spent for Clothing (Plus Jewelry),
United States, 1900–1990

Year	Share
1900	13.7%
1910	13.8
1920	17.1
1929	14.5
1940	12.5
1950	12.4
1960	9.9
1970	9.0
1980	7.0
1990	6.4

Source: Appendix A.

The U.S. share for clothing had peaked in 1916 as the last great wave of immigrants to the United States finally replaced their native dress with American clothing. A brief restocking boom followed the end of World War I. Clothing's share then declined remorselessly, through prosperity in the 1920s, depression in the 1930s, war in the 1940s. It continued its fall during the 1950s and 1960s—though that decline was then attributed to a search for simplicity by students in sandals and jeans. They merely continued the twentieth-century trend, however.

The decline did mask a rising share for women's clothing (see Table II.11). A probable reason for the rise was a change in the economic role of women. In 1900, two-thirds of clothing purchases

Table II.11

Percentage of Total Clothing
Expenditures Spent for Women,
United States, 1899–1990

Year	Women's Share
1899	38%
1909	48
1919	52
1929	61
1939	60
1949	64
1959	65
1969	64
1980	65
1990	66

Source: For 1899–1919: Shaw, *Value of Commodity Output since 1869* (1947), 115–17; for 1929: Kuznets, *Commodity Flow and Capital Formation* (1938), 84; for 1980 and 1990: unpublished U.S. Bureau of Economic Analysis revision, May 1992.

Note: The proportions shown do not include spending for shoes, jewelry, and accessories.

were made for men; women made nearly all their own clothing. As time passed, women turned that chore over to factories. The cost of factory cutting and sewing, however, accounted for only 20 percent of the entire 1900–1929 rise in women's clothing expenditure. Around 80 percent went for more clothing.[33] By 1929 the housewife no longer made most of her own clothing. The Great Depression did not change women's share of total clothing expenditures at all. Nor did postwar prosperity and inflation. Nor, most strikingly, did the massive entry of women into the labor force.

---

[33] Value added in women's clothing manufacture ran to $89 million in 1899, $676 million in 1919, and $914 million in 1929. Data from U.S. Bureau of the Census, 10, *Manufactures, 1905* (1907–8), 13, and idem, *Manufactures, 1919*, 327, 372, 385, summing figures for corsets and women's clothing, not elsewhere classified.

Of the entire 1900–1980 increase in clothing expenditure, how much provides better protection against the elements? And how much provides display, convenience, and luxury? Amid so many changes in style and design, the answer is hardly obvious. An empirical guide does exist, however. Congress buys clothing for the Navy. It surely provides every American seaman, rating or officer, with decency, safety, and protection against the elements (not to mention gold braid). Expenditures to clothe navy personnel rose somewhat between 1900 and 1929, thanks to rising wages and material costs (annual reports of the War Department). But gains for civilians far surpassed that standard. A 16 percent gain in Navy expenditures contrasts sharply with the 150 percent gain for civilian males—and 492 percent for females. Those excesses point to the satisfactions consumers sought from style and variety, particularly in women's clothing. The tradition was not halted by moralists or those who urged a tight budget.

Hudson Maxim, a leading American inventor, described his boyhood in Maine at the beginning of this century: "I didn't have a pair of shoes until I was 13 years old. I sometimes tied old bags around my feet when I was going out to help in the barn." Going to school in winter, "we ran with all our might as long as our feet could endure the cold and then climbed on a fence . . . to rub our feet and ankles with our hands; and then we'd rush on again."[34] The South had an equally widespread problem associated with lack of shoes: hookworm. That debilitating disease was contracted by walking barefoot on infected soil.

Such factors help explain why American consumers spent more for shoes as workers' incomes rose, even though shoe prices fell.[35]

[34] Maxim, *Reminiscences* (1924), 52.
[35] Ending hookworm in fact required public-health programs sponsored and financed by Rockefeller Foundation money.

Resources devoted to shoe production could indeed have been carefully economized, as they once were. When barrels of shoes for slaves arrived at plantations, they were filled with large brogans, having neither lefts nor rights. But by the 1850s luxury began to creep into mass markets, at least in the North. For factories had begun to make "crooked shoes"—i.e., rights and lefts.[36] In time sizes multiplied, and styles. By the 1950s some major manufacturers stocked ten to thirty thousand lasts.[37] Each represented a different size and style.

Scholars have premised that "shoes are . . . a fundamental basic need for most people in developing countries." No doubt they were thinking of dirt and injuries. But a recent study of Ghana discovered a wide "variety of shoe designs using many different materials."[38] Consumer surveys there gave unexpected results. For it was "the high income group [that] most appreciated durability." "Fashion and finish [proved] much more important in low-income households." The reason? "The most important use of footwear . . . was for ceremonial occasions . . . family gatherings, community meetings, funerals, etc."[39] "Superfluities" that enraged Veblen thus appeared in Ghana. So did the "wasteful variety" so troubling to later commentators. The "problem" was not limited to the United States or even to rich nations in general. A footwear criterion that excludes the vulgarities of the uncouth and the superfluities of the elite from judicious consumption is no straightforward matter. Nor are the gains from applying such a criterion.

[36] Hazard, *Organization of the Boot and Shoe Industry* (1921), 76.

[37] Bright, *Automation and Management* (1958), 34.

[38] Baron and van Ginneken, "Appropriate Products and Egalitarian Development" (1982), 671.

[39] Ibid., 680–81.

· H O U S I N G ·

Relatively large and well appointed house room is . . . at once

"a necessary for efficiency" and the most convenient and obvious way

of advancing a material claim to social distinction.

—ALFRED MARSHALL, *Principles of Economics*

The American "way of life" is significantly distinguished from that of other nations by the American "way of housing." Americans spend some 70 percent of their lives in and around their homes.[40] Their commitment of real resources to housing exceeds that of other nations. The United States is also near the peak of the international league in its share of all consumption expenditure going to housing. Its share had been fully as great in 1900.

Is it so high because Americans require sturdier housing than those who live at the equator? Not obviously. The climate in the Netherlands, Germany, and Ireland is no warmer most of the year. But their housing shares are smaller. Was a concentration of U.S. population in major cities the explanation? Land costs, and rents, are surely higher at such high densities. Yet land rent accounts for less than a tenth of U.S. residential rent.[41] Nor did America's housing share increase from 1900 to 1980, though more and more of the nation's population concentrated in cities.

More powerful forces explained the high share for housing. The deep current of American individualism was perhaps most significant. Americans sought greater privacy and more living space than Europeans. That goal led to persistent conflicts between immigrant and American modes of life.

Immigrants had been accustomed to living close together. Twenty percent of London's families lived with over two persons per room.

[40] See chapter 8, n. 1 above.

[41] Land accounts for 10 percent of residential asset values, according to Grebler, et. al., *Capital Formation in Residential Real Estate* (1956), 454. I assume that the same percentage would apply to the charge for services from these assets.

In Berlin and Vienna, 28 percent did so.[42] Europeans in rural villages had lived in close proximity to one another.[43] Even large families shared one- or two-room houses with a cow, pigs, and poultry. They removed the manure only in the spring, when it was spread on the fields.[44] European hospital patients typically shared a bed with one other patient, sometimes two.

When European and Asian immigrants arrived in the United States, they naturally continued to crowd their large families into one or two rooms.[45] Reliable data are available for 1910, a peak immigration year. The difference between American and immigrant housing behavior was striking. Fully one-third of the foreign born took boarders and lodgers into their homes, more than double the 14 percent for native whites. (Of the Lithuanians, some 77 percent had boarders and lodgers.[46]) Almost no native white family shared its lodgings with another family—but 9 percent of those from Italy did so. While 17 percent of the native white families squeezed three (or more) persons into each sleeping room, 39 percent of the foreign born did (Table II.12). An incredible 66 percent of the Bulgarians did so, and 81 percent of the Romanians. All told, the foreign born crammed about 40 percent more persons into each room than native white Americans. So did Blacks.

That crowding, that tolerance of life in cellars, of tenement privies, intolerably affronted Jacob Riis and an immense battery of housing reformers. Bessie Pierce described the "disgusting" housing condition of the slums near Hull House, where "large undigested groups of foreigners" lived.[47] The progressives described how immigrants from Europe, as black migrants from the rural South, "kept coal in bathtubs," allowed both sexes to share the same bedroom, and created other housing outrages. Their investigations

[42] Weber, *Growth of Cities* (1899), 416.

[43] Arensberg, *Irish Countryman* (1937), has emphasized the concentrated pattern in rural Irish living.

[44] Cf. Estyn, *Irish Folk Ways* (1957), 86–87, 33–34, 41.

[45] An average of three persons per bed in the early eighteenth-century homes of Maryland's poorest (20 percent) young fathers indicates early American precedents. Main, *Tobacco Colony* (1982), 219, 242.

[46] The data on boarders and lodgers are from Lebergott, *American Economy*, 252–56.

[47] Pierce, *History of Chicago* (1937–), 3:55. Presumably "digested" foreigners were not associated with such conditions.

Table II.12

U.S. Household Congestion (More than Three Persons
per Sleeping Room) in 1910, 1970, and 1989

	1910	1970	1989
Native white	17%	3%	n.a.
Negro	34	11	1%
Foreign born	39	6	n.a.
English	13	0	n.a.
Irish	16	4	n.a.
German	22	1	n.a.
Bohemian	39	n.a.	n.a.
Hebrew	43	n.a.	n.a.
Italian	44	2	n.a.
Polish	50	1	n.a.
Slovak	55	4	n.a.
Bulgarian	66	0	n.a.
Romanian	81	0	n.a.
Greek	n.a.	6	n.a.
Indian	n.a.	9	n.a.
Latin and Mexican	n.a.	16	n.a.
Chinese	n.a.	24	n.a.
Albanian	n.a.	50	n.a.
Jordanian	n.a.	50	n.a.
Total	23%	4%	1%

Sources: For 1910: Lebergott, *American Economy*, 256. For 1970:
Tabulation of computer tapes for U.S. Bureau of the Census,
Population 1970 (5% percent sample, county group tapes). For
Slovak in 1970—data for Yugoslav. For 1989: U.S. Bureau of the
Census, *American Housing Survey for the United States in 1989*,
tables 2-17, 5-17.

provided the basis for complaint, and then for action by
government.

During the peak years of immigration, American reformers laid
down the law and arithmetic of proper housing. By 1920, "health
and decency" required a definite minimum of one room per person
in every housing unit.[48] By 1937, the nation's leading housing expert

[48] *Monthly Labor Review* (June 1920), 11. Thus the Bureau of Labor Statistics "health
and decency" budget for a worker's family.

declared it "has been accepted in the United States that 20 percent of income is a normal proportion to devote to rent."[49] To alter persistent "abnormal" housing expenditure, zoning developed, regulations proliferated. These pushed up housing costs for immigrants. They also increased property values, made jobs for construction workers, and increased wages and profits in the construction material industries.

During the twentieth century, aberrant housing behavior was steadily reduced. Rising incomes helped bring the foreign born into line with progressive standards. American mores, law, and the construction industry all pressured immigrants to increase their "abnormal" rent expenditures. Together, as Table II.12 shows, they brought migrants into conformity by 1970. Only a handful of newer ethnic groups still followed ancient crowding patterns.

Why was it urgent that immigrants and blacks spend a "normal proportion" for rent? Congress had never committed itself to such a percentage, nor even to "large and well-appointed houses." And even the population at large (white, native) failed to meet some implicit goal of more space per family. Rooms per family actually declined between 1900 and 1970.[50]

Three quite different goals were sought by American consumers. One goal, in Virginia Woolf's words, seemed to be "a room of one's own." In 1900, half of all families crowded more than one person into each room. By 1970, only 8 percent, and by 1980, 4.5 percent did so. Family size fell along with birth rates. But there was a second force: families sharing their homes with lodgers fell—from 25 percent to 2 percent.[51] Persons per room also fell, as did the percentage sharing toilets or water supply, and the percentage bringing in-home work (other people's washing, factory sewing, etc.) (see Table II.13). Family members then achieved still more privacy, since the number of rooms occupied did not decline as precipitously. Some commentators saw that outcome as desirable: more persons had their "own" room. Others worried about an increase in isolation, in "anomie."

---

[49] Wood, in *Encyclopedia of the Social Sciences*, vol. 7 (1937), 512. She did not specify by whom 20 percent had "been accepted [as] normal."

[50] Grebler et al., *Capital Formation in Residential Real Estate*, 120.

[51] Lebergott, *American Economy*, 252, 253, 258; U.S. Bureau of the Census, *General Housing Characteristics, 1980, U.S. Summary* (1981), table 1. Persons per room declined from 1.13 in 1910 to 0.62 in 1970.

Table II.13

Congestion, Water Supply, and Employment in U.S. Urban Households,
1910 and 1989

	Persons per room		Shared		Gainful employment in home
	2+	3+	toilet	water supply	
1910					
Native					
White	6%	1%	46%	10%	4%
Black	12	3	71	26	33
Foreign born					
All	28	5	72	16	5
Hebrew					
Russian	27	4	70	3	3
Other	22	3	72	7	4
Irish	10	*	57	18	2
Italian					
Northern	14	3	56	8	8
Southern	43	10	74	27	8
Polish	34	7	75	22	2
Slovenian	43	4	68	32	*
Swedish	1	*	36	*	4
Syrian	36	12	95	50	6
1989					
White	1	*	*	*	n.a.
Black	1	*	*	1	n.a.
Hispanic	1	*	*	*	n.a.

Sources: For 1910: U.S. Congress, Immigration Commission, *Immigrants in Cities* (1911), 48, 99, 97, 96. For 1989: U.S. Bureau of the Census, *American Housing Survey for the United States in 1989*, tables 2-4, 2-6, 2-17, 5-17.

*Less than 1%.

Perhaps the search for privacy, even individuality, was more intense in the United States than other nations. By 1970, the typical U.S. household had five rooms (compared to only one in the Soviet Union).[52] A leading British economist nonetheless decided that

[52] U.S. Bureau of the Census, *Space Utilization of the Housing Inventory, 1970* (1973), table A-4. For U.S.S.R.: U.S. Congress, Joint Economic Committee, *Soviet Economy in a Time of Change*, vol. 1 (1979), 794. The Soviet Union had 23 percent more households

Americans spent too little on housing. "Beyond the obvious needs of food, clothing and amusement," she declared, "a decent house ranks highest" to a proper bourgeois. Yet "the wealthy capitalist democracies have a great struggle to impose this scale of values upon their pattern of production."[53]

A second goal appeared to be piped water in the household. The percentage of American households with running water rose from about 25 percent to 99 percent between 1900 and 1970 (see Table II.14). Indeed, plumbing made up the largest single cost in rising housing expenditures. Housewives thereby reduced their task of first pulling up buckets from a well, or pumping water, and then carrying over 10,000 gallons a year into the kitchen, laundry, or bath.[54]

To achieve the third goal, indoor toilets were built in each new dwelling unit (Table II.15). An ancient Athenian writer found the most succinct way of describing how unbelievably rich Thebes was: "Every man has a privy right at the door; he does not have to go a long way to relieve himself." In 1900, half of U.S. farmhouses did not even have privies.[55] Half did, while most city dwellers used earthen privies, often clustered in tenement courtyards. (Even at that they were far better off than Europeans. Two-thirds of the French even lacked privies.[56]) But running water and flush toilets

---

than dwelling units (ibid., 797). Fewer than 1 percent of the U.S. units had nonrelatives living with them. U.S. Bureau of the Census, *Housing Characteristics by Household Composition, 1970* (1973), table A-1, p. 7, and table A-2, p. 10.

[53] Joan Robinson in C. H. Feinstein, ed., *Socialism, Capitalism, and Economic Growth* (1967), 178. This statement is prefaced by a description of the scale of values of "a middle class family with an income considerably above the national average, sufficient education and self-confidence to resist advertisements and ignore the Joneses. In their notion of a comfortable standard of life beyond the obvious needs of food, clothing and amusement, a decent house ranks highest."

[54] Household family consumption of water in Boston and middle-sized New England towns was about 25 gallons a day, or 9,125 gallons a year. Turneaure and Russell, *Public Water Supplies* (1911), 11, 22, and Waring, in *Journal of Social Science* (1879), 183. With 4.76 persons per household, per capita consumption was thus about 5 gallons per day. In 1975, the average person consumed about 100 gallons a day. U.S. Geological Survey, *Estimated Use of Water in the United States in 1985*, Circular 1004, (1988), 15, Water Withdrawals and Deliveries.

[55] Athenaeus, *Deipnosophistae* 10:417.

Stiles of the U.S.D.A. reports a survey of 4,825 farmhouses in six states: 55 percent had no privies of any kind (35 percent for whites; 77 percent for blacks). Cited in Howard, *House Fly* (1911), 204.

[56] Zeldin, *France 1848–1975*, 622.

Table II.14

U.S. Homes with Running Water, 1890–1989

	Total			Urban			Rural		
Year	All	White	Black	All	White	Black	All	White	Black
1890	24%	n.a.	n.a.	58	n.a.	n.a.	1	n.a.	n.a.
1920	n.a.	n.a.	n.a.	n.a.	n.a.	n.a.	10	n.a.	n.a.
1930	n.a.	n.a.	n.a.	n.a.	n.a.	n.a.	16	18	1
1940	70	74	39	94	96	68	37	41	6
1950	83	84	57	96	97	81	58	61	12
1960	93	94	80	99	99	95	79	83	28
1970	98	98	92	99+	99+	99	91	93	55
1980	99	99+	98	99+	99+	99+	96	97	85
1989	99+	99+	99+	99+	99+	99+	99+	99+	98

Source: For 1890–1970: Lebergott, *American Economy,* 272. For 1980: U.S. Bureau of the Census, *General Housing Characteristics, 1980, U.S. Summary,* tables 3, 6, 7. For 1989: U.S. Bureau of the Census, *American Housing Survey for the United States in 1989,* tables 2-6, 5-6.

were steadily added in the 1910s and 1920s, and even during the Great Depression (Table II.14). By the 1950s, three American families in every four had indoor plumbing and water closets.

Some scholars nonetheless mourned the passing of the privy. One specialist in American studies noted with regret:

> Technological advances during the end of the nineteenth century brought unprecedented comfort . . . to the more privileged sectors of the urban bourgeoisie. . . . Indoor plumbing, central heating and canned foods were pleasant amenities, but made life seem curiously insubstantial . . . [these] "modern conveniences" . . . insulated people from the primary experience. [It all] added to the thinness of things.[57]

The redolent aspects of outdoor plumbing were surely "primary experience." Chic Sale regretted their end, as did T. Jackson Lears. But millions of housewives preferred indoor plumbing, to reduce both the "primary experience" and the odds of dying from typhoid.

[57] Lears, "From Salvation to Self-Realization," 7.

Table II.15

U.S. Households with Inside Flush Toilets, 1800–1989

Year	Total	By location		By race	
		Urban	Farm	White	Nonwhite
1800	—ᵃ	n.a.	n.a.	n.a.	n.a.
1860	1%	n.a.	n.a.	n.a.	n.a.
1880	7	34%	0%	n.a.	n.a.
1890	13	46	0	14%	5%
1900	15	n.a.	n.a.	n.a.	n.a.
1914–16	n.a.	n.a.	—ᵇ	n.a.	n.a.
1920	20	n.a.	n.a.	n.a.	n.a.
1925–26	n.a.	82	n.a.	n.a.	n.a.
1930	51	85	8	54	23
1940	60	85	9	63	26
1950	71	87	28	n.a.	n.a.
1960	87	94	62	88	69
1970	96	99	87	97	89
1980	98	99	94	99	96
1989	99+	99+	99+	99+	99+

Source: For 1800–1970: Lebergott, *American Economy,* 272. For 1914–16: U.S. Department of Agriculture, *Yearbook of Agriculture, 1926,* 587; Howard, *The House Fly,* 204.

For 1980: U.S. Bureau of the Census, *General Housing Characteristics, 1980 U.S. Summary,* tables 3, 6, 7. These figures are underestimates as they relate to "complete plumbing facilities including baths, showers, hot water." For 1989: U.S. Bureau of the Census, *American Housing Survey for the United States in 1989,* table 2-4.

ᵃLess than 1 percent.

ᵇLess than 1 percent. Half even lacked a privy.

There were, of course, alternatives to massive consumer spending for indoor plumbing. Sidney Webb (socialist, scholar, and future member of the House of Lords) urged one for the United States. Dirty people, he told Americans, were not appropriate in modern society. "It becomes more and more imperative, in the public interest, to enforce the fulfilment of personal and parental and marital responsibility on every adult." The state must make "the negligent and recalcitrant" citizen fulfill his obligations. How? By "experiments on volition." These would be planned to alter "the mind of the ordinary man. . . . By the provision of public baths and cleansing stations he [would then] find it more easy for him to keep his family free from vermin, and more disagreeable to let them remain neglected and dirty." How would Webb "experiment on volition"?

> It is principally on economic and political science that the world is dependent in the deliberate corporate action which is ever increasingly typical of the present age. Individual decision may come from impulse and intuition; but what is done by Cabinets and Legislatures, Municipal Councils and Co-Operative Committees has to be the outcome of deliberate concert which . . . plainly needs to be informed . . . by all the science that each generation possesses.[58]

Guided by "all" of science, cabinet ministers would thus wave the wand of Progress. (Only his fellow Fabian, George Bernard Shaw, could do justice to such rhetoric.)

Public baths appealed to upper-class Englishmen well before "Municipal Councils" and "Science." As early as 1844, Lord Normanby and Lord Manners helped organize an Association for Promoting Cleanliness amongst the Poor. It was to promote by building public baths and wash-houses.[59] American philanthropists had helped support public baths in New York City.

But few Americans cared for the faint menace of a "deliberate concert," even a concert of "Cabinets, Legislatures and Co-Operative Committees." Following "impulse and intuition," they simply rented housing with private baths. By 1900, two U.S. urban homes in every three had running water. By the time Webb was urging "experiments on volition," 95 percent did (and perhaps 70 percent of rural families[60]). Meanwhile, the most "cultured" nation in Europe had about 1 percent.[61]

Kerosene lamps, almost universal in 1900, were replaced by electricity. Wood heating had been commonplace in 1900. By the 1920s central heating by coal had replaced it. A further drift, from coal to oil or gas, marked the 1930s.

---

[58] Webb, "Labor," (1928), 135–36.

[59] Tarn, *Five Per Cent Philanthropy* (1973), 3. "What white skins they have," one British officer marvelled when he saw the lower ranks bathing in France during World War I.

[60] Nearly all of whom had wells in addition. Lebergott, *American Economy*, 264, 272.

[61] Zeldin, *France 1848–1975*, 622.

Of today's house value, or rent, one-quarter is accounted for by its electrical and plumbing work.[62] The far greater U.S. expenditure on facilities for housewives than high-income European nations stands out (see Table II.17).

Ever greater privacy in American living arrangements altered the family in unexpected ways. It stimulated independence, increased anomie and rudderlessness, broke family bonds. The vast increase in housing expenditure reduced heavy household chores by women (and some men). Time was freed for television and for work outside the home.

The legend of Prometheus emphasizes how ancient was the importance of fire. Humans may have been accustomed to freezing, but they were never reconciled to doing so. Early Americans used their endless forests to provide warmer homes than Europeans could hope for. In 1800, they burned about one cord of wood per person per year, far more than Europeans.[63]

By 1900, Americans had more than doubled their usage. Kitchen stoves alone consumed eight cords per year.[64] Fireplaces took six cords more in the South, or thirty in New England.[65] On "many

[62] Grebler et al., *Capital Formation in Residential Real Estate*, 118.

[63] *Niles Register*, June 28, 1817, p. 278.

[64] U.S. Department of Agriculture, *What the Farm Contributes Directly to the Farmer's Living*, Farmers' Bulletin 635 (1914), 15. The bulletin indicates that three-fifths of the wood consumption in southern states "was used in cookstoves," reporting totals of 14 cords a year in North Carolina and 18 in Georgia. This implies 8 cords, say, for the stove and 6 to 8 for the fireplace. I do not use data for southern states that relied on coal, nor for northern states, since their totals might reflect greater use in fireplaces.

[65] Jefferson, in 1792, noted that "Mr. Remsen tells me that 6 cord of hickory last a fire place well the winter." Betts, ed., *Thomas Jefferson's Farm Book* (1953), 83. An average of 30 cords per winter was estimated for Hadley, Massachusetts about 1765. Cf. Schumacher, *Northern Farmer* (1975), 5.

western farms when firewood was wanted a tree was cut down and hauled bodily to the kitchen . . . giving the servant and the wife green wood with which to kindle and keep up their fires."[66] Where the housewife had no servant, and she usually did not, she and the children loaded each fireplace with six or so additional cords of wood. (Merely collecting firewood took poor U.K. families "three hours more or less every day" in the winter.[67])

From 1620 to 1900, few Americans heated the whole house during the winter. Cutting trees, splitting them, carrying firewood in, and loading the fireplaces took far too much labor for that. Most families heated only their kitchens, and few living rooms were "lived in during the winter." By 1919, that had changed. The Bureau of Labor Statistics then declared that "it is reasonably certain that the American family [now] consume[s] abundant fuel, so that the living room can be lived in during the winter."[68]

The development of central heating in the 1920s has often been instanced as one more example of how American materialism overwhelmed the simple life. Indeed it did. It ended the simple family chore of cutting and hauling fifteen to twenty tons of wood for stove and fireplace, with the housewife then having to carry much or all of it into the house. (As late as 1919 half of all farm women carried in their firewood.[69] Many also had to chop logs or branches into kindling.)

By 1900, coal was in wide use. One Boston study measured coal consumed by the kitchen stove. The housewife lifted 7-1/2 tons of coal and kindling a year into her stove.[70] Many also filled their coal scuttle from a pile in the basement, or outside the farm house, and carried that tonnage to the kitchen. By the 1920s, coal largely replaced wood. With central heating more common, husbands and/or older sons became accustomed to shoveling six tons of coal into the furnace each winter, then removing cans full of ashes and clinkers.[71]

[66] U.S. Commissioner of Agriculture, *Agricultural Report 1863* (1863), 463.

[67] *A Treatise on Coal Mines*, 1769, quoted in Ashton and Sykes, *Coal Industry of the Eighteenth Century* (1929), 148–49.

[68] Meeker, "What Is the American Standard of Living?" (1919), 8.

[69] 54 percent according to a Department of Agriculture survey of 10,000 families. Kirkpatrick, *Farmer's Standard of Living* (1929), 152.

[70] Commonwealth of Massachusetts, *Labor Bulletin*, 75. The figure understates the average week: Sunday meals were surely more complex and would have taken more coal.

[71] I estimate 6 tons on the basis of the proportion of rural nonfarm families using

In the 1930s Americans switched again, this time to gas and oil. For the Federal Power Commission began to hold down the price of natural gas. Americans then adopted gas, happily ending two objectionable chores. Men no longer shoveled tons of coal and ash each year. Women no longer spent six hours every week dusting floors, furniture, and sills, and more hours still washing wood ash or coal dust from curtains, blankets, and clothing.[72] During the 1920s and 1930s, they also cut their time caring for the stove fire, and cleaning the kitchen stove, by more than four hours a week. They did so by switching from wood and coal to gas and electricity.[73] By 1989, only one in twenty families remained dedicated to simple living by reliance on wood. Indeed, 25 percent insisted on the newer convenience of electricity (see Table II.16).[74]

The share of American income spent for fuel showed a remarkable trend this century. Nearly every major supply and demand force tended to increase it. Coal and oil became scarcer. Capitalist owners of coal mines and oil wells charged all the economic rent they could. Truck drivers and miners joined unions and increased their wages. Americans began to heat every room in the house, not just the kitchen. And by 1987, 63 percent of all households were air conditioned.[75]

Yet American families spent no more of their incomes to heat their homes in 1990. Despite all the factors driving up expenditures for

---

bituminous or anthracite coal, and the quantities of each. Cf. U.S. Department of Agriculture, *Rural Family Spending and Saving in Wartime*, Miscellaneous Publication 520 (1943), table 19. New York City and Boston averaged 6 tons per home owner in 1935–36. Averages for the Midwest ran 4.6 tons (Cleveland), 3.7 tons (Detroit), 5.3 tons (Milwaukee), 5.7 tons (Columbus), and 8.6 tons (Indianapolis). Data on expenditures computed from Bureau of Labor Statistics, *Money Disbursements . . . in the East North Central Region* Bulletin 637, vol. 1, p. 133; vol. 2, p. 314; idem, *Money Disbursements . . . in the North Atlantic Region*, Bulletin 636, pp. 265, 269, 275. Price data from *Monthly Labor Review* (March 1936).

[72] I include time spent cleaning floors (except kitchen and bathroom) and rugs and dusting furniture. See Rowe, "Time Necessary to Do the Work," 571.

[73] Stove tending and cleaning time for a coal stove took 5-1/2 versus 1-1/2 hours for gas stoves in 1900–1901. Commonwealth of Massachusetts, *Labor Bulletin*. Cf. also Berk, ed., *Women and Household Labor* (1980), 37. Cleaning stoves in 1990, except for the most incompetent cooks, could hardly average 1-1/2 hours a week.

[74] U.S. Bureau of the Census, *American Housing Survey for the United States in 1989* (1991), Table 2–5.

[75] U.S. Department of Energy, *Housing Characteristics, 1987* (1989), 85.

Table II.16

American Homes by Heating Fuel, 1880–1989

	Wood	Coal	Oil	Gas	Electricity
1880	65%	35%	0%	0%	0%
1908	36	63	1	*	0
1940	23	55	11	11	0
1950	11	35	23	29	*
1960	5	12	32	48	2
1970	2	3	26	61	8
1980	3	*	18	59	18
1987	6	*	12	60	20
1989	5	*	13	53	25

Source: For 1880–1940: Lebergott, *American Economy,* 276; for 1950–80: U.S. Bureau of the Census, *Statistical Abstract, 1987,* 713; *Reports;* for 1987: U.S. Department of Energy, *Housing Characteristics, 1987,* 59; for 1989: U.S. Bureau of the Census, *American Housing Survey for the United States in 1989,* table 2-5.

*Less than 1 percent.

fuel, despite OPEC and the frenetic Carter energy program, they actually spent less than 3 percent—compared to 3 percent in 1900.[76] The explanation? Persistent productivity advance by businesses that mined fuel and produced electricity.[77]

[76] Expenditures for fuel oil, coal, gas, and electricity in 1990 were 2.5 percent of personal income. Since one-half of household spending on electricity was for lighting, the aggregate for fuel would have been 1.7 percent.

[77] More precisely: even greater advances in these industries than in the rest of industry and government.

·DOMESTIC SERVICE·

I want to send my cook to learn of her. Poor people with four children

like us, you know, can't afford to keep a good cook.

—GEORGE ELIOT, *Middlemarch*

Veblen's magnificent diatribes on conspicuous consumption gave pride of place to attacks on domestic service. With modern appliances, he declared, "body servants, or indeed domestic servants of any kind, would now scarcely be employed by anybody except on the ground of a canon of reputability carried over by tradition from earlier usage." Why so? Because he believed personal contact with servants was "commonly distasteful" to their employers.[78] "The presence of domestic servants, and of the special class of body servants in an eminent degree, is a concession of physical comfort to the moral need of pecuniary decency." Servants perform duties "not so much for the individual behoof of the head of the household as for the reputability of the household taken as a corporate unit."[79] Moreover, "idle man-power embodied in the servant class is sorely needed for present use in productive industry," he contended in 1918. He instanced the "two able-bodied man servants, coachman and footman, in waiting at the curb while their patriotic and spendthrift mistress within the gates sits in self-appointed council on the state of the republic at large."[80]

Would one infer from all this that less than 1 percent—indeed, less than a thousandth of 1 percent—of the entire U.S. labor force were coachmen? Or that the entire nation had a mere 296 footmen?[81]

---

[78] Veblen's was no coruscating attack on domestic service by a woman who did her own chores. It was by a man who did not. Veblen hired graduate students to cook and clean in return for room rental. Cf. Duffus, *Innocents at Cedro* (1944).

[79] Mitchell, ed., *What Veblen Taught*, 259–61.

[80] Veblen, *Essays in Our Changing Order* (1934), 272.

[81] U.S. Bureau of the Census, *Occupations, 1910*, 430 gives data for individual occupations, including a U.S. figure of 2,436 for valets. The labor-force estimate of 37,380,000 is from Lebergott, *Manpower* (1964), 510.

Perhaps Veblians were morally outraged even by 296 footmen if they served women's convenience (rather than the "behoof" of household heads). Yet how infinitesimal a share of national resources was thus diverted, even during the still well-dramatized era of Bradley Martin and William Vanderbilt.

By 1910, when Veblen was working out these views, the United States had 2 million domestic servants (for 20 million households). Precious few were on display in elegant uniforms to demonstrate "the reputability of the household." Most worked in back halls, cellars, kitchens. There, quite hidden from visitors' view, they filled fireplace baskets with wood, cleaned floors, blacked stoves, washed clothes, and cooked. (Female farm laborers performed such tasks as well.) Their efforts helped millions of housewives before electric appliances provided mechanical help. Their jobs enabled foreign-born and black women to earn income despite wide discrimination against their broken English or color.

Between 1910 and 1930, the number of domestic servants actually fell, though the number of families more than doubled. In part they declined because demand for servants may have weakened. Some upper-class women vigorously tried to "blot out from our domestic life the SERVANT ELEMENT! . . . Those outrageous little kingdoms of insubordination, ignorance, lying, waste, sloth, carelessness, dirt." These were to "be merged (as the good-for-nothing little German states are being swallowed by Prussia) into a thoroughly organized, well-balanced despotism . . . where lynx-eyed matrons . . . note that each servant does exactly the right thing at the right moment." (The quotation is from Melusina Pierce, "a writer and feminist, one of the many women who burst into militancy in the sixties and seventies."[82])

From 1910 to 1930, however, mass immigration was closed off. Immigrant and black workers began to earn higher wages, reducing the supply of domestics. When World War II expanded job opportunities for unskilled women, the number of servants fell further— far more swiftly than the number of appliances rose. Rising wages to unskilled workers in factories and shops further cut supply. By 1970, fewer than 1 percent of the nation's 46,000,000 families could have been gilded with "reputability" by their live-in servant.[83] One could

---

[82] See Dudden, *Serving Women*, 184–88, and Lichtman and Challinor, *Kin and Communities* (1979), 286.

[83] U.S. Bureau of the Census, *Occupational Characteristics, 1970* (1973), table l. To be

assert an American commitment to "chastity and poverty" as persuasively as one to "reputability": for the nation had at least as many nuns and monks as chauffeurs and live-in servants.

·HOUSEHOLD OPERATION·

One well-known economist has found it impossible to believe "that sustained attempts to harness the greater part of man's energies . . . to amassing ever larger amounts of material possessions—fashion goods, gimmickry, motorized implements, novelties and tasteless inanities—can add much to people's happiness."[84] His olympian judgment aimed at two targets. One was very vague—novelties and "tasteless inanities." (Tasteful inanities were acceptable, if not actually laudable.) But one target was quite specific—motorized implements. Families did spend more for such implements between 1900 and 1990, but allocated only 2 percent of their total expenditure increase.[85]

That small commitment enabled U.S. housewives to do their housework far more easily than women in other nations (Table II.17). French housewives, and Italian, produced gourmet meals without the refrigeration Americans demanded. But they shopped every day to do so. They did turn an elegant seam. But to do so they sewed for hours by hand, or pushed their sewing machines by hand or foot treadle. Most of them also lifted tons of coal or wood into the

---

exact, less than 1 percent of the families with incomes of $25,000 and over had live-in servants, even including nurses for the aged and ill.

[84] Mishan, "Wages of Growth," 85. Earlier he observed: "Insofar as this [keeping up with the] Jones['s] effect is operative, society has been collectively gulled into struggling on, accumulating, destroying, innovating, to no intelligent purpose. The goods proliferate, but society feels no better off" (p. 85).

[85] In 1982 prices. By including "kitchen appliances" and all "other durable furnishings" I overstate the gain. Attacks on spending for automobiles (and airplanes) appear in Mishan's earlier analysis.

Table II.17

Nations with Specified Conveniences, 1960

	United States	Great Britain	Netherlands	Luxemburg	France	West Germany	Belgium	Italy	Soviet Union
All households	100%	100%	100%	100%	100%	100%	100%	100%	100%
With hot running water	93	77	67	57	41	34	25	24	n.a.
With washing machine	55	45	69	74	32	36	52	8	15
With refrigeration (electric or gas)	96	30	23	57	41	52	21	30	5
With sewing machine									
electric	45	12	24	15	14	10	13	5	n.a.
hand/foot powered	(*)	34	55	47	42	50	34	51	n.a.
With stove (coal or wood)	n.a.	7	2	67	54	50	45	44	n.a.
With automobile	77	35	26	48	40	26	30	20	n.a.

Source: Readers' Digest, *European Common Market and Britain*, tables 1, 22, 32 (the European data include hand-powered washing machines); and U.S. Bureau of the Census, *Statistical Abstract, 1979*, 788. Data for the Soviet Union are from Shumilova, 1964, quoted in Swafford, "Sex Differences in Soviet Earnings" 1978, 665.

*Less than 1 percent.

Table II.18
U.S. Households with Appliances, 1900 and 1987

		1987	
	1900	All	Family income over $50,000
Refrigerator	0%	100%	100%
Radio	0	100	100
Television	0	93	99
Washing machine	0	73	92
Microwave oven	0	61	81
Air conditioner	0	62	n.a.
Dishwasher	0	43	79
Freezer	0	35	41

Source: U.S. Department of Energy, *Housing Characteristics*, *1987*, table 30; and unpublished data kindly provided by the Department of Energy.

kitchen stove every year, when American housewives had already switched to gas or electricity. By 1987, major appliances had invaded home after home in the United States. Their growth, decade after decade, seemed remorseless (see Tables II.17, II.18, II.19).

By what specific incentives had American families been "gulled into" spending even 2 percent of their income for "motorized implements"? Spending more even during the decade of the Great Depression? I focus on two expensive, widely desired implements—washing machines and refrigerators.

WASHING MACHINES

From 1620 to 1920, the American washing machine was a housewife. As late as 1900 the family laundry took about seven hours a week.[86] The typical housewife washed some 40,000 diapers for her four children.[87] Lacking running water, she carried 9,000 gallons of water

[86] A 1917 household of three adults and no children, with running water and a washing machine, needed five hours weekly for laundry. Rowe, "Time Necessary to Do the Work," 571–72.

[87] As of 1990, a yearly estimate of 4,420 cloth diapers per child in diapers, plus 8,060 gallons of water to rinse and wash them and 2-1/2 years in diapers appears in

Table II.19

U.S. Families with Electricity and Appliances, 1900–1989

	Electric lighting	Refrigerators		Washing machines	Vacuum cleaners
		Ice	Mechanical		
1900	3%	n.a.	0%	n.a.	0%
1910	15	18%	0	n.a.	0
1920	35	48	1	8%	9
1930	68	40	8	24	30
1940	79	27	44	n.a.	n.a.
1950	94	11	80	n.a.	54
1960			90	73	73
1970	99	1	99	70	92
1984	100	*	100	73	n.a.
1987	100	*	100	75	n.a.
1989	100	*	100	75	n.a.

Source: For 1900–1970: Lebergott, *American Economy, 101, 280, 286–88, 195. For 1984: U.S. Department of Energy, Housing Characteristics, 1984,* 12. For 1987 and 1989: U.S. Department of Energy, *Housing Characteristics, 1987,* 29, 83, and unpublished tabulations kindly provided by the Residential and Commercial Branch of the Energy Information Administration. For washing machines, 1989: U.S. Bureau of the Census, *American Housing Survey for the United States in 1989,* table 2-4.

*Less than 1 percent.

into the house each year, then boiled most of it.[88] And she relied on a scrub board, not a washing machine.

Yet in the tradition of heroic conservatism, two leading sociologists opposed "motorized implements" in a classic 1937 study. They warned that American culture "has been hypnotized by the gorged stream of new things to buy." What "new things" merged into a gorged stream to accomplish that fascinating feat? "Electrical equipment for the home," said Robert and Helen Lynd; also "radios, automatic refrigerators and all but automatic ways to live."[89]

Arthur D. Little, Inc., *Disposable versus Reusable Diapers* B-8, B-9. The average family had four children in 1900, and I estimate 4,420 diapers per child for thirty months (ibid., II-20). Between 1900 and 1990, electric washing machines, piped hot water, and diaper service had all been widely adopted.

[88] Cf. note 54 above.

[89] Lynd and Lynd, *Middletown in Transition,* 46. A host of analytically similar but more recent critiques are summarized in Horowitz, *Morality of Spending* (1985).

The 1900 housewife relied on a nonautomatic (and fuel-efficient) wash board. It cost only 12 cents, included a "Globe crimp as shown in cut." Of course, the housewife with a good strong back and shoulders could get several hours of healthy exercise each week washing clothes. She would be independent of "motorized implements," and perhaps would clean the clothes more thoroughly than by using a high-priced machine.

The housewife's task was indeed simple. She first carried water in from the well or tenement faucet. (Less than a third of all homes had cold running water.) She then filled a wash boiler (only $1), carried gallons of boiling water to the wash tub, and began her work. Effete and well-to-do housewives persuaded their husbands to spend $2.50 for an "Anthony Wayne" washer. By cranking its center post around and around they could wash a full load (four shirts). They then had only to carry away several pails of dirty water, fill with pails of clean water, and get on with the next load. Some housewives indulged in an "Electric Washer." That cost $1 more—a day's pay for most workers—because it had "electrically welded" bands. But it rarely leaked on the floor. And it also retained the heat. The housewife did not, therefore, have to boil and add water as frequently as for an ordinary washer. (Its tight seal also locked in the "odor of foul steam.")

Once the wash was done, the housewife could wring the clothes out by hand or lift them straight up, heavy with water, and put them through a separate wringer. Handy turnbuckles could be loosened (if the clothes coming out of the murky water proved to be towels or overalls) or screwed tight (if they were housedresses or socks). Some women, however, felt that "the ordinary tub wringer [required] about as much work to hold the tub as to turn the wringer." They therefore spent an extra $1 on a better wringer.

By 1929, the housewife's obsession with "motorized implements" led her to buy wringers directly attached to the tub. Metal rollers (or vulcanized covers) readily squeezed out the water. Since they occasionally squashed a finger, many women were "gulled into" buying safer machines with rubber rollers. Nor was that the end. Power wringers promised to end the creative task of cranking the wringer. Consumers Union then found "a great many . . . women catching hands, sleeves and hair in power wringers while drying clothes. . . . Wringers are very dangerous [and] we strongly urge anyone who can afford it to purchase a machine which removes water by some means other than a wringer."[90]

Major advances took place during the prosperous and technological 1920s, and apparently even during the Depression (Table II.20). By 1960, nearly every American family had its own mechanical washing machine.[91] (But only 12 percent of French households, and 27 percent of English ones, did.[92])

Table II.20

U.S. Households Using Scrub Boards and Washing Machines, 1900–1987

	Scrub board	Hand and water powered machine	Electric washing machine	Commercial laundries
1900	98%	(1)%	(0)%	(1)%
1920	n.a.	(8)	8	n.a.
1924	(17+)	n.a.	n.a.	n.a.
1930	n.a.	n.a.	24	n.a.
1960	n.a.	n.a.	73	n.a.
1987	n.a.	n.a.	75	n.a.

Sources: Electric: Lebergott, *American Economy*, 281; and U.S. Bureau of the Census, *Statistical Abstract, 1984*, 755, and *Statistical Abstract, 1991*, 729.

Note: For 1920 I assume that the proportion using hand and water power washing machines about equalled that for the electrical machines. That asumption rests on a large scale survey of schoolchildren by the American Home Economics Association. Hastie and Gorton, "What Shall We Teach Regarding Clothing and Laundry Problems?" (1926), 133. These 1924 data show much the same percentages for hand as for electric machines. (Their levels, however, are well above those I use for 1920.) I assume that although their survey percentages are biassed, the ratio of the percentages is not. Hastie and Gorton, charts 5 and 6, indicate that 53 percent of U.S. households used washing machines. Since 70 percent of the housewives did all the laundry, the figures imply that 17 percent used scrub boards. Given the survey's income bias, this figure is surely an understatement.

[90] *Consumers Union Reports* (May 1937): 23–24.

[91] In that year 74 percent of all households were families (i.e., two or more persons). Cf. U.S. Bureau of the Census, *Population, 1980; U.S. Summary PC-80-1-B1*, table 46. And separate surveys show three households out of four had a washing machine. I assume that nearly all families did, but not single persons living alone.

[92] These figures are for 1958. Pyatt, *Priority Patterns* (1964), 38; di la Gorce, *La France* (1965), 181.

By 1960, the housewife had indeed abandoned the wringer. But only for another machine. She no longer carried dripping wash from wringer to clothesline, having chosen a still more expensive implement. It filled its tub with water, emptied it, ran the rinse water in, emptied that, and spun the clothes, leaving them damp/dry. The housewife had then only to hang up all those clothes. (Unless she had bought yet another motorized implement to dry them.)

The American housewife's washing equipment had cost her husband a day's pay in 1900. By 1990, the cost amounted to two to three weeks' pay—or 10 minutes' pay per day of its useful life. It reduced the housewife's work far more than proportionately. Could anyone but upper-class critics who never washed clothes by hand describe such changes as "innovating to no intelligent purpose"?

REFRIGERATORS

When the Lynds warned Americans against hypnosis by "the gorged stream of new things to buy" in 1937, three in every four housewives had already bought "electrical equipment for the home." Why had those housewives yielded to the hypnotic pull of the "automatic refrigerator"? Most surely could have sawed ice in frozen ponds and hauled it home. Nearly all could afford unmechanized iceboxes. After all, 80 percent of French housewives managed without refrigerators as late as 1957, and 87 percent of British housewives.[93]

Perhaps most U.S. housewives were less heroic than Helen Lynd. Less willing to shop every day for fresh food. Perhaps they preferred the reliable temperatures that "automatic refrigerators" provided but ice did not. (Leftovers spoiled less frequently.) Fewer trips to the grocery were necessary. Nor did floors have to be mopped after dripping 25- or 50-pound cakes of ice were carried across them. Melting ice no longer drained into a container beneath the icebox, the foul accumulation having to be lifted carefully, and the container emptied and cleaned.

"Hypnotized" by such considerations, or weak willed, housewives bought motorized, electrical, automatic refrigerators. Even then they had to use pans of hot water to remove ice frozen around

93 Pyatt, *Priority Patterns*, 38; di La Gorce, *La France*, 181.

the coils, and (inevitably) mop the floor. Most therefore moved on to buy still more automatic, self-defrosting refrigerators. Not, however, without professors of geology doubting whether "ever-larger frostless refrigerators are needed, and whether the host of kitchen appliance really means less work or only the same amount of work to a different standard."[94] (What principle of geology determines the proper size of refrigerators is not mentioned. Nor the names of volunteers who would bring in pots of hot water for defrosting because it was "only the same amount of work.")

As of 1960, Western Europe continued to uphold the tradition of hard labor for women commended by the Lynds (see Table II.17). Most American families, however, had given up the spartan simplicity of the window box or ice.

· W A T E R ·

Survival in North America depends on a few items. Of these, clean water is most critical, for no one could live a week without it. Perhaps that very essentiality explains the intense emotion generated by water supply. Thus D. H. Lawrence found that "every time we turn on a tap to have water, every time we turn a handle to have fire or light, we deny ourselves and annul our being."[95]

Obviously some gentlemen preferred earlier societies, in which the average housewife pulled up 10,000 gallons of water yearly in buckets from a well, or carried them from a stream. But American behavior did not heed their sensitivities.

The average urban resident consumed about 20 gallons of water per day in 1900. Rural families had virtually no piped water; 55 percent did not even have privies. Not surprisingly, both rural and

[94] The geological analysis appears in Steinhart and Steinhart, "Energy Use" (1974), 315.

[95] Quoted by Brenda Maddox in *The New York Times Book Review*, Apr. 9, 1989, p. 26.

urban families drew their washing water from typhoid- and cholera-ridden wells and streams. By 1990, American families devoted two days' worth of their annual income to get about 100 sanitary gallons every day, piped into the home.[96]

The reasons for that expenditure rise were simple: In 1900, the American housewife carried many thousands of gallons of water a year into the house from river, brook, or well (with some help from the children). Water was free. So was the work. (Carrying took perhaps an hour a week.[97]) By the 1980s, only a handful of hippies expected their womenfolk to haul water from the brook or well.

Spending for water increased massively as Americans sought to cut the death rate from typhoid. That rate fell precipitously (75 percent in Albany, and 79 percent in Lawrence, Massachusetts) when they began filtering their water (about 1900). A few years earlier, Zurich and Hamburg achieved similar declines.[98] If drinking water had not been chlorinated, and 1900 death rates had persisted, 79,000 Americans would have died from typhoid in 1990—five times as many as died from AIDS in that year.[99]

Further, nearly half of all American families in 1900 drew water from farm wells for washing clothes, for baths, or for gardens. By 1990 almost none did. Many more automobiles were washed by 1990, but many fewer miles of dusty city streets were sprinkled, and few paved streets were still hosed down.

[96] Cf. note 54 above.

[97] A *Farmers Alliance* paper estimated a sixty-yard carry, six times a day—or 2.86 miles a week. Berk, ed., *Women and Household Labor*, 43.

[98] Turneaure and Russell, *Public Water Supplies*, 460.

[99] U.S. Centers for Disease Control, *HIV/AIDS Surveillance* (Dec. 1990): 13. The national death rate from typhoid in 1900 was 31.3 per 100,000. (U.S. Bureau of the Census, *Historical Statistics*, 1:58.)

· L I G H T I N G ·

What folly, to have a diamond necklace or a Corregio, and not to light

your house with gas! . . . How pitiful to submit to a farthing candle

existence, when science puts such intense gratification within your

reach! . . . Better to eat dry bread by the splendor of gas than to

dine on wild beef with wax candles.

—SYDNEY SMITH, 1820

According to one widely held view, the human drama began with a tremendous opening statement: "Let there be light." Since then, society has supplemented natural light by fire and other artifices. Smith's gay paean to gas light, only recently introduced into Britain, describes the joy a new lighting technology could bring. The twentieth century steadily replaced darkness with light by increased spending for gas and electricity.

Safety had much to do with that increase. Many knew how Fanny Longfellow—wife of the nation's most popular nineteenth-century poet—had been burned to death: Her dress caught fire from the candle she used to seal a packet of her children's curls.)[100] And only a few years before the century began, Lady Salisbury, wife of one of the most powerful and richest men in England, died when her dress caught fire from her bedroom candle. The similar death of the Duchesse de Maille in France was still remembered. When even the rich were menaced in their brick or stone mansions, the average family had still greater reason to fear its wooden house going up in flames. One third of New York's tenement fires in 1900 were attributed to candles, matches, or kerosene lamps.[101]

---

[100] Gorman, *A Victorian American* (1926), 289–90.

[101] Rumbold, *Recollections of a Diplomatist* (1902), 1:47. Charles V, king of Spain, was one of their many predecessors who died of fire in their own bedrooms. Robert W. De Forest and Lawrence Veiller, *The Tenement House Problem* (New York, 1903), 1:266.

Table II.21

Primary Lighting Sources for U.S. Families, 1900–1990

	Kerosene, coal oil	Gas	Electricy			Kilowatt hours per family
			All areas	Urban	Farm	
1900	88%	9%	3%	8%	0%	150
1920	27	35	35	47	2	339
1940	*	21	79	96	31	952
1960	*	1	99	—	—	3,854
1990	*	*	99+	—	—	(10,000)

Source: For percentages, 1900–1960: Lebergott, *American Economy*, 279–80. For 1990: author's estimate.

For 1920 I revise the gas estimate as follows. U.S. Bureau of the Census, *Fourteenth Census*, 10:722, reports 8.25 million consumers. Gould, *Output and Productivity in the Electric and Gas Industries* (1946), 84, estimates 204 b. cu. ft. to households. Dividing gives 24,718 ft. per household, in line with 1929 and 1900 figures. Hence 35 percent of the 23,873,000 households used gas. I allow 3 percent for families relying on candles or without lighting—as in 1900—and take the kerosene and coal oil percentage in 1920 as a residual.

For kilowatt hours per family with electricity, 1900: Lebergott, *American Economy*, 394. For 1920–60: U.S. Bureau of the Census, *Historical Statistics*, 827. For 1990: assuming 99 percent of households had electricity, I extrapolate the 1970 figure by data from U.S. Bureau of the Census, *Historical Statistics*, and idem, *Statistical Abstract, 1990*, 45.

*Less than 1 percent.

Kerosene and coal oil had become common in the United States by 1900, for they were fifteen times as bright as candles.[102] In time, gas lighting, four times as bright as kerosene lamps,[103] took over. Electricity then superseded both. It was no more expensive. (Edison priced it to be competitive with gas.) But was far safer, brighter, and much more versatile (Table II.21).

"Cultural historians" see a darker side:

> With a public gas supply, domestic lighting entered its industrial—and dependent state. No longer self-sufficiently producing its own heat and light, each house was inextricably tied to an industrial energy producer. . . . Being connected . . . as consumers made people uneasy. They clearly felt a loss of personal freedom.[104]

[102] Bell, *Art of Illumination*, 82–89.
[103] With a welsbach mantle. See ibid.
[104] Schivelbusch, *Disenchanted Night* (1988), 28–29.

Who lost "personal freedom"? Dr. Schivelbusch sees each house —not each housewife—"each house [being] inextricably tied to an industrial energy producer." He thus ignores millions of women who made their own candles, trimmed their oil lamps, lugged tons of wood and coal into their homes. Certainly they, and not their "houses," did so before gas, electricity, and central heat became common.

The low cost of electricity led to its generous use, apparent in the last column of Table II.21. By 1990, American households consumed 10,000 kilowatt hours per capita, over forty times as much as Soviet households. Did that profusion help explain the excessive cheerfulness that foreign visitors attributed to Americans?[105]

If the rich could hire the poor to die for them what a living

the poor would make.

—Anonymous

The twentieth century may seem the century of death. It has already had two overwhelming world wars, the Holocaust, plus the nearly endless slaughter of tribes and nationalities killing one another once the colonial era was past. But, if due proportion be kept, it is also the century of life. Its immense reduction in death rates is without precedent. Many more lives were saved, and years of life, than were destroyed by its massive slaughters.

[105] For the U.S.: U.S. Bureau of the Census, *Statistical Abstract, 1991,* 571, indicates 9,776 KWH for 1987.

For the U.S.S.R.: U.S. Congress Joint Economic Committee, *U.S.S.R.: Measures of Economic Growth and Development, 1950–80* (1981), 74, 345.

U.S. consumer spending to improve health, and defer death, increased with unprecedented speed. Rising incomes permitted that change, but did not dictate it. Health had indeed long been a superior good. But the elasticity of demand for health expenditure never before reached the level it did during the twentieth century. Between 1900 and 1929, spending for physicians, dentists, etc., nearly doubled (in constant dollars). Drug spending quadrupled; that for hospitals rose tenfold. Those unprecedented gains were then all dwarfed by the increase after 1945. I consider each in turn.

MEDICINES

The desire to take medicine is one feature which distinguishes

man, the animal, from his fellow creatures.

—SIR WILLIAM OSLER, *Aequanimitas*

In 1905, Sir William Osler observed that "we may safely say (reversing the proportion of fifty years ago) that for one damaged by dosing, one hundred were saved."[106] In the first decades of the twentieth century, medicines began to save more lives than they destroyed. Patent medicines were increasingly replaced by pharmaceuticals that chemists, physicians, and bacteriologists developed. As these proved their superiority, consumers began to rely on them. Table II.22 details that consumer choice by contrasting expenditures for medicines (to help the living) and those for funerals (to honor the dead).

The rise for medicines was clear and persistent. From about 60 percent of funeral expenditures in 1900 it reached to over 100 percent by 1929. Only then did the rise really become dramatic. For pharmaceuticals could at best alleviate pain, and cure minor illness, before the 1930s. Few new and significant drugs were part of civilian supply before 1945. But then the magic sulfanilimides (discovered in the late 1930s) and penicillin came to market with a rush. A staggering possibility appeared: deaths from ancient, widespread, and

---

[106] Osler, *Aequanimitas* (1932), 124.

Table II.22
U.S. Expenditure for Medicines, 1900–1990

	Medicines[a] (millions)	Funerals (millions)	Ratio: medicines to funeral expenditures
1900	$ 114	$ 195	58%
1929	700	600	117
1945	1,400	700	200
1980	23,500	4,400	534
1990	69,900	8,200	852

Source: Appendix A.
[a]Includes opthalmic goods.

overwhelming causes—influenza, tuberculosis, diarrhea, measles —could now be ended. And the death rate for infectious disease today is one-tenth what it was in 1900.[107] For the first time, the lower-income families could, in some real sense, buy the gift of life.

Medicines, of course, do more than strike at specific organisms of infection. Their psychosomatic contribution alters those symptoms which constitute so troubling and debilitating a part of illness.[108] That element is surely one significant reason why prescriptions rose from 1.4 per capita per year to 6.2 between 1929 and 1974.[109] U.S. prescriptions per capita in 1969 (5.9) actually exceeded the figure for the United Kingdom (5.7). Yet the latter nation offered "free" medical care.[110] Apparently Britons relied on drugs as much as Ameri-

[107] American Chemical Society, *Chemistry in the Economy* (1973), 171. The estimate is 500 deaths per 100,000 population in 1900 and 50 in 1970. The reduction in morbidity and suffering, of course, provided further inducement to medication.

[108] Placebos "have an average significant effectiveness of 35%" in altering "subjective responses and symptoms . . . through their effect on the reaction component of suffering." Beecher, "Powerful Placebo" (1955), 1602–6.

[109] An estimate of 165 million prescriptions written in 1929 appears in Rorem and Fischelis, *Cost of Medicines* (1932). Estimates of 1.197 and 1.366 billion, from the National Prescription Audit, appear in the *Pharmacy Times* (Apr. 1970): 32 and (Apr. 1980): 31. They are presumably more reliable than an estimate of 1.877 million for 1969 in U.S. Congress, Senate, *Competitive Problems in the Drug Industry* (1967), pt. 21, p. 8282.

[110] In 1968, U.K. physicians wrote 5.7 prescriptions per capita. Dunnell and Cartwright, *Medicine Takers, Prescribers and Hoarders* (1972), 1.

cans: "Fifty-five percent . . . had taken some pill or potion during the 24 hours previous to interview."[111]

The difficulty in actually getting to see a physician apparently contributed to such reliance on medication in the United Kingdom, as the direct cost of paying physicians did in the United States.[112]

MEDICAL PERSONNEL

His wife's affiliation with "the best people" brought him a good many of

those patients whose symptoms are, if not more interesting

in themselves than those of the lower orders,

at least more consistently displayed.

—HENRY JAMES, *Washington Square*

For the first third of the twentieth century, spending on medical care was restricted by the height of income, or depth of hypochondria. Treatments for fractures, smallpox, and breech births existed. For these, physicians were called in. But for a wide range of illnesses, physicians could provide only emotional support.

Between 1900 and 1930, the number of physicians increased somewhat less than the population (Table II.23). That did not reflect any lessened appreciation of emotional help. It revealed, instead, the triumphant restriction of supply by the Flexner report and the American Medical Association. Physicians could now be recruited only from "first-class" medical schools. As a result, the United States—which had nearly twice as many physicians per capita as Britain in 1910—had only 30 percent more by 1930.

The pattern of medical practice had, however, changed significantly. By 1988, the typical British physician collected fees for 1,999 patients on the "list" he regularly served. The typical U.K. physician dealt with 20 patients a day (plus about 3 hospital contacts). Few U.S. physicians pretended to cope with the health problems of more than 23 patients a day. They averaged only 13.[113]

[111] *New Society* (U.K.) (November 2, 1972).

[112] See Dunnell and Cartwright, *Medicine Takers*, 96.

[113] The patients per physician—i.e., "average list size of unrestricted principals"—appears in U.K. Central Statistical Office, *Annual Abstract of Statistics,*

Table II.23

Medical Care, United States and United Kingdom, 1900–1987

Year	U.S. physicians in private practice	Active physicians per million population		U.S. expenditures on medical care[a]
		U.S.	*U.K.*	
1900	100,000	1,315	n.a.	$ 7.2
1910	119,000	1,293	654	11.3
1929	117,000	1,104	649	22.8
1930	126,000	1,024	745	22.0
1950	222,000	1,461	987	45.6
1965	290,000	1,495	1,156	104.9
1976	394,000	1,833	1,400	193.4
1987	586,000	2,207	1,511	268.2

Source: For U.S. active physicians, 1900–1930, see unpublished estimates described in Lebergott, *Manpower*, 457. For 1965 and 1976, the count of "all physicians" minus inactive doctors of medicine is from U.S. Bureau of the Census, *Statistical Abstract, 1978*, 105. The 1950 figure is extrapolated from 1965 by the percentage change in the total number of physicians, from *Statistical Abstract, 1978*, 104.

Constant dollar expenditures on physicians, dentists, and other professional personnel, 1900–1929. For U.K. active registered civilian doctors: U.K. Department of Health and Social Security, *Medical Manpower—The Next Twenty Years* (1977), 46, and U.K. Central Statistical Office, *Annual Abstract of Statistics, 1990* (1991), 6, 64. Data for 1988.

[a]In billions of 1982 dollars. Data in Appendix A are in 1987 prices.

1990, 53. This study shows figures for 1961ff. ranging from 2,257 to 2,431 in various years. For 1988 the figure was 1,999. See also Great Britain, *Hospital In-Patient Enquiry—1979–1985* (n.d.).

The yearly contact figure is from U.S. Department of Health and Human Services, *Physician Contacts by Sociographic and Health Characteristics, 1982–83*, PHS 87–1589 (1987), table 7. But it omits contacts with hospital inpatients. The U.S. Bureau of the Census, *Statistical Abstract 1991*, 109, shows 38 million patients discharged and an average stay of 6.6 days. If there were only a single contact per day, that would increase the 5.1 to 6.2. The 447,000 active non-Federal U.S. physicians (in 1983) thus averaged 12.6 contacts a day.

The number of U.S. physicians rose after 1930. They became able to treat many illnesses with new drugs such as the antibiotics, and with the newer insights of physiology. Family incomes had risen, and medical care was a preferred good. Most important, health-insurance coverage expanded. The increasing number of physicians during the 1960s and 1970s made no evident dent in the trend of death rates. Nor did additional spending for physicians and hospitals. But together these factors led to quicker diagnosis, less pain, shorter hospital stays, and more assurance.[114] Unless the psychosomatic component of illness did not matter, nor life extension, these were tangible advances.

HOSPITALS

Few secular services offer anything as valuable as the gift of life, which hospitals apparently provide. It may, therefore, be somewhat surprising that as U.S. incomes rose from 1900 to 1950, hospital charges rose little faster than the cost of living. From 1893 to 1935, hospital rates increased about as fast as consumer prices. Between 1935 to 1950 they tripled, while prices generally rose by one-half. But in the next quarter-century, they rose elevenfold, while the Consumer Price Index barely doubled (Table II.24). The human desire to live longer did not obviously begin after 1950. And the concurrent decline in death rates hardly demonstrated that hospitals could provide miraculously effective services.

But two other elements changed. One was the way hospital services were produced. X-rays, laboratory tests, and many drugs other than opiates were now required. Second, and increasingly important since 1950, was expanded insurance and federal payments. Since such payments were routinely made within the annual contract or appropriation period, their impact was similar to cost-plus contracts: costs soared.

There were, of course, alternatives. But Americans did not choose Great Britain's alternative, where, for example, one-fourth of all

---

[114] Cross-section studies indicated small differences in mortality and even morbidity resulting from differences in physicians per capita. Cf. Fuchs, *Who Shall Live?* (1974); Belloc and Breslow, "Relationship of Health Practices and Mortality" (1973). The further lack of relationship to measures of health status is noted in Newhouse and Friedlander, "The Relationship between Medical Resources and Measures of Health" (1980), 200–218.

Table II.24
U.S. Hospital Expense
per Patient Day, 1893–1988

1893	$ 1.25
1923	3.45
1935	5.42
1950	15.62
1960	32.23
1970	81.00
1980	245.00
1988	586.00

Source: In 1893, the daily rate for the Pennsylvania Hospital, Philadelphia, ran $1.36; for the Presbyterian Hospital, Chicago, $1.27. Billings and Hurd, eds., *Hospitals, Dispensaries and Nursing* (1894), sec. 3, pp. 61, 125–26. The rates for other cities appear in U.S. Congress, *Joint Select Committee to Investigate Charities in the District of Columbia*, pt. 2 (1898), 61.

For 1923: U.S. Bureau of the Census, *Hospitals and Dispensaries, 1923*, 8, 19. For 1935: idem, *Business Census of Hospitals, 1935*, 13, 22. Idem, *Historical Statistics*, 1:81, gives hospital expense per patient-day (non-Federal short term) for 1950–70. For 1980–87: idem, *Statistical Abstract, 1991*, 108, provides data for "community hospitals."

patients going to a hospital with heart disease waited three months to be admitted, and 15 percent with acute myocardial infarction (heart attack) waited 8.1 weeks; nor the Canadian, where the average waiting time for heart surgery was 108 days.[115] Unit costs in the United States were not kept down by such fuller utilization of facilities.

[115] Great Britain, Department of Health and Social Security, *Hospital In-Patient Enquiry*, 36, 48; Jacobs and Hart, "Admission Waiting Times" (1990), 32. A study for Australia does not provide data by diagnostic group, but concluded that vigorous efforts to reduce these [waiting] lists are still urgently needed . . . given the deterioration in health . . . in some patients (14 percent of those interviewed) whilst on surgical waiting lists." Cf. "Surgical Waiting Lists" (1991), 328.

· TRANSPORT ·

What are my wants? First . . . a fine day in Dublin . . . and
second . . . the power of unimpeded movement . . . a Baby Ford.
—OLIVER ST. JOHN GOGARTY, *As I Was Going Down Sackville Street*

Has any image been more durably attractive than Mercury's sandals, or the magic carpet? Each promised a miraculous escape from
nature's restraints (e.g., gravity) or civilization's (e.g., responsibility). Yet for thousands of years, only rulers and priests had
ready access to transport—on the backs of their followers, in sedan
chairs or rickshaws, or on domesticated animals. The rest of the
human race patiently walked. Without magic they could not travel
whenever need, or whim, seized them.

In 1900 the United States led most nations in wealth. With so
much open land, it fed horses at low cost. Yet only one urban family
in five had its own horse and could therefore travel at need, or whim
(see Table II.25).[116] Fewer still had carriages, enabling several family
members to travel together. Most Americans still walked to work,
living within a mile of their workplaces.[117]

The rise of incomes after 1900 did not increase the percentage of
families with horses. Had it done so, every major city would have
had to stable thousands of horses. How could they find the space?
Or clean up after them? Or cart away the thousands who fell dead
each year? Only the mass production of automobiles removed such
problems.

By the middle of the Great Depression, most farm families, and
nearly half of all urban families, enjoyed the freedoms provided by
automobile ownership. Western Europe did not even reach a 44

---

[116] Most farmers owned a ploughhorse or a mule. But neither was suited to recreational travel, or to long distances.

[117] Hershberg, *Philadelphia* (1981), 136–38, 152–53, presents data for Philadelphia
in 1880. Although the city had 300 route miles for its streetcars, five workers out of six
walked to work.

Table II.25

U.S. Urban Families with Horses
and Automobiles, 1900–1989

Date	Percentage
With a horse	
1900	20
With a car	
1935	44
1977	84
1989	87

Sources: For 1900: U.S. Bureau of the Census, *Statistics of Agriculture, 1900*, pt. 1, vol. 5, table 41. For each population size group, the ratio of horses to population was computed, then applied to population counts for each group from idem, *Supplementary Analysis, 1900, 25.* The resultant total is 1,438,487. In that year, 38 percent of all households were urban (idem, *Historical Statistics*, 11, 43), or, say, 6 million out of 16 million. To allow for urban horses used by livery stables and small business, I reduce the implicit ratio of 25 percent to 20 percent.

For 1935: Lebergott, *American Economy,* 290.

For 1977: Survey data indicate that 80 percent of all U.S. households, and 81 percent of those in metropolitan areas, owned autos; U.S. Bureau of the Census, *Statistical Abstract, 1978,* 45, 649.

For 1989: Idem, *American Housing Survey, 1989,* table 2-7.

percent ownership rate until a third of a century later.[118] Even then only 20 percent of the Portugese and 30 percent of the Spaniards had cars, and less than 2 percent of those in Eastern Europe or most of the rest of the world. By the 1960s, second-hand cars cost so little that few Americans went without one except in cities that subsi-

[118] Readers' Digest, *Survey of Europe Today* (1970), table 39.

Table II.26

U.S. Families with Automobiles, 1900–1989

		Location		Race	
Year	Total	Urban	Farm	White	Black
1900	0%	0%	0%	0%	0%
1910	1	n.a.	n.a.	n.a.	n.a.
1920	26	35	29	n.a.	n.a.
1930	60	n.a.	n.a.	n.a.	n.a.
1935–36	55	44	n.a.	59	15
1942	58	55	69	n.a.	n.a.
1960	75	69	77	n.a.	n.a.
1970	79	73	87	83	53
1983	86	n.a.	n.a.	n.a.	n.a.
1989	84	83	89	86	69

Source: For 1900–1970: Lebergott, *American Economy,* 290; urban-rural data for 1971 are used for 1970. For 1983: U.S. Energy Information Administration, *Consumption Patterns of Household Vehicles, 1983,* 2. For 1989: U.S. Bureau of the Census, *American Housing Survey for the United States in 1989,* table 2-7; includes trucks and vans regularly used by household.

dized local transit (Table II.26). Indeed, by 1987 the typical very low income family (income below $5,000) owned an automobile.[119]

When the twentieth century opened, the automobile appeared to be only a plaything for the rich and reckless. In the 1920s it became the center of a new society. Its promise of instant mobility made it "essential" for millions. Between 1900 and 1980, the number of cars increased from 8,000 to 100,000,000.

When Robert and Helen Lynd spoke of America's "gorged stream of new things to buy," they put the automobile first on their list.[120] Expanding demand pushed up the cost of buying and operating a car (Table II.27). But two quite different sets of cost changes can be distinguished in the first two-thirds of the century, 1900–1967, prior to OPEC—private and public.

---

[119] According to the unpublished U.S. Bureau of Labor Statistics expenditure survey for that year.

[120] Lynd and Lynd, *Middletown in Transition,* 46.

Table II.27

U.S. Cost of Automobile Operation, 1900 and 1967

(cents per mile)

	1900	1967
Private	7.4	6.6
Depreciation	4.4	2.8
Gasoline	1.1	1.5
Oil and accessories	1.3	0.5
Repairs and tires	0.6	1.8
Public and insurance	0.0	4.4
Taxes	0.0	1.2
Insurance	0.0	1.4
Parking, tolls	0.0	1.8
Total	7.4	11.0
Addenda		
Speed (miles per hour)	17	60
Miles per year	4,000	10,000
Average horsepower	27	269

Sources: For 1900: Norman, "Can I Afford an Automobile?" (1903), 3502. For 1967: U.S. Department of Transportation, *Energy Statistics: A Supplement* (1976). The purchase price was $1,750 in 1900; $2,806 in 1967. Data estimated for a 10-year life. For 1967, a 10,000-mile-a-year figure is used. For horsepower: U.S. Bureau of the Census, *Manufactures, 1910,* 818; and information provided by the staff of *Automotive News,* 1967.

Since oligopolies developed in the industries that manufactured automobiles, the prices of gasoline and tires inevitably changed. But they did not rise. They fell.

The number of automobile producers fell from 1900 to 1967. The cost per mile charged by auto manufacturers (i.e., depreciation) inevitably changed. Since an oligopoly developed, profit presumably rose. Wage rates in the industry also rose for decades. Yet cost per mile did not. It actually fell, about one-third.[121] And the industry delivered an even safer car to the consumer. The car was also far better equipped than its more costly predecessors. It had a unitized,

[121] The Norman estimate in Table II.27 assumes 4,000 miles a year. The Department of Transportation figures assume 10,000 miles.

closed, steel body instead of an open body of wood. Safety glass had replaced glassine curtains. Hydraulic brakes superseded mechanical ones. And electric starters replaced hand cranks.

Gasoline costs changed as well. Consumers shifted from the simple models of 1900 to heavy, complicated "gas guzzlers." (Horsepower by 1967 was almost ten times as great.) They drove at 60 miles per hour instead of cruising along at 17 miles per hour. Both changes inevitably increased gasoline costs. Yet those rose less than a penny a mile.[122] Increasing efficiency in the oligopoly that dominated gasoline production had substantially offset the increase in costs as consumers drove bigger cars, faster.

The really significant increase in automobile costs per mile after 1900 came because ownership was democratized. When millions of lower- and middle-class families began to buy automobiles, they created externalities. These forced costs up.

Taxes rose, to provide more and better roads. They represented public action for a larger public. (The analogy with yachts is suggestive. When only the rich owned power boats, little was spent for public marinas and facilities.)

Insurance became universal. It helped compensate for the damages that escalated along with auto ownership. The handful of cars driven in 1900 averaged 16 to 18 miles an hour and rarely encountered one another. But when 100 million autos competed for road positions, at 60 miles an hour, accidents escalated. Had only "the rich" owned autos in 1967, as they did in 1900, accident rates would have been far lower. So would insurance costs. And parking charges.

The automobile found fierce critics on each side of the "two cultures," as had earlier transport improvements. Wordsworth interrupted his nature walks to write fervent letters urging the prime minister to halt railroad development. Ruskin interrupted his art criticism for some intense comment on the first railways in Britain:

[122] As late as the inflation of 1920, gasoline cost only 20 cents a gallon, and oil, 7 cents. See U.S. Department of Agriculture, *Yearbook of Agriculture, 1921* (1922), 807. A 1965 price of 20 cents and a 1967 price of 23 cents—exclusive of tax—are reported in U.S. Department of Transportation, *Energy Statistics, Annual Report* (1967). Gasoline costs rose from 1.1 to 1.5 cents per mile. Gas prices rose only 10 percent. Hence $1.5 - (1.1 \times 110\%) = 0.003$ additional cents per mile because of increased size of car and motor, and increased speeds.

We have just paid men [a hundred and fifty millions] for digging ground from one place and depositing it in another. We have formed a large class of men, the railway navvies, especially reckless, unmanageable, and dangerous. We have maintained besides . . . a number of ironfounders in an unhealthy employment . . . we have, in fine, attained the power of going fast from one place to another. . . . suppose, on the other hand, that we had employed the same sums in building beautiful houses and churches?[123]

In 1977, a distinguished American physicist added his voice:

Though scientific advance . . . increase[s] the number of alternatives available for our choice . . . we can choose foolishly; we can seize one item out of the mass of new knowledge and transform it into an overspecialized technology that distorts our whole society—as we have done with the automobile.[124]

Did the early critics prefer walking to using the railroad? Or the later ones, the railroad to the automobile? Perhaps. Each system nonetheless had its costs. If Ruskin had to walk across Europe from Calais he would never have contemplated the stones of Venice. Instead he took the coach and stage. But those too created "distortions." As Robert Mills pointed out (in 1826):

Stage proprietors . . . find it more profitable sometimes to double the quantity of labor assigned to a horse, though they are aware that, in so doing, they will destroy the animal in three or four years. But in a large business, stage proprietors do not hesitate sacrificing one-third of their stock of horses every year on this account. For the difference between the interest that will return the excess of capital expended in the purchase of the first horses, and the annual expense of keeping a great number, is too great for them to hesitate to make the sacrifice.

This is a melancholy truth; may we not hope, however, . . . that railroads will, in some degree, lessen the evil, and diminish the quantity of animal torture?[125]

How many peasants, anywhere in the world, willingly shortened their lives (by working longer and harder) to extend the lives of their draught animals? How many literary men? Humans consistently

[123] Quoted in Sherburne, *John Ruskin*, 40–41.
[124] Morse, *In at the Beginnings* (1977), 365.
[125] Mills, *"Three Papers on Railroads,"* (from *The American Farmer* n.p., n.d.) p.5.

allocated resources to cut their own transport time and effort. They did so under feudal regimes, as under capitalist ones. (That "over-specialized" railroads and automobiles actually reduced "animal torture" is, however, beyond the concern of economics.)

Critics of U.S. "auto worship" have urged smaller cars, less luxury, less speed. One intuited that by limiting speed to between 15 and 25 miles per hour we would even create a more "convivial society."[126] But most auto trips are made to work or by housewives shopping or chauffeuring their children. Americans kept down such uninteresting and tiresome transit hours—by speed (paying, as noted, less than 1 cent a mile for greater speed in 1967 than in 1900). Moreover, they sped along with greater safety and comfort—thanks to the addition of windshield wipers, heaters, electric self-starters, steel bodies, unit construction, four-wheel brakes, and a host of other conveniences. Yet they paid Detroit less per mile for the use of their cars (i.e., depreciation) than did their grandparents.[127]

Public transport also helped increase mobility between 1900 and 1990. But its share of consumer expenditure drifted downward for decades because auto transport proved so much more convenient (Table II.28). Individualistic Americans preferred to leave and return when they chose, not when the utility (or even airline) schedule permitted.

Table II.28
Percentage of U.S. Personal
Consumption Expenditure for Public
Transport, 1900–1990

1900	3.0%
1910	3.6
1920	3.0
1929	2.1
1980	1.1
1990	0.9

Source: Appendix A.

---

[126] Ivan Illich, quoted in Pirages, *Sustainable Society* (1977), 166. In 1900, a top speed of 35 miles an hour was achieved only occasionally.

[127] The inflation after 1967 inevitably changed the dimension of all prices.

At the beginning of the twentieth century, Americans made few contacts outside their family. If youngsters left home to live in another state, they rarely saw their parents again. But by 1990, contact with other families, other modes of belief and behavior, was almost incessant. Cheap transport, more than almost any other force, made "the melting pot" a reality.

·RECREATION·

"What signifies," says some one, "giving halfpence to common beggars?

They only lay it out in gin or tobacco." And why should they be denied

such sweeteners of their existence (says Johnson)? It is

surely very savage to refuse them every possible avenue to

pleasure reckoned too coarse for our own acceptance. Life

is a pill which none of us can swallow without gilding.

—HESTER THRALE, *Thraliana*

For eleven consecutive years, the Peking Capital Orchestra was "allowed" to perform only three pieces of music—The Yellow River Concerto and two cantatas.[128] That political episode emphasizes how important the surrounding culture is in determining the resources devoted to any recreational activity. Far more than income is involved, or mere economic considerations.

In the dim Western past, recreation was infrequent at best.[129] Festivals came so rarely that celebrants ate, drank, and abandoned themselves, "seeking to compensate themselves for the parsimony which dominates their existence throughout the rest of the year."[130]

[128] According to its conductor, Li Teh-Lun, quoted by Andrew Davis, conductor of the Toronto Symphony, in Hart, *Conductors* (1979), 61–62.

[129] Obligatory holidays involved church attendance, not revelry.

[130] "Plaintes à gassendi" (1838), 10:93.

American families lived under harsh, dangerous conditions for centuries. They therefore devoted little time, and few resources, to recreation. Even by 1900, when holidays were still more frequent in Europe, it was "a common saying that there are only two holidays in the United States—Independence Day and Christmas."[131] Vacations were rare. Less than 2 percent of American families took them.[132] And recreational expenditure accounted for only 3 percent of consumption in 1900.

By 1990 that share had more than doubled. It increased decade after decade (apart from the 1929-39 decline). Surprisingly, the share did not rise most in the era of Victor Herbert and the Floradora girls, nor when motion pictures developed, nor even during the television and boom-box era. The great increase came between 1920 and 1929. The radio and the automobile then created an unprecedented set of new recreational possibilities—within the home and the other outside (Table II.29). These were later supplemented in multifarious ways.

Economists from the largest nation in the world saw such increases as reflecting "a degeneration in ideology and culture. . . . In the capitalist world, strange clothing, modern dances, and 'Beatles' music bands have been common, and exhibitions of 'impressionist' art painted by monkeys have been much in vogue . . . culture and art under imperialism have been rotten to the core."[133]

Some American historians also voiced doubts about art under capitalism:

The Steinway was billed "as the best in the piano maker's art." Indeed, Wagner called it a "noble work of art." Those purchasing a Steinway thus were not buying merely a piano but something akin to great painting or sculpture. References to touch and tone—that is, the pi-

---

[131] According to an officer of a leading steel company, quoted in Jeans, ed., *American Industrial Conditions and Competition*, 78.

[132] Even after the custom had spread, a 1922-24 survey showed that less than 27 percent of farm families took any days of vacation from work. Some 4 percent took two weeks or more. (And farmers—unlike wage earners—did not lose any income by being away from work.) Cf. U.S. Department of Agriculture, *Farmer's Standard of Living* (1926), 51.

[133] Fundamentals of Political Economy Writing Group, *Fundamentals of Political Economy* (1977), 189.

ano's USEFUL functions—were nothing compared to the basic USELESS-
NESS that allowed Steinway to thrive in the consumer's imagination.[134]

Scholars undoubtedly preferred their own phrases for advertising
copy. But could even five-day-a-week psychoanalytic sessions describe how a "basic uselessness . . . thrive[d] in the . . . imagination" of several million consumers?[135]

Table II.29

U.S. Households Containing Pianos, Phonographs, Radios, Televisions,
1920–90

	Homes with			
	Pianos	Phonographs	Radios	Televisions
1920	13%	16%	—	—
1925	n.a.	n.a.	10%	—
1930	n.a.	n.a.	46	—
1940	n.a.	n.a.	81	—
1946	n.a.	n.a.	88	(0.002)
1950	13	13	95	9
1960	14	31	95	87
1970	n.a.	n.a.	99	95
1980	n.a.	n.a.	99	98
1990	n.a.	n.a.	99	98

Source: For radio and television 1925–70: U.S. Bureau of the Census, *Historical
Statistics,* 2:796, 1:41; for 1980–90: U.S. Bureau of the Census, *Statistical Abstract, 1991,*
556. For piano and phonograph, 1920: Percentage of families purchasing "music" and
"records" respectively. U.S. Bureau of Labor Statistics, *Cost of Living in the United
States,* Bulletin 357, 451, 399; for 1950 and 1960: U.S. Bureau of Labor Statistics,
Monthly Labor Review (Oct. 1964): 1135.

In any event, "degeneration" and "uselessness" helped increase
recreational spending this century. So did charges by performers.
They rose, as they have since Phidias, and Bach. And critics were

[134] Roell, *Piano in America* (1989), 50.
[135] But grant this scholarly psychoanalysis of what went on in the minds of two
million purchasers of this brand during the 1920s. What are the criteria of
"uselessness" to the consumer? If only "touch and tone" matter, portable keyboards
do provide a far cheaper substitute for the average consumer.

exasperated. Did Rachel, the great actress, need to be paid so much, asked Proudhon? Did Michael Jackson really need enough income to drive a gold Camaro? The artists, of course, answered as most wage earners would. When an outraged manager cried, "Even the President of the United States doesn't make as much money!" Callas replied: "Then let him sing."[136] Singers (and artists and athletes) continue to collect high rates in both Russia and the United States. Field marshals, party chairmen, and presidents make a less remunerative living, not singing. They may be liked, but they are rarely adored.

Throughout this century technical advance persistently cut the cost of each hour of "recreation." It has, of course, been argued by Baumol and others that technological advance in services is necessarily sluggish. After all, the Haydn Quintenquartette took 19 minutes playing time two centuries ago. It can be performed no faster today. Yet what about economics, not musicianship? In 1900 it was played to audiences of at most a few hundred. In 1990 radio and satellites beam it to millions. Similar changes for baseball games, opera, and tennis matches cut recreation costs this century, even ignoring records and videocassettes. Thus recreation experience increased more this century than the constant dollar figures report.

Eventually, American men devoted as much time to television and other recreation as to jobs (Table II.30). Women devoted about as many hours as men to television, and to recreation in general.[137] That switch was unprecedented in human history. It did little to confirm forecasts of "immiseration" under capitalism. As alternative routes to pleasure multiplied, time devoted to recreation increased.

---

[136] Wechsberg, *Red Plush and Black Velvet* (1961), 114. When Catarina Gabrielli asked Empress Catherine of Russia for 3,000 ducats for one concert, the scandalized empress told "the diva that none of her field marshals received as much money. Gabrielli suggested sweetly that her Majesty let her field marshals sing for her." It is noteworthy that some of the highest paid workers in the equalitarian Soviet state were artists.

[137] Exactly comparable data are not available for women with full-time jobs. Total hours of work in the home plus time on the job were similar for women (47) and men (47). Juster and Stafford, *Time, Goods, and Well-Being*, 173.

Related data show married women and men working about as long each week, if one adds work both on the job and at home (481 versus 467 minutes a week). But women spent less time in leisure than men (233 versus 258 minutes). (Ibid., 270, 272–73.) Juster and Stafford suggest that the "secular decline" from about 60 hours in 1900 may have ended in 1975, not continuing to 1981 (p. 260).

Table II.30

Weekly Hours of Recreation and Work, United States, 1975

	Men (hours)	Women (hours)
Working on the job	33.1	16.9
Working in the house and shopping	13.5	30.1
Total Recreation	33.3	31.9
Television	14.8	14.0
Sports, entertainment, travel, hobbies	14.0	13.9
Meals out, gardening, driving to movies, taverns[a]	4.5	4.0

Source: Juster and Stafford, *Time, Goods, and Well-Being*, 173, based on the I.S.R. National Time Budget Survey.

Note: For "job" I exclude lunch and coffee time.

[a]This includes time for meals out (2.7 hours), fraternal organizations (0.16), gardening and pet care (0.94), driving to movies, etc. (0.7).

Social analysts who kept talking of America's "Puritan Ethic" were clearly wide of the mark. "The Book of Sports" would be more to the point. In 1900, American workers almost never took a vacation. They had neither television nor radio, bought few books, and spent little for sports, music, or the theatre. By 1990 they were following Herrick's advice:

> While the milder fates consent
> Let's enjoy our merriment.

· WELFARE ·

Charity was explained by the two Smiths. According to the Reverend Sydney Smith:

> Benevolence is a natural instinct of the human mind; when *A* sees *B* in distress his conscience always urges him to entreat *C* to help him.[138]

According to Adam Smith, the economist:

> How selfish soever man be supposed, there are evidently some principles in his nature which interest him in the fortune of others, and render their happiness necessary to him, though he derives nothing from it except the pleasure of seeing it.[139]

A laborious literature has recently developed to demonstrate that humans are moved by motives other than "self-interest."[140] It has broken through a largely open door. For even economists specializing in self-interest have never doubted it.[141] Adam Smith spoke of "the natural effort of every individual to better his own condition," and added that "the principles of common prudence do not always govern the conduct of every individual, [but] they always influence that of the majority of every class or order."[142]

As Hahn put it, "A relevant description of the domain of choice includes the welfare . . . of other[s]; this is simply to aver that we live in society. The interesting question is not: 'Do we care about others?' but, 'How much do we care and for which others?'"[143]

---

[138] *Bon Mots of Sydney Smith and Robert Brinsley Sheridan* (1893), 59.

[139] Adam Smith, *Theory of Moral Sentiments* (1976), 1.

[140] See, among others, Hirschman, *The Interests and the Passions* (1977); and Jane Mansbridge, ed., *Beyond Self-Interest* (1990), in particular the chapter by Stephen Holmes, "The Secret History of Self-Interest."

[141] Cf., e.g., Becker, *Economic Theory*, 25–26. Rational "behavior with utility maximization" does not mean "that people are necessarily selfish 'economic men' solely concerned with their own well-being. This would rule out charity and love" and would be "grossly inconsistent with actual behavior."

[142] See George Stigler's "Smith's Travels on the Ship of State" (1975), which begins, "The Wealth of Nations is a stupendous palace erected upon the granite of self-interest.

[143] Hahn, "Benevolence" (1991), 8.

How much indeed? One answer is given by anecdotes, recent and resounding. They declare that a more elysian, more altruistic era surely preceded "the rise of selfishness in America."[144] But a more systematic measure of "the rise of selfishness" exists: the share of income spent by Americans to "better their own condition" versus "the welfare of others." I contrast in Table II.31 expenditures oriented to the family versus those to outsiders. (The "self," of course, includes members of the family,[145] for evolution has inextricably mixed up individual and family behavior.)

Table II.31
Percentage of Personal Expenditures
Used for Welfare, United States,
1900–1990

1900	0.0064%
1910	0.0036
1920	0.0042
1929	0.0038
1980	0.0048
1990	0.0178

Source: Appendix A.

As American incomes rose, the share devoted to welfare of others rose—from two-thirds of 1 percent, to almost 2 percent: Over 98 percent of total expenditure was, and continued to be, "self-regarding."

Psychologists and philosophers assert that empathy indeed provides "the chief motive for altruism."[146] In recent years, economists have frequently defined A's altruism as an argument in his utility function.[147] They portray A as deriving potent satisfactions from

[144] Collier, Rise of Selfishness in America (1992). Did other cultures also show a rise? Or had they always been selfish? Or saintly?

[145] The percentage of family income in "cash contributions . . . to relatives and others" runs about 3 percent for income groups reported in Bureau of Labor Statistics surveys. Cf. U.S. Bureau of Labor Statistics, Consumer Expenditure Survey, 1987 (1990), table 2.

[146] The quotation is from Mussen and Eisenberg-Berg, Roots of Caring, Sharing and Helping (1977), 127. Thomas Nagel ("Comment" [1975], 64) observed that "this capacity to put oneself in another person's shoes is behind most altruistic behavior."

[147] Cf., for example, Phelps, ed., Altruism. Developments in sociobiology do not

altruistic behavior, whether mere politeness or arduous self-sacrifice.

Sydney Smith observed A entreating B to help C. But A could help indirectly by making other people contribute million of pennies, via the government, for each one given by A. Once the income tax was enacted in 1913 the American "A" satisfied his altruism readily.

Did public expenditure increasingly substitute for private benevolence after the income tax, the New Deal, JFK, and the poverty programs? Hardly. Spending on public welfare, public housing, and Medicaid did increase: amounting to less than 1 percent of personal income in 1902, it rose after 1929, reaching 3 percent by 1982.[148] But that rise did not, as many believe, depress the private share. Consumers no longer allocated half a penny of each dollar to welfare, but almost two cents. (Data for benevolence in other nations are lacking, except for the Soviet Union—where charity was officially forbidden. It was unnecessary in a "well-planned" state.)

· RELIGION ·

In earlier generations, parishioners who failed to give a tenth of their income to the church could be excommunicated. Priests could

> curse them by the authority of the Court of Rome, within and without, sleeping and waking, going, sitting and standing, lying down on the earth and under the earth. . . . Curse them by the Father and Son and

---

controvert such a position, focusing as they do on the origins of the individual's utility.

[148] U.S. Bureau of the Census, *Historical Statistics*, 2:1120. (I assume that all of "public welfare" and one-half of "hospitals" in 1902 were spent for welfare); U.S. Bureau of Economic Analysis, *National Income and Product Accounts of the United States, 1929–82* (1986), tables 2.1, 3.15 (I do not include transfer payments for education, urban renewal, old-age assistance. Such items chiefly return to the givers, and their families).

Holy Ghost. Curse them angels and archangels and all the nine orders of heaven . . . the pains of hell be their lot.[149]

Surely a tenth of one's income was a tiny sum compared to the present value of hell. But belief in the afterlife attenuated remarkably over the decades. Pascal's wager found fewer and fewer takers. Nineteenth-century biblical scholarship "robbed many pious souls of their hope of eternal damnation." Secularism completed the task for others.

In 1900, Americans were devoting closer to one than ten percent of their income to religious endeavor. Even that share was cut by 1929. By 1990 they still spent less than one percent.[150] (Ministers earned more than the average American in 1900. By 1980 they earned less.[151] Hence their share declined, in part, because their services were relatively cheaper.) The things of this world had come to dominate the prospect of eternity. With unconscious humor (or heavy irony), a British scholar pigeonholed twentieth-century spending on religion in the "late out-moded stage"—along with spending for horse-drawn carriages.[152] But belief that buying indulgences, or giving money in this world, would moderate purgatory, or pave the route to salvation, had nearly disappeared by 1990.

[149] Peacock, ed., *Instruction for Parish Priests by John Myrc* (1898), 64, 67.

[150] Unpublished data for 1990 kindly provided by the U.S. Bureau of Economic Analysis.

[151] Earnings of Methodist and Congregational ministers for 1900 are reported in Douglas, *Real Wages in the United States* (1930), 386. Earnings for all workers appear in Lebergott, *Manpower*, 523. For 1970, data are available in U.S. Bureau of the Census, *Occupational Characteristics, 1970*, table 1. Comparisons with data for men only at both dates would have shown a greater relative decline.

[152] Ironmonger, *New Commodities and Consumer Behavior* (1972), 159.

·POSTSCRIPT·

JEFFERSON, that indefatigable record keeper, left a single note of his activities the day American independence was declared: "July 4, 1776—paid for 7 pair of women's gloves, 27 shillings."[1] The "ordinary business of life" continued, even then.

This inevitably brief survey of how Americans spent their increased incomes in the twentieth century reveals how American materialism was implemented. The official Communist breviary declares:

> The higher the level of civilisation, the wider and more diverse the range of things and services that people need. The conception of well-being today includes . . . convenient and spacious homes, high quality beautiful clothes . . . TV sets, musical instruments, athletic gear and many other things. Communism aims at fully satisfying peoples' needs for all these things and services.[2]

The U.S. record lacks detail on spending for "spacious homes, high quality beautiful clothes . . . athletic gear and many other things." But the broader trends are clear. Increased income was chiefly used to reduce household chores—preparing food, washing clothes, keeping the family and dwelling free from lice and dirt. Greater housing expenditure did not add more space, but provided more privacy for each child. It also added the safety and comfort of clean water and indoor plumbing, replacing privies and schoolroom toilets. The convenience of hot water from pipes substituted for the labor of hauling wood indoors, boiling tubs of water for washing. Electric lighting substituted for smoking oil and kerosene lamps. Spending for medical care reduced suffering, brought faster recov-

---

[1] Record from his *Account Book*, 1776–78, quoted in Betts, ed., *Thomas Jefferson's Garden Book* (1944), 69.

[2] Kuusinen, *Fundamentals of Marxism-Leninism* (1961), 857.

ery from illness. It also helped millions of ordinary human beings to extend their lives—more important, surely, than better publicized examples of how persons were saved from collapsed mines or buildings.

Spending increases for recreation, clothing, or nondurable household items after 1900 were hardly "essential." Critics of such expenditure were on target. But few spoke from monasteries, or even adopted the simpler life that the Amish and Hutterites still manage in America. Spending to enhance "the sweetness of life" continues to draw on resources, not least for roads, automobiles, gas, and airplanes to reach wilderness areas and parks.

As always, temperaments patrol the approaches to consumption. Some Americans seek Priestly's vision of life after the revolution:

> Nature will be more at our command; men will [be] abundantly more easy and comfortable . . . and daily grow more happy each in himself, and more able . . . to communicate happiness.[3]

Others agree with Santayana:

> All living things pursued the greatest happiness they could see their way to; but they were marvelously short sighted. . . . If you asked for little, it was more probable that the event would not disappoint you. It was important not to be a fool, but it was very hard.[4]

[3] Quoted in Lucas, *Greatest Problem* (1961), 250.
[4] Santayana, *Three Philosophical Poets* (1953), 33.

· A P P E N D I X A ·

Key to Appendix Table A
Personal Consumption, per Capita, by Major Group and by Item, United States, 1900–1990
(1987 prices)

Food, clothing, personal care	
1900–1929	148
1929–1956	152
1956–1985	157
1986–1990	162
Housing, household operation	
1900–1929	149
1929–1956	153
1956–1985	158
1986–1990	162
Medical, personal business	
1900–1929	150
1929–1956	154
1956–1985	159
1986–1990	162
Transportation, recreation, education	
1900–1929	150, 151
1929–1956	155, 156
1956–1985	160, 161
1986–1990	163
Religion, welfare, travel	
1900–1929	151
1929–1956	156
1956–1985	161
1986–1990	163

Source: For 1900–1928: Stanley Lebergott, *Consumer Expenditures: New Measures, Old Motives* (forthcoming). For 1929–1990: U.S. Bureau of Economic Analysis, *National Income and Product Accounts of the United States, 1929–1988,* and *Survey of Current Business* (January 1992).

Appendix Table
Per Capita Personal Consumption by Type of Expenditure (1987 Dollars)

Year	TOTAL PCE	Food, Alcohol, Tobacco							Clothing					Personal Care		
		TOTAL	Purch. food, mls., bevs.	Food fur-nished	Food on farms	Al-cohol (legal)	To-bacco	TOTAL[a]	Shoes	Total civilian	Jewelry	Clean-ing	TOTAL	Toi-letries	Barber, beauty
1900	3266	1416	1049	24	105	169	69	272	79	116	13	64	28	6	22
1901	3462	1494	1112	21	111	176	73	354	89	122	12	71	30	7	24
1902	3477	1505	1123	21	105	185	71	354	87	130	14	62	31	7	24
1903	3512	1496	1118	17	100	189	73	375	91	141	14	66	32	7	25
1904	3562	1509	1133	17	99	190	69	384	93	144	13	69	32	7	25
1905	3729	1585	1197	18	102	199	70	398	93	150	15	71	35	8	27
1906	3817	1581	1176	17	98	213	76	439	95	178	20	74	36	8	28
1907	3782	1572	1158	19	102	216	78	436	93	172	19	76	38	9	28
1908	3681	1560	1161	17	101	207	74	419	94	171	15	68	36	8	27
1909	3866	1652	1248	19	102	205	79	446	90	187	22	71	38	8	29
1910	3891	1670	1254	19	101	213	83	442	93	180	22	72	38	8	29
1911	3816	1564	1163	17	89	214	81	467	95	197	22	76	39	9	30
1912	3892	1584	1181	18	90	215	80	473	94	202	21	77	39	9	30
1913	3954	1614	1203	18	91	216	86	478	94	203	20	81	40	9	31
1914	3912	1636	1237	19	88	202	90	446	83	187	15	82	39	9	31
1915	3775	1476	1098	17	90	188	85	429	80	174	14	82	39	10	30
1916	4039	1517	1129	19	90	188	91	492	98	207	17	88	41	10	31
1917	4081	1529	1147	21	101	171	90	469	88	222	12	67	40	9	31
1918	4019	1439	1048	73	94	120	104	465	94	217	9	56	42	12	31
1919	3829	1249	999	21	85	56	88	424	77	188	17	54	43	12	31
1920	3667	1121	929	16	77	0	98	410	74	179	13	57	44	13	31
1921	3404	1017	854	15	62	0	86	408	69	169	9	71	45	12	33
1922	3687	1119	947	16	65	0	91	509	80	228	13	86	50	15	36
1923	3972	1163	991	17	59	0	96	544	89	249	13	84	54	16	38
1924	3981	1191	1012	17	59	0	103	506	83	214	12	85	56	16	39
1925	4155	1192	1008	17	63	0	103	533	80	238	14	84	58	17	41
1926	4285	1225	1041	18	62	0	105	541	81	240	15	84	60	17	43
1927	4289	1229	1047	17	58	0	107	561	79	251	15	89	64	19	45
1928	4564	1229	1041	17	59	0	111	566	73	252	15	90	68	21	47
1929	4561	1247	1057	18	57	0	115	437	75	260	15	86	71	22	49

[a] Includes military: 1917–1, 1918–5, 1919–2. All other years—less than 1.

		Housing				Household Operation														
Year	TOTAL	Non-farm owned	Non-farm rented	Farm	Other	TOTAL	Furniture	Kitchen appliances	China, glass	Other durables	Semi-durables	Cleaning supplies	Stationery	Electricity	Gas	Water	Fuel	Telephone	Domestic serv.	Other
1900	256	123	80	45	8	465	37	5	30	24	10	10	3	*	7	20	96	1	212	12
1901	261	124	82	46	8	474	41	5	34	25	10	11	3	*	8	19	90	1	213	13
1902	265	122	86	48	9	475	41	5	35	29	10	11	3	*	9	20	88	1	211	11
1903	266	122	88	47	9	482	42	5	37	29	10	11	4	*	10	21	90	1	208	13
1904	278	125	90	54	9	481	42	5	36	28	10	11	6	*	11	20	91	1	207	13
1905	279	127	95	47	9	495	46	6	45	30	9	13	4	*	11	21	88	1	207	13
1906	288	130	100	50	10	494	51	7	46	21	11	13	4	1	12	21	90	2	203	13
1907	293	132	104	48	10	499	44	6	39	31	9	14	4	1	13	21	97	2	205	13
1908	295	131	107	48	10	477	36	5	35	25	9	13	5	1	13	22	95	2	204	13
1909	307	137	111	48	11	497	46	5	36	30	11	13	5	1	14	22	94	3	202	14
1910	310	137	113	48	12	495	44	5	35	32	12	13	5	1	15	24	92	3	200	12
1911	317	139	117	49	12	495	40	6	38	30	13	13	5	1	16	25	93	3	198	14
1912	324	141	118	52	12	504	40	7	41	32	13	14	5	2	16	25	96	4	195	14
1913	323	137	121	53	12	517	48	7	39	33	15	14	6	2	17	24	103	4	191	14
1914	328	139	123	53	12	489	36	6	36	29	15	14	6	2	18	23	97	4	188	14
1915	331	139	124	55	13	474	35	6	40	27	14	16	5	3	20	24	93	4	175	14
1916	342	144	127	56	14	496	44	7	38	31	14	19	5	3	21	24	110	5	161	14
1917	345	150	125	54	15	502	45	9	33	32	14	17	5	3	23	25	127	5	151	13
1918	355	158	127	53	17	480	44	8	20	28	13	16	5	4	24	26	131	6	142	12
1919	359	164	125	51	19	477	52	9	24	26	14	15	6	5	26	22	120	7	140	12
1920	353	166	126	42	19	486	37	10	27	28	14	16	5	6	27	22	136	8	139	11
1921	342	151	126	50	16	458	35	6	27	22	18	15	5	6	25	22	115	8	142	12
1922	323	128	130	50	15	508	43	7	27	32	19	19	6	6	26	23	132	9	146	13
1923	361	160	133	53	15	528	47	8	32	38	21	21	8	8	27	24	121	9	150	13
1924	368	163	137	53	14	524	54	8	23	35	20	20	7	8	28	24	121	9	153	14
1925	381	170	142	54	14	558	56	9	32	39	23	20	7	10	28	25	128	10	156	14
1926	399	179	150	54	16	588	59	10	39	39	28	20	6	10	30	26	134	11	160	15
1927	408	184	153	54	17	574	59	10	35	39	26	22	6	12	31	25	118	12	163	15
1928	424	191	159	54	19	610	60	10	41	43	25	23	7	13	30	26	136	12	168	16
1929	430	199	156	55	21	622	57	10	40	44	28	23	7	15	30	25	136	15	176	16

* Less than 1.

(continued)

Appendix Table (continued)

Year	Medical						Personal Business			Transportation							
	TOTAL	Drugs	Ophth., ortho. prods.	Drs., other profs.	Hos-pitals	Health ins.	TOTAL	Bro-kerage	Other	TOTAL	Motor veh.	Tires, access.	Re-pair	Gas, oil	Ins., tolls	Purch. local	Purch. inter city
1900	171	8	1	143	19	1	248	117	131	141	3	*	*	*	*	100	38
1901	179	9	1	148	21	1	311	158	153	150	4	*	*	*	*	104	41
1902	180	8	1	149	21	1	304	148	155	152	4	*	*	*	*	102	46
1903	184	9	1	153	21	1	308	142	166	160	4	*	*	*	*	108	47
1904	186	9	1	153	22	1	309	142	167	176	5	*	*	*	*	122	48
1905	192	10	1	155	25	1	353	173	180	191	4	*	*	*	*	136	50
1906	199	10	1	157	30	1	383	191	192	202	4	*	*	1	*	144	52
1907	215	10	1	163	39	1	341	162	179	202	5	1	1	1	*	142	54
1908	207	9	1	164	31	1	302	146	156	204	5	*	1	1	*	142	54
1909	206	8	1	161	34	1	322	158	163	214	10	*	2	1	1	148	54
1910	210	8	1	154	47	1	312	149	163	227	13	*	2	2	1	151	57
1911	209	9	1	154	45	1	300	134	166	240	13	*	3	3	1	161	58
1912	215	9	1	159	43	1	308	130	178	263	22	1	4	3	1	174	58
1913	220	9	1	161	47	2	307	116	191	271	26	1	5	3	1	174	57
1914	224	9	2	165	46	2	281	99	181	279	32	1	6	9	2	175	55
1915	230	9	2	166	50	2	315	116	200	286	44	1	8	9	2	172	49
1916	238	10	3	162	61	2	386	133	253	319	75	2	11	9	3	171	49
1917	237	10	3	155	67	3	378	119	259	323	82	2	16	12	3	158	51
1918	268	11	4	153	96	3	434	101	333	263	58	3	16	12	3	125	46
1919	227	11	4	145	63	3	506	161	345	287	80	4	17	14	3	125	47
1920	240	19	7	137	74	3	477	164	313	278	88	4	13	12	3	117	41
1921	212	9	4	148	49	2	433	134	299	262	66	2	11	21	3	121	38
1922	204	12	5	136	48	3	447	164	283	325	111	4	19	24	4	126	36
1923	222	13	4	144	56	4	493	178	315	401	166	6	30	28	6	128	38
1924	232	13	4	150	60	4	501	177	324	393	144	7	36	40	6	125	35
1925	235	14	4	151	62	4	546	212	333	429	177	9	42	38	7	124	33
1926	258	13	4	162	74	5	528	200	327	453	197	9	44	39	7	125	32
1927	253	14	4	157	72	6	558	205	352	408	149	12	43	46	7	122	29
1928	264	17	4	160	78	6	577	243	334	433	168	13	42	59	7	118	26
1929	280	18	5	166	87	6	614	258	356	455	176	13	43	74	8	117	24

* Less than 1.

Year	Recreation								Education				Religion, Welfare			Travel		
	TOTAL	Books maps	Mags. news.	Non-dur. toys	Dur. equip.	Video, audio	Plants, flowers	Rec. serv.	TOTAL	Higher ed.	Nurs.–12th	Other	TOTAL	Re-ligion	Wel-fare	NET	Foreign, by U.S. res.	In U.S., nonres.
1900	83	14	14	3	3	1	7	42	38	5	19	15	131	96	35	15	17	2
1901	90	14	15	4	3	1	7	46	39	5	18	16	125	91	34	15	17	2
1902	99	15	16	4	3	1	8	52	40	5	17	17	119	87	32	15	17	2
1903	103	16	16	4	3	1	8	55	40	5	18	17	114	84	30	15	17	2
1904	107	16	17	4	3	1	8	59	41	6	18	17	109	81	29	14	17	3
1905	112	17	18	4	3	1	8	62	42	6	18	18	104	77	27	13	17	4
1906	114	16	19	4	3	1	8	63	42	6	18	18	101	75	26	11	16	5
1907	115	16	20	3	3	1	8	63	42	7	17	18	94	72	23	10	16	7
1908	110	15	15	3	2	1	8	64	44	8	17	18	91	70	22	9	16	7
1909	119	17	20	4	3	1	8	66	44	8	18	18	88	67	21	9	16	7
1910	121	16	20	4	3	1	8	70	45	9	19	18	85	64	21	10	16	6
1911	125	16	19	5	3	1	8	74	47	9	19	19	81	62	19	9	16	6
1912	128	17	21	5	3	2	7	73	47	9	20	18	78	61	18	8	16	7
1913	135	20	21	5	4	2	7	76	48	9	20	18	76	59	17	8	15	7
1914	133	17	22	5	4	1	6	77	50	9	22	19	75	57	18	10	15	6
1915	135	18	22	6	4	1	6	78	50	10	22	18	74	56	18	12	16	3
1916	151	19	29	7	6	2	6	82	51	10	21	19	73	55	18	15	18	3
1917	167	22	33	9	9	2	5	86	49	10	20	19	103	54	49	18	22	3
1918	172	25	36	4	5	2	6	94	48	9	19	19	118	55	63	22	26	4
1919	187	31	37	5	5	3	5	101	51	12	19	20	80	55	24	23	27	4
1920	184	28	36	4	4	2	5	105	53	12	19	21	88	55	33	21	25	4
1921	164	18	37	5	3	2	6	94	52	13	19	20	80	54	26	20	25	6
1922	163	18	38	6	3	2	6	89	52	15	18	20	67	55	11	22	26	5
1923	174	17	41	6	4	2	7	96	53	16	18	19	69	58	11	20	25	5
1924	180	18	41	6	4	3	8	100	54	17	18	18	71	60	11	18	24	6
1925	184	19	44	7	4	3	7	100	56	19	19	18	80	61	19	20	25	6
1926	195	18	45	8	4	3	8	109	58	20	19	19	83	64	20	18	25	7
1927	205	20	46	9	4	3	9	115	58	21	19	18	82	62	20	17	24	8
1928	220	20	46	10	5	4	10	126	60	23	19	18	82	63	19	16	24	8
1929	231	22	46	11	5	4	9	134	62	24	20	18	83	63	20	15	24	9

(continued)

Appendix Table (continued)

Year	TOTAL PCE	Food, Alcohol, Tobacco						Clothing								Personal Care		
		TOTAL	Purch. food, mls., bevs.	Food furnished	Food on farms	Alcohol (legal)	Tobacco	TOTAL	Shoes	Total civilian	Women's civilian	Men's civilian	Military	Jewelry	Cleaning	TOTAL	Toiletries	Barber, beauty
1929	4561	1247	1057	18	57	0	115	437	75	260	150	110	*	15	86	71	22	49
1930	4227	1207	1030	18	56	0	104	390	65	232	136	96	*	14	79	68	19	48
1931	4037	1206	1027	17	59	0	104	367	66	226	133	93	*	9	67	64	19	44
1932	3656	1121	955	16	59	0	91	320	66	193	112	81	*	7	53	57	16	40
1933	3562	1085	877	16	63	34	96	285	59	173	97	76	*	5	48	49	12	36
1934	3647	1130	868	17	60	84	102	303	65	179	101	79	*	6	52	56	16	40
1935	3830	1172	886	18	55	106	107	324	64	197	112	85	*	7	56	60	16	44
1936	4170	1312	991	20	56	131	115	353	70	213	117	96	*	7	63	64	17	48
1937	4302	1374	1032	22	55	144	121	357	74	206	112	94	*	10	67	67	18	50
1938	4174	1397	1064	21	55	135	121	355	73	208	117	91	*	10	64	64	18	46
1939	4342	1429	1088	22	56	140	123	374	71	227	129	98	1	10	65	66	20	46
1940	4491	1479	1134	23	55	142	125	385	72	231	133	99	1	11	70	67	21	46
1941	4705	1546	1174	31	52	155	135	414	76	241	135	105	6	13	78	70	24	47
1942	4667	1575	1168	47	50	164	146	428	80	236	137	99	15	14	83	73	26	47
1943	4788	1618	1167	73	53	171	153	467	75	255	156	99	23	17	97	78	30	48
1944	5009	1746	1267	101	51	177	151	461	74	248	151	97	23	17	100	82	33	49
1945	5353	1888	1373	111	53	194	158	488	81	256	153	103	24	19	109	85	36	49
1946	5536	1885	1412	54	51	194	169	493	86	260	152	108	7	23	117	80	33	47
1947	5503	1775	1330	37	45	193	171	462	76	247	145	103	4	20	115	75	30	45
1948	5540	1733	1304	33	42	180	173	455	73	248	146	102	3	20	112	73	29	43
1949	5568	1719	1301	33	39	175	171	445	73	243	142	101	3	19	107	73	30	43
1950	5741	1713	1294	32	37	180	170	446	76	243	139	103	4	20	104	76	33	43
1951	5812	1748	1314	41	36	183	174	436	67	243	140	103	6	19	101	75	32	44
1952	5905	1783	1349	43	34	179	178	449	66	256	151	105	4	21	102	79	35	45
1953	6055	1814	1384	42	31	184	173	447	66	255	152	103	2	21	102	84	36	47
1954	6099	1806	1396	40	30	177	163	442	63	253	151	103	1	22	102	89	37	52
1955	6343	1842	1433	38	28	180	162	452	67	260	155	105	1	24	101	111	58	53
1956	6418	1867	1457	37	27	182	164	453	65	263	157	106	1	24	99	99	43	56

* Less than 1.

	Housing					Household Operation													Do-	
Year	TOTAL	Non-farm owned	Non-farm rented	Farm	Other	TOTAL	Furniture	Kitchen appliances	China, glass	Other durables	Semi-durables	Cleaning supplies	Stationery	Electricity	Gas	Water	Fuel	Tel. & tel.	mestic serv.	Other
1929	430	199	156	55	21	622	57	10	40	44	28	23	7	15	30	25	136	15	176	16
1930	421	191	156	54	20	576	46	9	29	38	24	22	7	16	32	27	132	15	163	16
1931	413	184	157	54	18	540	44	9	31	35	25	22	6	17	32	27	119	14	144	15
1932	401	176	156	52	17	483	34	6	31	29	23	19	4	17	31	26	113	12	122	14
1933	391	177	147	51	16	466	30	7	28	23	23	19	5	17	29	27	118	11	116	12
1934	409	178	163	50	18	495	30	9	28	25	23	22	6	18	29	30	121	11	130	13
1935	410	177	164	49	20	520	40	11	26	27	24	23	7	19	29	29	125	12	135	13
1936	414	177	167	48	21	575	48	13	31	35	30	26	7	20	30	29	134	13	143	15
1937	419	177	172	49	22	591	48	14	34	34	31	28	8	22	31	30	132	14	150	15
1938	422	177	175	49	22	554	44	12	31	32	31	27	7	23	30	30	122	13	136	16
1939	429	179	179	49	22	597	51	13	31	35	38	29	8	25	30	31	131	14	145	16
1940	437	181	184	49	23	629	55	15	33	36	40	31	9	26	32	32	139	15	150	16
1941	457	193	191	49	25	655	62	19	39	41	42	33	10	28	32	32	142	17	140	18
1942	474	206	196	48	24	641	50	11	36	37	39	35	11	29	35	33	145	19	142	19
1943	491	221	195	47	27	607	41	4	30	36	40	36	13	30	37	34	147	21	117	21
1944	514	242	195	47	30	602	36	2	28	33	40	36	14	33	38	34	147	23	113	24
1945	528	259	189	46	33	630	38	4	34	34	39	33	17	35	41	35	157	25	112	26
1946	543	277	188	44	34	715	52	19	50	48	46	38	17	39	42	35	161	26	98	44
1947	578	301	191	45	41	746	56	30	51	50	37	46	15	42	47	36	165	26	102	43
1948	597	319	196	46	36	735	56	31	53	53	39	26	14	47	50	36	163	28	99	44
1949	623	338	204	47	34	736	55	28	49	51	44	49	15	51	50	37	141	29	97	42
1950	652	362	210	47	33	794	61	35	49	56	48	54	15	57	56	37	149	30	103	44
1951	692	391	219	48	34	795	57	32	47	56	47	53	14	63	63	38	147	32	101	45
1952	726	418	224	49	35	785	61	31	45	51	47	52	15	68	67	38	140	34	91	45
1953	753	438	229	49	35	793	64	32	44	50	46	56	16	73	69	38	134	36	88	47
1954	775	459	231	50	36	794	64	33	43	46	44	57	17	78	75	38	134	37	81	47
1955	798	481	231	49	36	853	73	37	44	51	46	61	17	82	80	38	139	41	95	49
1956	822	504	232	49	376	872	74	40	42	53	46	63	16	87	86	38	137	43	97	50

(continued)

Appendix Table (continued)

Year	Medical						Personal Business								
	TOTAL	Drugs	Ophth., ortho. prods.	Drs., other profs.	Hospitals	Health ins.	TOTAL	Brokerage	Exc. brokerage	Bank svc. chgs.	Fin. svc. w/o pay	Life ins.	Legal serv.	Funeral	Other
1929	280	18	5	166	87	6	614	258	356	14	141	72	71	47	10
1930	275	16	5	153	94	6	515	169	346	11	136	76	69	45	9
1931	269	15	4	145	98	6	468	119	349	10	133	80	74	44	9
1932	253	14	3	133	97	5	425	96	329	8	119	87	66	43	6
1933	235	14	3	121	92	5	470	150	320	9	104	92	67	42	7
1934	240	15	5	127	89	5	376	51	325	10	100	89	72	43	10
1935	242	16	5	126	90	5	436	91	345	10	109	97	74	43	11
1936	254	17	5	136	91	5	450	99	351	11	115	94	74	46	12
1937	261	18	6	138	93	5	455	91	364	11	123	93	75	44	18
1938	257	19	6	130	97	6	421	63	357	10	119	93	74	42	20
1939	268	20	6	136	100	7	421	54	366	10	122	95	77	42	21
1940	273	20	7	138	102	7	409	45	364	10	120	93	77	42	22
1941	283	23	8	142	102	8	406	37	369	11	125	90	79	41	24
1942	297	26	9	146	108	9	387	29	358	11	123	81	79	40	24
1943	306	30	10	141	114	10	388	41	346	12	108	80	76	42	27
1944	328	32	11	155	118	12	378	41	337	14	104	78	73	41	26
1945	338	34	11	160	120	13	392	55	337	15	109	75	71	41	25
1946	368	35	12	187	121	13	391	47	344	14	129	72	73	30	25
1947	383	33	11	196	119	23	392	38	354	13	135	81	70	32	23
1948	409	34	11	213	124	26	394	37	356	13	134	80	74	32	22
1949	415	35	11	209	130	29	384	32	352	13	130	79	75	33	21
1950	431	38	12	213	136	33	402	48	354	15	130	81	74	32	21
1951	450	41	13	218	137	41	403	41	362	17	132	81	76	34	22
1952	465	42	13	222	146	42	392	34	359	17	134	79	72	35	21
1953	481	43	14	228	151	45	396	31	366	18	139	80	72	36	22
1954	499	42	13	242	158	43	412	39	374	19	143	80	74	36	22
1955	507	45	13	238	166	46	419	38	381	19	146	85	73	36	22
1956	531	48	14	246	175	49	413	31	382	19	146	92	68	36	22

Year	Transportation								Recreation					
	TOTAL	Motor veh.	Tires, access.	Repair	Gas, oil	Ins., tolls	Purch. local	Purch. intercity	TOTAL	Books, maps	Mags., news.	Non-durable toys	Durable equip.	Video, audio
1929	455	176	13	43	74	8	117	24	231	22	46	11	5	4
1930	385	128	12	35	74	9	108	19	220	19	44	9	4	5
1931	333	92	11	30	77	9	98	16	210	19	41	9	4	3
1932	273	59	9	26	70	9	87	13	171	12	37	8	3	3
1933	281	71	8	30	70	9	81	13	164	12	37	7	3	2
1934	307	87	9	33	74	8	81	15	175	13	39	7	3	2
1935	350	123	10	32	78	9	83	16	183	15	39	7	4	2
1936	399	158	11	36	84	10	79	20	201	17	42	8	5	3
1937	424	163	11	37	90	11	87	24	213	19	44	8	6	4
1938	361	107	10	35	92	11	83	22	202	17	42	8	6	3
1939	407	137	12	41	97	11	85	24	212	17	44	9	6	4
1940	446	162	14	44	101	13	88	24	224	17	46	9	6	5
1941	491	175	18	49	112	14	94	29	239	19	49	11	8	6
1942	376	79	8	35	84	11	120	40	252	21	52	10	7	5
1943	383	70	9	32	53	10	149	60	268	24	57	10	6	3
1944	403	64	10	40	55	11	162	62	271	29	58	10	7	2
1945	439	60	14	55	73	13	162	63	291	33	62	11	8	2
1946	575	103	27	89	126	18	158	54	327	34	65	16	15	8
1947	622	160	25	93	131	21	147	47	307	28	66	16	16	8
1948	652	193	23	97	136	22	137	44	296	27	66	18	15	7
1949	698	253	21	100	146	23	118	38	288	27	64	19	13	8
1950	751	312	25	102	148	26	104	34	291	28	64	22	14	11
1951	596	144	22	107	159	31	95	37	288	31	65	18	13	10
1952	714	254	22	109	170	30	89	39	293	29	65	24	14	12
1953	760	296	19	116	176	31	84	38	293	29	65	24	15	13
1954	754	301	17	113	179	34	75	35	292	28	64	23	16	14
1955	839	370	20	119	190	34	69	35	301	29	64	24	19	15
1956	805	318	22	122	198	40	70	35	308	30	62	25	21	15

(continued)

Appendix Table (continued)

Year	Recreation		Education				Religion, Welfare			Travel		
	Plants, flowers	Rec. serv.	TOTAL	Higher ed.	Nurs.–12th	Other	TOTAL	Religion	Welfare	TOTAL	Foreign, by U.S. res.	In U.S., by nonres.
1929	9	134	62	24	20	18	83			15	24	9
1930	8	131	63	26	21	17	87			16	25	8
1931	7	127	65	28	22	15	88			15	21	7
1932	7	102	56	26	17	13	81			14	19	5
1933	7	97	51	25	15	11	73			9	14	5
1934	6	104	51	25	16	11	69			9	15	6
1935	6	109	53	26	16	11	67			8	15	7
1936	8	119	56	27	18	12	68			10	18	7
1937	6	126	61	27	22	12	65			12	20	8
1938	8	118	63	27	24	12	69			9	17	9
1939	11	121	63	27	24	11	70			5	14	9
1940	10	130	63	28	24	11	74			1	7	6
1941	12	135	65	28	24	13	74			2	8	6
1942	9	147	69	29	24	16	77			−1	5	7
1943	8	159	72	30	24	18	86			−3	6	8
1944	9	156	70	30	25	15	97			−3	7	10
1945	10	165	69	31	26	13	99			−3	8	11
1946	10	179	66	31	22	14	96			−3	13	16
1947	9	164	74	37	23	13	84			2	17	15
1948	8	155	76	39	24	14	83			6	19	13
1949	9	148	79	41	25	14	80			6	21	15
1950	9	144	81	41	25	15	80			7	23	15
1951	9	142	82	40	27	16	79			6	23	17
1952	9	140	85	41	28	16	89			8	26	18
1953	10	137	88	42	29	17	90			8	27	19
1954	11	136	90	43	30	17	93			8	28	20
1955	10	139	95	45	31	19	93			9	31	22
1956	11	143	98	47	32	19	99			10	33	23

Year	TOTAL PCE	Food, Alcohol, Tobacco						Clothing								Personal Care		
		TOTAL	Purch. food, mls., bevs.	Food fur-nished	Food on farms	Al-cohol	To-bacco	TOTAL	Shoes	Total civilian	Women's civilian	Men's civilian	Mili-tary	Jewelry	Clean-ing	TOTAL	Toi-letries	Barber, beauty
1956	6418	1867	1457	37	27	182	164	453	65	263	157	106	1	24	99	99	43	56
1957	6453	1874	1467	36	24	180	167	442	63	257	155	102	1	24	97	102	45	58
1958	6446	1846	1442	35	22	177	170	436	65	253	155	98	1	25	93	104	46	58
1959	6656	1880	1474	32	20	179	176	447	65	263	161	102	1	25	93	107	46	61
1960	6698	1866	1468	31	18	175	175	440	64	260	160	100	1	24	90	110	50	61
1961	6740	1876	1474	31	17	175	177	438	63	262	162	100	1	24	89	118	54	64
1962	6931	1870	1468	31	15	181	175	448	64	270	168	102	1	25	88	126	58	68
1963	7089	1860	1459	31	14	182	174	449	63	272	171	101	1	26	87	128	61	67
1964	7384	1894	1496	30	13	185	169	474	67	290	181	108	1	27	90	134	65	70
1965	7703	1954	1552	31	11	189	171	491	67	300	187	113	1	31	93	141	70	71
1966	8005	1996	1585	35	10	196	169	519	70	317	197	120	2	38	94	154	77	77
1967	8163	2003	1593	37	10	195	169	520	70	315	193	122	2	40	94	159	80	79
1968	8506	2063	1650	35	9	203	166	537	73	325	199	126	2	42	95	164	84	80
1969	8737	2085	1673	34	8	208	162	539	75	327	201	126	2	42	94	162	85	77
1970	8842	2102	1682	31	8	217	163	525	70	323	200	123	1	41	89	166	87	79
1971	9022	2085	1666	28	8	220	162	534	70	336	209	127	1	43	84	162	87	75
1972	9424	2126	1698	27	8	229	164	561	74	356	219	137	1	45	85	167	90	77
1973	9752	2118	1671	27	7	241	172	596	78	379	233	146	1	54	84	172	97	75
1974	9602	2065	1611	30	9	243	173	582	73	373	231	142	1	59	77	168	97	71
1975	9711	2084	1630	31	8	244	171	593	72	383	238	145	1	63	74	161	93	68
1976	10121	2161	1689	33	8	250	180	621	74	399	249	150	1	74	74	160	96	64
1977	10425	2176	1703	32	8	261	172	647	77	416	259	157	1	80	74	167	100	67
1978	10744	2163	1686	33	6	264	174	691	84	450	283	167	1	84	72	171	104	66
1979	10876	2161	1681	34	6	270	171	700	88	463	292	171	1	81	68	171	107	64
1980	10746	2141	1660	34	5	271	170	690	87	465	295	170	1	74	63	167	106	61
1981	10770	2112	1634	35	5	268	171	711	91	485	312	173	1	75	59	162	104	58
1982	10782	2106	1640	34	5	265	162	705	88	488	317	171	1	74	55	154	100	54
1983	11179	2134	1674	35	4	265	156	746	91	515	338	178	1	81	58	165	103	62
1984	11617	2153	1699	35	4	260	155	795	95	553	364	188	1	91	56	172	109	62
1985	12015	2178	1724	36	4	262	152	820	98	567	375	193	1	97	56	178	113	65

(continued)

Appendix Table (*continued*)

		Housing										Household Operation								
Year	TOTAL	Non-farm owned	Non-farm rented	Farm	Other	TOTAL	Furniture	Kitchen appliances	China, glass	Other durables	Semi-durables	Cleaning supplies	Stationery	Electricity	Gas	Water	Fuel	Tel. & tel.	Domestic serv.	Other
1956	822	504	232	49	37	872	74	40	42	53	46	63	16	87	86	38	137	43	97	50
1957	848	524	237	49	39	866	69	40	37	53	45	66	17	92	88	37	133	45	93	51
1958	872	544	243	48	38	868	67	38	35	51	43	67	18	95	92	35	136	46	94	51
1959	902	568	249	47	38	888	71	40	35	54	45	72	19	100	95	38	128	48	90	53
1960	930	591	255	46	38	890	69	39	34	53	44	76	20	103	98	41	120	50	89	54
1961	958	611	264	45	38	895	67	39	33	53	46	84	19	107	102	42	112	52	85	54
1962	996	638	274	44	40	925	70	40	33	56	49	91	20	112	107	44	110	54	83	56
1963	1027	658	284	42	42	957	74	42	33	61	50	95	21	116	110	47	114	58	81	55
1964	1060	680	295	41	44	1007	82	45	35	68	54	102	22	121	114	49	117	61	79	58
1965	1104	710	307	40	47	1049	85	46	39	73	57	109	22	126	116	50	121	67	75	63
1966	1142	735	317	39	49	1102	89	50	44	78	61	118	25	133	119	50	123	73	71	68
1967	1180	762	327	39	53	1125	87	51	45	80	62	119	24	140	124	50	122	78	71	72
1968	1226	790	343	38	54	1151	90	56	46	84	64	123	26	147	127	51	114	84	67	72
1969	1278	828	357	37	56	1170	90	59	46	82	62	127	29	155	131	54	107	91	63	74
1970	1313	851	366	39	57	1166	87	61	44	79	59	129	28	163	132	57	99	97	58	73
1971	1352	882	378	37	54	1161	89	65	45	79	58	125	25	166	131	57	94	100	55	72
1972	1410	923	392	36	59	1225	98	72	46	85	60	130	27	175	135	62	102	106	52	75
1973	1466	962	407	35	62	1296	106	78	50	95	65	141	28	184	130	64	110	116	51	78
1974	1528	1018	413	34	63	1248	103	77	48	97	60	133	25	187	126	66	86	121	43	76
1975	1558	1041	418	33	66	1227	97	70	45	93	59	116	24	197	129	66	84	133	40	74
1976	1590	1063	424	32	71	1273	101	72	48	99	61	115	25	204	130	65	93	142	41	77
1977	1613	1083	427	31	72	1322	112	76	51	107	62	113	26	221	124	65	89	151	42	83
1978	1675	1142	430	30	73	1375	117	76	56	113	64	123	30	228	126	65	87	163	42	85
1979	1723	1190	429	29	75	1407	121	78	56	117	65	133	31	228	123	68	80	174	36	92
1980	1754	1224	431	28	71	1384	113	75	56	111	65	137	32	237	121	71	61	181	32	92
1981	1771	1236	440	26	69	1355	111	72	57	107	67	138	32	233	116	70	51	182	29	90
1982	1764	1233	441	24	67	1328	102	66	58	102	64	139	32	233	117	69	47	185	30	84
1983	1773	1235	445	23	70	1362	110	71	59	110	65	145	32	245	112	71	47	179	30	86
1984	1805	1258	453	23	71	1422	122	77	62	119	69	156	35	245	112	74	47	178	34	92
1985	1828	1263	470	22	72	1460	125	85	63	121	70	163	35	251	112	77	48	182	33	95

| Year | Medical | | | | | | Personal Business | | | | | | | | |
	TOTAL	Drugs	Ophth., ortho. prods.	Drs., other profs.	Hos-pitals	Health ins.	TOTAL	Bro-kerage	Exc. broker-age	Bank svc. chgs.	Fin. svc. w/o pay	Life ins.	Legal serv.	Funeral	Other
1956	531	48	14	246	175	49	413	31	382	19	146	92	68	36	22
1957	551	51	13	254	182	51	418	30	388	19	143	94	71	37	23
1958	567	52	13	268	197	37	433	33	400	19	150	94	75	38	24
1959	606	56	14	277	210	49	444	42	402	20	155	86	80	38	24
1960	618	60	14	281	214	49	447	36	411	20	159	92	78	38	25
1961	634	66	13	284	221	50	466	48	419	20	160	92	85	38	25
1962	678	72	15	303	236	52	460	37	423	20	160	92	87	38	25
1963	710	76	16	313	251	54	471	34	437	20	167	93	92	39	26
1964	771	78	17	355	264	57	489	38	452	22	174	100	91	38	27
1965	796	80	18	362	277	59	513	46	467	24	177	107	93	39	29
1966	825	83	19	361	303	60	532	49	482	26	181	105	100	39	31
1967	849	88	17	355	332	58	549	60	488	28	188	101	99	39	33
1968	909	96	19	364	369	62	564	58	507	29	198	104	99	41	36
1969	968	103	20	377	403	65	571	45	525	31	209	106	100	40	39
1970	1018	114	22	389	424	68	582	35	548	32	220	110	106	40	39
1971	1072	118	21	389	475	69	585	36	549	33	225	106	106	40	39
1972	1136	127	22	406	508	72	597	35	562	36	230	109	106	40	41
1973	1209	136	24	443	532	75	614	28	586	38	238	116	110	40	43
1974	1246	142	24	448	554	78	623	23	600	40	246	120	111	39	43
1975	1294	141	24	460	584	85	645	26	619	37	265	128	107	37	44
1976	1340	145	24	465	618	88	682	30	652	37	275	144	110	40	46
1977	1385	145	24	484	642	91	706	30	677	38	287	150	112	40	49
1978	1432	154	25	487	674	92	743	29	714	40	303	157	120	41	52
1979	1483	165	25	496	699	97	758	31	727	45	313	160	118	39	53
1980	1522	170	25	506	720	101	770	34	736	50	314	166	117	39	51
1981	1581	173	24	537	747	101	762	31	731	55	299	168	122	36	50
1982	1589	171	24	530	765	99	790	37	753	59	312	178	121	33	50
1983	1621	176	25	550	773	96	837	55	782	61	345	172	123	30	50
1984	1656	182	28	573	777	96	855	57	799	63	348	177	128	30	52
1985	1695	186	30	600	786	95	903	68	835	62	361	189	138	32	53

(continued)

Appendix Table (continued)

Year	Transportation TOTAL	Motor veh.	Tires, access.	Repair	Gas, oil	Ins., tolls	Purch. local	Purch. intercity	Recreation TOTAL	Books, maps	Mags., news.	Non-durable toys	Durable equip.	Video, audio
1956	805	318	22	122	198	40	70	35	308	30	62	25	21	15
1957	801	312	24	125	202	39	64	34	293	29	60	25	22	14
1958	758	272	25	126	208	37	58	31	284	28	58	26	23	14
1959	808	309	28	131	215	37	57	31	295	28	57	28	25	15
1960	816	310	29	135	218	38	56	30	297	29	56	28	23	15
1961	772	268	31	137	217	38	52	30	296	30	51	30	22	16
1962	817	300	33	142	222	39	50	31	311	31	56	31	22	17
1963	854	326	35	147	226	40	48	31	323	33	57	33	24	18
1964	883	334	37	153	235	42	46	35	338	39	55	35	28	21
1965	946	380	37	159	243	42	45	39	353	38	57	37	31	26
1966	970	377	39	165	255	46	44	44	387	41	64	41	38	32
1967	971	363	40	171	261	50	42	44	395	40	63	42	42	36
1968	1060	413	45	177	276	53	43	54	413	40	62	45	47	39
1969	1100	418	50	183	292	53	44	59	429	43	62	46	50	40
1970	1070	365	53	192	306	54	43	58	445	51	64	46	50	43
1971	1176	426	59	199	317	54	43	58	449	48	64	47	51	44
1972	1242	480	64	204	327	59	43	65	480	45	66	52	65	49
1973	1298	509	73	202	340	62	42	70	518	45	71	58	74	55
1974	1172	405	73	194	321	61	43	75	536	46	72	60	73	57
1975	1180	405	72	199	327	63	43	71	545	43	67	61	77	61
1976	1295	498	74	205	337	62	43	77	570	38	67	66	83	66
1977	1376	546	78	220	344	65	43	82	597	39	69	70	90	69
1978	1401	559	77	222	348	67	42	86	633	43	75	75	95	73
1979	1346	506	73	225	339	69	40	94	666	45	82	79	103	77
1980	1207	422	67	212	316	69	34	86	655	45	81	76	89	77
1981	1198	428	65	209	318	68	30	79	672	46	79	78	88	79
1982	1193	436	62	199	318	69	29	80	678	44	75	79	84	78
1983	1303	520	69	211	323	68	31	81	720	46	74	83	84	95
1984	1430	604	74	237	329	68	32	86	778	49	78	90	99	108
1985	1541	679	77	264	332	69	30	91	820	48	75	94	102	125

	Recreation (continued)		Education				Religion, Welfare			Travel		
Year	Plants, flowers	Rec. serv.	TOTAL	Higher ed.	Nurs.-12th	Other	TOTAL	Religion	Welfare	TOTAL	Foreign, by U.S. res.	In U.S., by nonres.
1956	11	143	98	47	32	19	99			10	33	23
1957	11	132	104	51	34	19	98			11	35	24
1958	10	127	108	54	34	19	101			13	37	24
1959	11	130	111	55	37	19	109			16	40	24
1960	12	133	116	57	39	20	116			19	43	24
1961	11	136	120	60	42	18	120			18	43	24
1962	13	140	126	63	44	19	126			22	45	24
1963	15	143	132	66	47	20	132			24	48	24
1964	15	146	141	72	49	20	141			21	48	27
1965	18	147	152	81	50	21	152			22	51	29
1966	19	152	164	88	52	25	164			21	53	32
1967	19	154	172	91	52	29	172			30	62	32
1968	20	161	185	96	55	34	185			25	58	33
1969	20	167	194	101	57	36	194			27	63	36
1970	20	171	203	109	57	37	203			32	70	39
1971	20	175	210	115	58	37	210			28	69	41
1972	21	182	217	119	60	38	217			31	75	43
1973	22	194	221	122	59	40	221			23	72	49
1974	23	206	213	119	57	37	213			13	65	52
1975	22	215	216	118	57	40	216			7	63	56
1976	23	227	218	119	56	44	218			3	66	62
1977	21	239	217	120	53	44	217			5	68	62
1978	25	248	225	121	59	46	225			4	69	65
1979	26	255	226	123	58	46	226			-2	67	69
1980	26	260	227	124	59	43	227			-10	65	74
1981	27	277	229	127	59	43	229			-33	65	98
1982	27	291	233	132	59	42	233			-19	71	90
1983	27	311	239	133	60	45	239			0	80	80
1984	29	325	242	134	61	47	242			10	117	107
1985	29	346	250	135	63	52	250			20	125	105

(continued)

Appendix Table (*continued*)

Year	TOTAL PCE	Food, Alcohol, Tobacco TOTAL	Purch. food, mls., bevs.	Food furnished	Food on farms	Alcohol	Tobacco	Clothing TOTAL	Shoes	Total civilian	Women's civilian	Men's civilian	Military	Jewelry	Cleaning	Personal Care TOTAL	Toiletries	Barber, beauty
1986	12336	2200	1751	36	4	262	147	876	104	603	402	201	1	111	57	185	118	68
1987	12568	2206	1766	37	3	256	144	887	106	612	404	208	1	111	58	195	123	72
1988	12903	2230	1800	38	2	255	135	904	107	622	411	212	1	109	65	203	125	77
1989	13027	2208	1782	38	2	253	133	933	112	647	430	217	1	105	68	208	128	80
1990	13051	2193	1773	39	2	249	129	920	113	636	420	216	1	100	70	209	129	80

Year	Housing TOTAL	Non-farm owned	Non-farm rented	Farm	Other	Household Operation TOTAL	Furniture	Kitchen appliances	China, glass	Other durables	Semi-durables	Cleaning supplies	Stationery	Electricity	Gas	Water	Fuel	Tel. & tel.	Domestic serv.	Other
1986	1837	1266	477	21	73	1501	133	91	64	130	74	171	36	251	105	80	50	183	35	98
1987	1863	1284	483	20	76	1544	136	94	62	141	74	176	38	260	105	82	49	195	34	98
1988	1884	1296	492	19	77	1600	134	98	66	150	79	180	41	267	111	84	49	208	36	98
1989	1896	1304	497	19	76	1636	144	103	70	155	81	180	43	266	114	86	46	212	38	99
1990	1898	1307	501	18	72	1626	143	108	70	152	79	182	44	265	104	87	40	216	37	100

Year	Medical TOTAL	Drugs	Ophth., ortho. prods.	Drs., other profs.	Hospitals	Health ins.	Personal Business TOTAL	Brokerage	Exc. brokerage	Bank svc. chgs.	Fin. svc. w/o pay	Life ins.	Legal serv.	Funeral	Other
1986	1744	190	32	615	811	96	933	84	849	70	374	176	144	30	56
1987	1813	196	33	657	829	99	964	94	870	74	385	173	151	30	57
1988	1860	195	36	687	843	100	985	83	902	76	378	194	163	30	61
1989	1881	195	35	700	849	101	989	94	895	79	367	189	167	29	63
1990	1928	195	35	724	871	102	993	94	899	79	369	190	166	29	66

		Transportation							Recreation					
Year	TOTAL	Motor veh.	Tires, access.	Repair	Gas, oil	Ins., tolls	Purch. local	Purch. intercity	TOTAL	Books, maps	Mags., news.	Non-durable toys	Durable equip.	Video, audio
1986	1615	726	77	264	344	71	34	99	866	49	75	98	109	147
1987	1584	678	77	271	349	72	33	104	921	53	78	105	116	161
1988	1646	712	83	288	351	72	33	107	979	57	81	107	118	185
1989	1653	710	83	302	350	71	31	105	1016	59	82	111	117	200
1990	1621	680	85	312	340	72	31	102	1026	62	83	113	111	210

(continued)

	Recreation (continued)		Education				Religion, Welfare			Travel		
Year	Plants, flowers	Rec. serv.	TOTAL	Higher ed.	Nurs.–12th	Other	TOTAL	Religion	Welfare	TOTAL	Foreign, by U.S. res.	In U.S., by nonres.
1986	32	357	257	137	63	57	257			−4	110	115
1987	35	373	264	139	64	61	264			−2	122	124
1988	37	393	276	141	66	69	276			−17	123	140
1989	39	407	287	143	71	74	287			−40	119	159
1990	39	409	298	147	73	78	298			−47	120	167

· A P P E N D I X   B ·

Estimating Details

SAVINGS: CHAPTER 5 DETAILS

A special Brookings study implies savings rates of 44 percent in 1928 and 41 percent in 1929. See Kuznets, *Shares of Upper Income Groups in Income and Savings* (1953), 228. That survey constitutes the basis for Kuznets's own savings ratios, which appear in footnotes to his table 47. Reference to somewhat more reliable data for families indicates an implicit savings rate of 50 percent for the top 1 percent. Cf. Maurice Leven, *America's Capacity to Consume* (1934), 260–61.

The Bureau of Labor Statistics field survey for 1972–73 yields a 37 percent rate for families with incomes of $25,000 and over. U.S. Bureau of Labor Statistics, *Consumer Expenditure Survey: Integrated Diary and Interview Survey Data, 1972–73*, Bulletin 1992, table 1. The B.L.S. estimated that 3 percent of all reporting units had incomes of $25,000 and over. I compute the ratio of current consumption expenses to family income after taxes. Later B.L.S. surveys yield improbable results. Thus in U.S. Bureau of Labor Statistics, *Consumer Expenditure Survey: Integrated Survey Data, 1984–86*, Bulletin 2333, (1989), table 2 those with incomes $50,000 and over had $72,757 in money income, and $60,404 in total expenditures plus personal taxes—implying a saving rate of only something like 17 percent. Moreover, the B.L.S. reported federal income tax paid by this group at only one-third of what they actually paid to the I.R.S.—$20,667. (U.S. Internal Revenue Service, *Individual Income Tax Returns, 1986*, 18.)

Families data for 1983 comes from Robert Avery et al., *Measuring Wealth with Survey Data: An Evaluation of the 1983 Survey of Consumer Finances* (May 15, 1987), table 7. net worth data from *Federal Reserve Bulletin (FRB)* (Mar. 1986): 166. income data from *FRB* (Sept. 1984):

680–81. A 65.6 percent ratio of consumer expenditures to income before tax is implicit in 1983 B.L.S. data for families with incomes of $40,000 and over, and 75 percent for the $30,000 to $40,000 group. (U.S. Bureau of Labor Statistics, *Consumer Expenditure Survey: Interview Survey, 1982–83*, Bulletin 2246, table 2.) I assume a 60 percent rate for those $50,000 and over.

ALCOHOL

In calendar year 1900, 100 million proof-gallons of spirits were consumed in the United States (U.S. Bureau of the Census, *Statistical Abstract, 1901*, 354). Approximately 48 percent of American adults consumed liquor in the late 1880s (U.S. Department of the Treasury, Bureau of Statistics, *Quarterly Report of the Chief of the Bureau of Statistics, Import, Exports . . . 1886* [1887], 395). I use a figure of 50 percent for 1900. The adult drinking population in 1900 is therefore taken to equal the 21.1 million males 21 and older (U.S. Bureau of the Census, *Population, 1900*, pt. 3, p. 2). In 1900, each gallon yielded some 120 drinks (U.S. Industrial Commission, *Hearings*, vol. 1, p. 119). From these data I estimate 4.73 gallons, or 568 drinks of hard liquor a year, per drinking adult.

In addition, 1,240 million gallons of beer were consumed in the United States in 1900 (U.S. Bureau of the Census, *Statistical Abstract, 1901*, 354). Using the same procedure as for spirits, and taking a glass of beer as 12 ounces in 1900, leads to an estimate of 626 glasses per year. For wine, a similar procedure, with 30 million gallons and 6 ounces per glass, leads to a figure of 30 glasses per year.

Similar procedures were applied to data for the United Kingdom that appear in Alan R. Prest, *Consumers' Expenditure in the United Kingdom, 1900–1919* (1954), 75, 76, 83, 177. Prest includes cider under the heading of alcoholic beverages—and allowance for 25 million gallons of cider and perry would increase the U.K. total still further.

HOURS OF WORK

I adjust Kendrick's standard 1900 estimates for two sectors.

Agriculture

Kendrick offers an astoundingly improbable weekly hours series for agriculture, with 1900 at 45.5—or 14 hours below his average for nonfarm workers (and 5 hours below the National Bureau of Economic Research estimates of Barger and Landsberg).[1] His estimate is derived, in unspecified fashion, from Department of Agriculture estimates of labor days required to produce different crops.[2] The ultimate U.S. Department of Agriculture source for data prior to 1939, U.S.D.A. Statistical Bulletin 233, like U.S.D.A. Technical Bulletin 1020 and Barger and Landsberg, relies on four W.P.A. monographs, summarized in the fourth—John A. Hopkins, *Changing Technology and Employment in Agriculture* (1941). Hopkins does summarily report "a small reduction—probably a half hour . . . in the average length of the farm workday since the pre-war years" (pp. 25–27). But his tabulation (p. 27) is used by Bulletin 233 to create figures by crop. It relies on the U.S.D.A. *Yearbook of Agriculture, 1926,* p. 785, for estimates of prewar hours. From that source Hopkins reports only the column for "farm operators," ignoring that for farm workers. Thus his only report for a southern farm (Texas cotton) is 2,024 hours—compared with almost 50 percent more for every other state shown. This difference points to a significant qualification.

The U.S.D.A. 1926 yearbook "include[d] only the physical labor performed . . . in the fields . . . and maintenance and repair work about the farm," excluding "duties incident to management of the farm . . . including . . . supervision." It thus excluded both hours of supervision and time for keeping farm records, going to town to sell crops, negotiating the sales, buying supplies, having repairs made to wagons and farm machinery, time going from one crop location to another, from home to one crop area and back. Such an omission was particularly important for farm operators in the South. Kendrick's results for the U.S. average are therefore biased, since the South employed at least half of all U.S. farm workers.

Evidence from a survey of farms by the U.S. Commissioner of Labor in 1893–95 is preferable. That survey reported not merely time taken to produce a given crop but the length of the workday. For all

[1] Kendrick, *Productivity Trends* (1961), 310. The Barger-Landsberg estimates are also used in Barger, *Distribution's Place in the American Economy since 1869* (1955), 11.

[2] Kendrick, *Productivity Trends,* 352.

major crops but tobacco, rice, cotton, and sugar, the workday on every farm reported was 11 hours. It was, however, only 10 hours for the four southern crops.[3] Weighting these crop averages by the number of farm workers in each region[4] yielded an estimate of 10.49 hours per weekday. To this I add 4 hours for Sunday chores (as reported in U.S.D.A. surveys of the 1920s),[5] giving a 67-hour work week. That figure exceeds Kendrick's by about 20 hours a week, and presumably estimates that rely on his figures.[6]

Manufacturing

Kendrick's N.B.E.R. study does not use or refer to Rees's basic N.B.E.R. study of manufacturing, published in the same year. Both arrive at much the same hours figure, but Kendrick treats it as scheduled hours, not an actual average. He therefore reduces his 9.92 to 8.78 on the basis of data for a later period.[7] Rees, however, made a classic and extremely careful study by procedures that he, unlike Kendrick, outlines in detail. I prefer Rees's actual hours figure, 9.98.[8]

I use the above hours estimates for agriculture and manufacturing in 1900, and Kendrick's for other nonfarm. These estimates are weighted by employment, giving a U.S. average of 62.3 hours a week for 1900.[9]

HOURS/PERSONAL CONSUMPTION EXPENDITURE

The share of consumption taken by wage earners was computed as follows. For 1900, average hours in agriculture (67) and nonfarm activities (60) were multiplied by the number employed in each sector, and by the average annual earnings in each, using data from

[3] U.S. Commissioner of Labor, *Thirteenth Annual Report*, vol. 2, *Hand and Machine Labor* (1899), 428–73.

[4] U.S. Bureau of the Census, *Occupations, 1990*, pp. xc, xcii. Hopkins, Barger and Landsberg, and presumably the U.S.D.A. and Kendrick, used acreage weights.

[5] Hutson in U.S. Department of Agriculture, *Yearbook of Agriculture, 1926* (1927), 786. Hopkins, adding other sources, gives some Sunday averages for individual surveys.

[6] John Owen, in *Working Lives* (1986), and *The Price of Leisure* (1969), 77–78, uses Kendrick's hours figures, but his estimates are only marginally affected by the 1900 farm estimate.

[7] Kendrick, *Productivity Trends*, 310, 445.

[8] Rees, *Real Wages in Manufacturing* (1961).

[9] Kendrick, *Productivity Trends*, 310, with weights from Lebergott, *Manpower*, 512–14.

Lebergott, *Manpower*, 512, 524–25.) The ratio of the resultant wage and salary total to current dollar consumption in that year (from Lebergott, *Consumer Expenditures: New Measures, Old Motives* [forthcoming]) was then applied to the constant dollar figure for personal consumption expenditures in that year, from the same source.

Similar calculations for 1929, 1960, and 1990 used average hours from U.S. Bureau of the Census, Current Population Reports, P-50, no. 13, p. 28; U.S. Bureau of Labor Statistics, Special Labor Force Report 14, table D-1; and U.S. Bureau of Labor Statistics, *Employment and Earnings* (Jan. 1992): 200, 201; employment of persons 14 and older from Lebergott, *Manpower*, 512, 524–25, with 1960 extrapolated to 1990 by data for those 16 plus (the *Economic Report of the President*, Feb. 1991, p. 322); and average earnings figures from U.S. Bureau of Economic Analysis, *National Income and Product Accounts of the United States, 1929–82* (1986), 106ff., 113ff., and *Survey of Current Business* (Jan. 1992).

· WORKS CITED ·

Allen, Robert. "The Growth of Labor Productivity." *Explorations in Economic History* 25 (1988).

Andreev, Aleksander. *Housing*. Moscow, 1978.

Andrusz, Gregory. *Housing and Urban Development in the U.S.S.R.* Albany, 1984.

American Chemical Society. *Chemistry in the Economy*. Washington, D.C., 1973.

Arensberg, Conrad. *The Irish Countryman*. New York, 1937.

Ashton, Basil. "Famine in China, 1958–61." *Population and Development Review* 10 (Dec. 1984).

Ashton, T. S., and J. Sykes. *The Coal Industry of the Eighteenth Century*. Manchester, 1929.

Athenaeus. *Deipnosophistae*. Edited by C. B. Gulick. Vol. 3. London, 1929.

Avery, Robert, Gregory Elliehausen, and Arthur Kennickell. "Measuring Wealth with Survey Data: An Evaluation of the 1983 Survey of Consumer Finances." Unpublished paper for the 20th Congress of the International Association for Research in Income and Wealth, 1987.

Baran, Paul. *The Political Economy of Growth*. New York, 1962.

Barger, Harold. *Distribution's Place in the American Economy since 1869*. New York, 1955.

Barger, Harold, and Hans Landsberg. *American Agriculture, 1899–1937*. New York, 1942.

Baron, C., and W. van Ginneken. "Appropriate Products and Egalitarian Development." *International Labour Review* (Nov.-Dec. 1982).

Bate, Walter Jackson. *Samuel Johnson*. New York, 1977.

Bebel, August. *Woman and Socialism*. New York, 1910.

Becker, Gary. *Economic Theory*. New York, 1971.

———. "On the New Theory of Consumer Behavior." In *The Economic Approach to Human Behavior*, pp. 131–49. Chicago, 1976.

Beecher, Henry K. "The Powerful Placebo." *Journal of the American Medical Association* (Dec. 24, 1955): 1602–6.

Bell, Louis. *The Art of Illumination*. New York, 1912.

Bellamy, Edward. *Looking Backward, 2000–1887*. 1887; reprinted Cambridge, Mass., 1967.

Belloc, Nedra, and Lester Breslow. "Relationship of Health Practices and Mortality." *Preventative Medicine* (Mar. 1973): 401–21.

———. "Relationship of Physical Health Statistics and Health Practice," *Journal of Preventive Medicine* (Aug. 1972): 401–21.

Benevolo, Leonardo. *Origins of Modern Town Planning*. Cambridge, Mass., 1985.

Benn, Ernest. *Confessions of a Capitalist*. New York, 1926.

Bentley, Jerome, Charles Ofori-Mensa, Michael Ransom, and Donald E. Wise. In Mathtech, *The Cost of Children: A Household Expenditure Approach*. Princeton, 1981.

Berk, Sarah, ed. *Women and Household Labor*. Beverly Hills, 1980.

Bernstein, Peter. *Price of Prosperity*. Garden City, N.Y., 1962.

Betts, Edwin M., ed. *Thomas Jefferson's Farm Book*. Princeton, 1953.

———. *Thomas Jefferson's Garden Book*. 1936; reprinted Philadelphia, 1944.

Billings, John S., and Henry Hurd, eds. *Hospitals, Dispensaries and Nursing*. International Conference on Charities. Baltimore, 1894.

Blackstone, William. *The British Constitution: or, An Epitome of Blackstone's Commentaries on the Laws of England*. 1765–69; reprinted Chicago, 1979.

Bon Mots of Sydney Smith and Robert Brinsley Sheridan. London, 1893.

Boothe, Viva. "Gainfully Employed Women in the Family." *Annals of the American Academy* (Mar. 1932): 75–85.

Bourke, Algernon. *The History of White's*. London, 1893.

Brandis, Royall. *Principles of Economics*. Homewood, Ill., 1972.

Braudel, Fernand. *Capitalism and Material Life, 1400–1800*. New York, 1967.

Bright, James. *Automation and Management*. Boston, 1958.

Brooke, Lord. *The Prose Works of Fulke Greville, Lord Brooke*. Oxford, 1986.

Brus, W. "Political System and Economic Efficiency: The East European Context." *Journal of Comparative Systems* 4 (1980): 40–55.

Bureau of Applied Economics. *Standards of Living*. Washington, D.C., 1920.

Butterfield, Fox. *China: Alive in the Bitter Sea*. New York, 1982.

Cancian, Frank. "Consuming Relationships." *Reviews in Anthropology* 6 (Summer 1979): 301–11.

Cantillon, Richard. *Essai sur la nature du commerce en general*. Edited by H. Higgs. London, 1931.

Chao, Kang. *The Construction Industry in Communist China*. Chicago, 1968.

Cibber, Colley. *An Apology for His Life*. London, 1938.

Cist, Charles. *The Cincinnati Miscellany*. Cincinnati, 1845.

Clark, Eleanor. *Rome and a Villa*. Garden City, N.Y., 1952.

Clavigero, Frances. *History of Mexico*. Reprint. New York, 1979.

Cockburn, J. S., ed. *Calendar of Assize Records, Kent Indictments, Elizabeth I*. London, 1979.

Cohen, Mark. *The Food Crisis in Prehistory*. New Haven, 1977.

Collier, James L. *The Rise of Selfishness in America*. New York, 1992.

Commission on Population Growth and America's Future. *Statements at Public Hearings*. Vol. 7. Washington, D.C., 1972.

————. *Demographic and Social Aspects of Population Growth*. Edited by Norman Ryder and Charles Westoff. Washington, D.C., 1972.

Commonwealth of Massachusetts. *Labor Bulletin*. No. 19. Boston, 1901.

Conrad, Josef. *Nostromo*. New York, 1904.

Constable, Giles. *Cluniac Studies*. London, 1980.

Consumers Union of the United States. *Reports*. New York, 1937.

Cowan, Ruth Schwartz. *More Work for Mother*. New York, 1980.

Cramp, Tony. "Pleasures, Prices, and Principles." In J.G.T. Meeks, ed., *Thoughtful Economic Man*, pp. 50–73. Cambridge, 1991.

Cunliffe, Barry. *The Celtic World*. New York, 1979.

Daly, Herman. "The Population Question in Northeast Brazil: Its Economic and Ideological Dimensions." *Economic Development and Cultural Change* 19 (July 1970): 536–74.

Davidson, J. Hugh. "Why Most New Consumer Brands Fail." *Harvard Business Review* (Mar./Apr. 1976): 117–22.

Day, Clarence. *Life with Father*. New York, 1935.

de Montchretien, Antoine. *Traicte de l'oeconomie politique*. 1615; reprinted Paris, 1889.

de Sismondi, J.C.L. Simonde. *Nouveaux principes d'economie politique*. Vol. 2. Paris, 1827.

di la Gorce, Paul-Marie. *La France pauvre*. Paris, 1965.

Douglas, Paul. *Real Wages in the United States, 1890–1926*. Boston, 1930.

Dudden, Faye. *Serving Women*. Middletown, Conn., 1983.

Duffus, R. L. *The Innocents at Cedro*. New York, 1944.

Duhamel, Georges. *Scenes de la vie future*. Paris, 1931.

Dunnell, Karen, and Ann Cartwright. *Medicine Takers, Prescribers and Hoarders*. London and Boston, 1972.

Durkheim, Émile. *Suicide*. Reprint. Glencoe, Ill., 1952.

Easterlin, Richard. "Does Economic Growth Improve the Human Lot?" In Paul David and Melvin Reder, eds., *Nations and Households in Economic Growth: Essays in Honor of Moses Abramowitz*, pp. 89–125. New York, 1974.

Economic Council of Japan. NNW Measurement Committee. *Measuring the National Welfare of Japan*. Tokyo, 1974.

Eisner, Robert. "Extended Accounts for National Income and Product." *Journal of Economic Literature* 26 (Dec. 1988): 1611–84.

Estyn, E. *Irish Folk Ways*. London, 1957.

Fisher, Franklin, and Karl Shell. "Taste and Quality Change in the Pure Theory of the True Cost of Living Index." In J. N. Wolfe, ed., *Value, Capital, and Growth*, pp. 97–139. Edinburgh, 1968.

Food and Agriculture Organization. *Production Yearbook, 1971*. Rome, 1971.

———. *Trade Yearbook, 1977*. Rome, 1977.

———. *Production Yearbook, 1990*. Rome, 1990.

Fortescue, Sir John. *De laudibus legum Angliae*. Edited by S. B. Chrimes. Cambridge, 1942.

Fourier, Charles. *Selections from the Works of Fourier*. Introduction by Charles Gide. London, 1901.

Frank, Robert. "The Demand for Unobservable and Other Nonpositional Goods." *American Economic Review* 75 (Mar. 1985): 101–16.

Franklin, Alfred. *La Vie privée d'autrefois*. Vol. 3, *La Cuisine*. Paris, 1888.

Fuchs, Victor. *Who Shall Live?* New York, 1974.

Fundamentals of Political Economy Writing Group. *Fundamentals of Political Economy*. Translated by George Wang. Shanghai, 1977.

Fusfeld, Daniel. *The Age of the Economist*. Glenview, Ill., 1990.

———. *Economics*. 1972.

Galbraith, John K. *The Affluent Society*. Boston, 1958.

———. *The Culture of Contentment*. Boston, 1992.

George, Henry, Jr. *The Menace of Privilege*. New York, 1905.

George, M. Dorothy. *London Life in the Eighteenth Century*. New York, 1964.

Georgescu-Roegen, Nicholas. *The Entropy Law and the Economic Process*. Cambridge, Mass., 1971.

Gilman, Charlotte Perkins. *The Living, An Autobiography*. New York, 1935; reprinted 1975.

———. "The Waste of Private Housekeeping." *Annals of the American Academy of Political and Social Science* 48 (1913): 92–93.

Girouard, Mark. *The Victorian Country House*. New Haven, 1979.

Godts, F. X., C.S.S.R. *De paucitate salvandorum quid docerunt sancti*. Brussels, 1899.

Gogarty, Oliver St. John. *As I Was Going Down Sackville Street*. New York, 1937.

Goldman, Marshall. *U.S.S.R. in Crisis*. New York, 1983.

Gonzalez Casovana, Pablo. "The Economic Development of Mexico." *Scientific American* (Sept. 1980): 192–204.

Gordon, Phyllis. *Two Renaissance Book Hunters*. New York, 1974.

Gorman, Herbert. *A Victorian American, Henry Wadsworth Longfellow*. New York, 1926.

Gould, Jacob. *Output and Productivity in the Electric and Gas Industries*. New York, 1946.

Great Britain. Department of Health and Social Security. *Hospital In-Patient Enquiry—1979–1985*. Series MB4, no. 29. London, n.d.

———. Royal Commission on Population. *Papers*. Report of the Economics Committee, vol. 3. London, 1950.

Grebler, Leo, David Blank, and Louis Winnick. *Capital Formation in Residential Real Estate.* Princeton, 1956.

Gummere, Amelia M. *The Quaker: A Study in Costume.* 1901; reprinted New York, 1968.

Hahn, Frank. "Benevolence." In J.G.T. Meeks, ed., *Thoughtful Economic Man,* pp. 7–11. Cambridge, 1991.

Hammond, John Hays. *The Autobiography of John Hays Hammond.* New York, 1935.

Hart, Philip. *Conductors, A New Generation.* New York, 1979.

Hastie, Mabel, and Geraldine Gorton. "What Shall We Teach Regarding Clothing and Laundry Problems?" *Journal of Home Economics* (Mar. 1926): 127–33.

Hayden, Dolores. *The Grand Domestic Revolution.* Cambridge, Mass., 1981.

Hazard, Blanche. *The Organization of the Boot and Shoe Industry in Massachusetts before 1875.* New York, 1921.

Hazlitt, William. "On Will Making." In *Table Talk,* pp. 113–21. 1821; reprinted London, 1903.

Heilbroner, Robert. Review of Fred Hirsch, *Social Limits to Growth. New York Review of Books* (Mar. 3, 1977): 10–12.

Hemardinquer, J.-J., ed. *Pour une histoire d'alimentation.* Paris, 1970.

Hering, Rudolph, and Samuel Greeley. *Collection and Disposal of Municipal Refuse.* New York, 1921.

Herms, William B. "How to Control the Common House Fly." *California State Board of Health Monthly Bulletin* (May 1910): 269–77.

Herodotus. *Histories.* Translated by Sir Henry Rawlinson. Book 2. London and New York, 1927.

Hershberg, Theodore. *Philadelphia.* New York, 1981.

Hicks, J. R. "Technology in the Developed Economy: Comment." In B. R. Williams, ed., *Science and Technology in Economic Growth,* pp. 48–49. New York, 1973.

Higgs, Robert. "Wartime Prosperity." *Journal of Economic History* 52 (Mar. 1992): 41–60.

Higham, T. F., and C. M. Bowra, eds. *The Oxford Book of Greek Verse in Translation.* Oxford, 1938.

Hirsch, Fred. *Social Limits to Growth.* Cambridge, Mass., 1976.

Hirschman, Albert. *The Interests and the Passions.* Princeton, 1977.

Hobsbawn, Eric. "The British Standard of Living, 1709–1850." In *Labouring Men.* Garden City, N.Y., 1964.

Hoffman, Frederick L. *History of the Prudential Insurance Company of America.* Newark, 1900.

Holmes, Oliver Wendell, Jr. "Economic Elements." In *Collected Legal Papers,* pp. 279–82. New York, 1920.

Holmes, Stephen. "The Secret History of Self-Interest." In Jane Mansbridge, ed., *Beyond Self-Interest*, pp. 267–86. Chicago, 1990.

Hopkins, John A. *Changing Technology and Employment in Agriculture*. Washington, D.C., 1941.

Horowitz, David. *The Morality of Spending*. Baltimore, 1985.

Howard, L. O. *The House Fly*. New York, 1911.

International Labour Office. *Yearbook of Labour Statistics 1991*. Geneva, 1992.

Ironmonger, D. S. *New Commodities and Consumer Behaviour*. Cambridge, 1972.

Jacobs, Philip, and Warren Hart. "Admission Waiting Times: A National Survey." *Dimensions* (Canadian Hospital Association; Feb. 1990): 32–35.

James, William. *The Will to Believe*. 1896; reprinted Cambridge, 1979.

Jeans, J. Stephen, ed. *American Industrial Conditions and Competition*. London, 1902.

Juster, F. Thomas, and Frank P. Stafford. *Time, Goods, and Well-Being*. Ann Arbor, 1985.

Kaldor, Nicholas. *An Expenditure Tax*. London, 1955.

———. "Equilibrium Theory and Growth Theory." In Michael Boskin, ed., *Economics and Human Welfare*, pp. 273–91. New York, 1979.

Katsenelinboigen, Aron. *Studies in Soviet Economic Planning*. White Plains, N.Y., 1978.

Kendrick, John. *Productivity Trends in the United States*. Princeton, 1961.

Keynes, J. M. *The General Theory of Employment, Interest, and Money*. New York, 1936.

Kirkpatrick, E. L. *The Farmer's Standard of Living*. New York, 1929.

Knowles, Dom David. *The Monastic Orders in England*. Cambridge, 1949.

Koopmans, Tjalling. "Objectives, Constraints, and Outcomes in Optimal Growth Models." *Econometrica* 35 (Jan. 1967): 1–15.

Krishna, Raj. "The Economic Development of India." *Scientific American* (Sept. 1980): 166–78.

Kuusinen, O. W. *Fundamentals of Marxism-Leninism*. Moscow, 1961.

Kuznets, Simon. *Commodity Flow and Capital Formation*. New York, 1938.

———. *Shares of Upper Income Groups in Income and Savings*. New York, 1953.

Lappe, Frances. *Diet for a Small Planet*. New York, 1975.

Larkin, Paschal. *Property in the Eighteenth Century*. New York, 1930.

Lears, T. Jackson. "From Salvation to Self-Realization." In Richard W. Fox and T. Jackson Lears, eds., *The Culture of Consumption: Critical Essays in American History, 1880–1930*, pp. 1–38. New York, 1983.

Lebergott, Stanley. *Manpower in Economic Growth*. New York, 1964.

———. "Labor Force and Marriage as Endogenous Variables." In J. Duesenberry, E. Kuh, and G. Fromm, eds., *The Brookings Quarterly Econometric Model of the United States*, pp. 335–71. Chicago, 1965.

———. *The American Economy*. Princeton, 1976.

———. *Wealth and Want*. Princeton, 1976.

———. *The Americans*. New York, 1984.

———. *Consumer Expenditures: New Measures, Old Motives*. Forthcoming.

Lee, Richard, and Irven de Vore. *Man the Hunter*. Chicago, 1968.

Leeds, John B. *The Household Budget*. Germantown, Pa., 1914.

Leven, Maurice. *America's Capacity to Consume*. Washington, D.C., 1934.

Lévi-Strauss, Claude. *From Honey to Ashes: Introduction to a Science of Methodology*. Vol. 2. New York, 1973.

Lewis, H. C., and P. H. Peng. "The Three-Consideration Diet Revisited." *Journal of the American Dietetic Association* (Mar. 1977): 270–74.

Lichtman, A. J., and J. R. Challinor. *Kin and Communities*. Washington, D.C., 1979.

Arthur D. Little, Inc. *Disposable versus Reusable Diapers*. Brochure. Cambridge, March 16, 1990.

Locke, John. *An Essay Concerning Human Understanding*. Book 2. Reprint. London, 1961.

Lucas, F. L. *The Greatest Problem*. New York, 1961.

Lynd, Robert, and Helen Lynd. *Middletown in Transition*. New York, 1937.

Machiavelli, Niccolo. *Discourses*. London, 1975.

Mackenzie, Compton. *My Life and Times, Octave 3*. London, 1964.

[McLane Report]. *Documents Relative to the Manufactures in the United States*. Washington, D.C., 1833.

Main, Gloria. *Tobacco Colony*. Princeton, 1982.

Malthus, Thomas. *An Essay on the Principle of Population*. 2d ed. Book 2. Homewood, Ill., 1963.

Mansbridge, Jane, ed. *Beyond Self-Interest*. Chicago, 1990.

Marshall, Alfred. *Principles of Economics*. New York, 1948.

Marshall, John. "Population Policies in the Light of the Papal Encyclical, *Humanae Vitae*." In International Union for the Scientific Study of Population, *International Population Conference, London 1969*, 2:1407–14. Liege, 1971.

Marx, Karl. *Capital*. Translated by Samuel Moore and Edward Aveling. Vol. 1. Chicago, 1919.

Matthaei, Julie A. *An Economic History of Women in America*. New York, 1982.

Mauss, Marcel. *The Gift*. Glencoe, Ill., 1954.

Maxim, Hudson. *Reminiscences*. Garden City, N.Y., 1924.

Meeker, Royal. "What Is the American Standard of Living?" *Monthly Labor Review* 8 (July 1919): 1–13.

Mennell, Stephen. *All Manners of Food*. Oxford, 1985.

Mez, Adam. *The Renaissance of Islam*. London, 1937.

Mills, Robert. "Three Papers on Railroads." Pamphlet reprinted from *The American Farmer* (1827).

Mingay, E. F., ed. *The Agrarian History of England and Wales*. Cambridge, 1989.

Mishan, E. J. "The Wages of Growth." In Mancur Olson and Hans Landsberg, eds., *The No-Growth Society*, pp. 63–87. New York, 1973.

Mitchell, Wesley, ed. *Income in the United States, Its Amount and Distribution, 1909–1919*. New York, 1922.

———. *What Veblen Taught*. New York, 1936.

Mittelberger, Gottlieb. *Journey to Pennsylvania*. Reprint. Cambridge, 1960.

Mokyr, Joel. *Why Ireland Starved, 1800–1850*. London, 1983.

Moorman, Mary, ed. *Journal of Dorothy Wordsworth*. London, 1971.

Morishima, Michio. *Marx's Economics*. Cambridge, 1977.

Morse, Phillip M. *In at the Beginnings*. Cambridge, Mass., 1977.

Mountford, C. P., ed. *Records of the American-Australian Expedition to Arnhem Land*. Vol. 2. Melbourne, 1960.

Mulhall, Michael. *The Progress of the World*. London, 1880.

Muller, Herbert J. *In Pursuit of Relevance*. Bloomington, Ind., 1971.

Mussen, Paul, and Nancy Eisenberg-Berg. *Roots of Caring, Sharing, and Helping*. San Francisco, 1977.

Myrdal, Gunnar. *Economic Theory and Underdeveloped Regions*. London, 1957.

Nagel, Thomas. "Comment." In Edmund Phelps, ed., *Altruism, Morality and Economic Theory*, pp. 63–67. New York, 1975.

National Opinion Research Center. *General Social Surveys, 1972–1980, Cumulative Code Book*. Chicago, 1980.

Newhouse, J. P., and L. J. Friedlander. "The Relationship between Medical Resources and Measures of Health." *Journal of Human Resources* (Spring 1980): 200–218.

Nordhaus, William, and James Tobin. "Is Economic Growth Obsolete?" In James Tobin, ed., *Essays in Economics: Theory and Policy*, 360–439. New York, 1982.

———. "Is Growth Obsolete?" In M. Moss, ed., *The Measurement of Economic and Social Performance*, pp. 509–45. London, 1973.

Norman, Henry. "Can I Afford an Automobile?" *World's Work* (1903).

Ogburn, W. O., and C. Tibbitts. "The Family." In Wesley Mitchell, ed., *Recent Social Trends*, pp. 661–708. New York, 1934.

Okun, Arthur. *Equality and Efficiency*. Washington, D.C., 1975.

One Hundred Years' Progress of the United States. Hartford, Conn., 1870.

Origo, Iris. *The Merchant of Prato*. New York, 1957.

Osler, William. *Aequanimitas*. 1905; reprinted Philadelphia, 1932.

Owen, John. *The Price of Leisure*. Rotterdam, 1969.

———. *Working Lives*. Lexington, Ky., 1986.

Owen, Robert. *A New View of Society*. 1813; reprinted London, 1927.

Packard, Vance. *The Waste Makers*. London, 1960.

Peabody, James B., ed. *The Holmes-Einstein Letters*. New York, 1961.

Peacock, Edward, ed. *Instruction for Parish Priests by John Myrc*. London, 1898.

Pechman, Joseph, ed. *Setting National Priorities*. New York, 1978.

Penn, William. "The Great Case of Liberty of Conscience." In *A Collection of the Works of William Penn*. London, 1726.

———. "No Cross, No Crown, a Discourse. . . ." In *A Collection of the Works of William Penn*. London, 1726.

Phelps, Edmund, ed. *Altruism, Morality and Economic Theory*. New York, 1975.

Pierce, Bessie Louise. *A History of Chicago*. 3 vols. New York, 1937–.

Pirages, Dennis. *The Sustainable Society*. New York, 1977.

"Plaintes à gassendi." In C. Leber, ed., *Collection des meilleurs dissertations . . . à l'histoire de France*, vol. 10. Paris, 1838.

Pollack, Robert, and Terence Wales. "Welfare Comparisons and Equivalence Scales." *American Economic Review* (May 1979).

Pomper, Philip. *Lenin, Trotsky, and Stalin*. New York, 1990.

Pospisil, Leopold. *Kapauku Papuan Economy*. New Haven, 1963.

Potter, George. *To the Golden Door*. Boston, 1960.

President's Research Committee on Social Trends. *Recent Social Trends*. New York, 1934.

Prest, Alan R. *Consumers' Expenditure in the United Kingdom, 1900–1919*. Cambridge, 1954.

Pyatt, Graham. *Priority Patterns and the Demand for Household Durable Goods*. Cambridge, 1964.

Rawls, John. *A Theory of Justice*. Cambridge, Mass., 1973.

Readers' Digest. *The European Common Market and Britain*. Pleasantville, N.Y., 1963.

———. *A Survey of Europe Today: The Peoples and Markets of Sixteen European Nations*. London, 1970.

Rees, Albert. *Real Wages in Manufacturing, 1890–1914*. Princeton, 1961.

Robinson, Joan. *Economic Philosophy*. Chicago, 1962.

———. In C. H. Feinstein, ed., *Socialism, Capitalism, and Economic Growth: Essays Presented to Maurice Dobb*, pp. 176–88. London, 1967.

Roell, Craig. *The Piano in America, 1890–1940*. Chapel Hill, 1989.

Roemer, John. *Free to Lose—An Introduction to Marxist Economic Philosophy*. Cambridge, Mass., 1988.

Rohrabaugh, W. J. "Estimated U.S. Alcoholic Beverage Consumption, 1790–1860." *Journal of Studies on Alcohol* 37 (1976): 357–64.

———. *The Alcoholic Republic*. New York, 1979.

Rorem, C. Rufus, and Robert Fischelis. *The Cost of Medicines*. Committee on the Costs of Medical Care, abstract of Publication 14. Washington, D.C., 1932.

Rosaldo, Renato. *Ilongot Headhunting, 1883–1974*. Stanford, 1980.

Roscher, William. *Principles of Political Economy*. New York, 1878.

Rowe, Mary. "The Time Necessary to Do the Work in a Seven-Room House for a Family of Three." *Journal of Home Economics* 9 (Dec. 1917): 569–73.

Rumbold, Horace. *Recollections of a Diplomatist*. Vol. 1. London, 1902.

Ryder, Norman, and Charles Westoff. "Wanted and Unwanted Fertility in the United States: 1965 and 1970." In Commission on Population Growth and America's Future, *Demographic and Social Aspects of Population Growth*, pp. 467–88. Washington, D.C., 1972.

Sahlins, Marshall. *Stone Age Economics*. Chicago, 1972.

Saintsbury, George. *Notes on a Cellar-Book*. London, 1920.

Samuelson, Paul A. *Economics*. New York, 1961.

Samuelson, Paul A., and S. Swamy. "Invariant Index Numbers and Canonical Duality: Survey and Synthesis." *American Economic Review* 65 (Sept. 1974): 566–93.

Santayana, George. *Three Philosophical Poets*. Garden City, N.Y., 1953.

Schivelbusch, Wolfgang. *Disenchanted Night: The Industrialization of Light in the Nineteenth Century*. Translated by Angela Davies. Berkeley, 1988.

Schor, Julie. *The Overworked American*. New York, 1991.

Schumacher, Max. *The Northern Farmer and His Markets*. New York, 1975.

Scitovsky, Tibor. *The Joyless Economy*. New York, 1976.

Seneca, J. J., and M. K. Taussig. "Family Equivalence Scales and Personal Income Tax Exemptions for Children." *Review of Economics and Statistics* 53 (Aug. 1971): 253–62.

Sentry Insurance Company. *Consumerism at the Crossroads, A Survey*. Conducted by Louis Harris and Associates. Stevens Point, Wis., 1976.

Shaw, William. *Value of Commodity Output since 1869*. New York, 1947.

Shearman, Thomas G. *Natural Taxation*. New York, 1911.

Sherburne, James C. *John Ruskin, or the Ambiguities of Abundance*. Cambridge, Mass., 1972.

Sherman, Howard. *Radical Political Economy*. New York, 1972.

Sidgwick, Henry. *Elements of Politics*. London, 1891.

Simon, Julian. *The Economics of Population Growth*. Princeton, 1977.

Smith, Adam. *The Theory of Moral Sentiments*. 1759; reprinted Oxford, 1976.

———. *The Wealth of Nations*. Homewood, 1963.

Smith, Hedrick. *The Russians*. New York, 1976.

Smith, Nowell. *The Letters of Sydney Smith*. Oxford, 1953.

Sorrels, Charles. In Joseph Pechman, ed., *Setting National Priorities*. Washington, D.C., 1978.

Steinhart, John S., and Carol E. Steinhart. "Energy Use in the U.S. Food System." *Science* (Apr. 19, 1974): 307–16.

Steuart, Sir James. *Political Economy*. In *Works*, vol. 1. London, 1805.

Stewart, C. S. *A Residence in the Sandwich Islands*. Boston, 1839.

Stigler, George. "Smith's Travels on the Ship of State." In Andrew Skinner and Thomas Wilson, eds., *Essays on Adam Smith*, pp. 237–46. Oxford, 1975.

Stokes, Whitley, ed. *Sir Henry Maine*. New York, 1892.

Summers, Robert, and Alan Heston. "A New Set of International Comparisons . . . 1980–1985." *Review of Income and Wealth* (Mar. 1988): 1–25.

Summers, Robert, Irving Kravis, and Alan Heston. "International Comparison of Real Product and Its Composition: 1950–77." *Review of Income and Wealth* (Mar. 1980): 19–66.

"Surgical Waiting Lists in Victorian Hospitals." *Medical Journal of Australia* (Mar. 4, 1991): 326–28.

Swafford, Michael. "Sex Differences in Soviet Earnings." *American Sociological Review* (Oct. 1978): 657–73.

Szalai, Alexander, ed. *The Use of Time*. The Hague, 1972.

Tarn, John. *Five Per Cent Philanthropy*. London, 1973.

Tawney, R. H. *The Acquisitive Society*. New York, 1920.

———. *Equality*. New York, 1931.

Taylor, Jeremy. *The Whole Works*. Vol. 3, *The Rules and Exercises of Holy Living and of Holy Dying*. London, 1862.

Theobald, Robert. *Free Men and Free Markets*. New York, 1962.

Tobin, James. *Essays in Economics: Theory and Policy*. Cambridge, Mass., 1982.

———. "Comment." In D. Worswick and J. Trevithick, eds., *Keynes and the Modern World*, pp. 28–37. Cambridge, 1984.

Toutain, J. C. *La Consommation alimentaire en France, de 1789 à 1964*. Geneva, 1971.

Train, John. "Reflections on the Revolution in Russia." *Harvard Magazine* (Sept.-Oct. 1988): 8–13.

Turneaure, F. E., and H. L. Russell. *Public Water Supplies*. New York, 1911.

Turner, Michael. "Agricultural Productivity in England." *Economic History Review* 35, ser. 2 (Nov. 1982): 489–510.

U.K. Central Statistical Office. *Annual Abstract of Statistics, 1990*. London, 1991.

U.K. Department of Health and Social Security. *Medical Manpower—The Next Twenty Years*. London, 1977.

U.S. Bureau of Economic Analysis. *The National Income and Product Accounts of the United States, 1929–82*. Washington, D.C., 1986.

U.S. Bureau of Labor Statistics. *Cost of Living in the United States*. Bulletin 357. Washington, D.C., 1924.

———. *Money Disbursements of Wage Earners and Clerical Workers in Eight Cities in the North Atlantic Region, 1934–36*. Bulletin 637. Washington, D.C., 1939.

———. *Money Disbursements of Wage Earners and Clerical Workers in Eight Cities in the East North Central Region, 1934–36*. Bulletin 636. Washington, D.C., 1940.

———. *Family Spending and Saving in Wartime*. Bulletin 822. Washington, D.C., 1942.

———. *Workers' Budgets in the United States: City Families and Single Persons, 1946 and 1947*. Bulletin 927. Washington, D.C., 1948.

———. *Consumer Expenditure Survey: Integrated Survey Data, 1972–73*. Bulletin 1992. Washington, D.C., 1978.

———. *Consumer Expenditure Survey: Interview Survey, 1982–83*. Bulletin 2246. Washington, D.C., 1986.

———. *Consumer Expenditure Survey: Interview Survey, 1984*. Bulletin 2267. Washington, D.C., 1986.

———. *Consumer Expenditure Survey*. Unpublished. Washington, D.C., 1988.

———. *Consumer Expenditure Survey: Integrated Survey Data, 1984–86*. Bulletin 2333. Washington, D.C., 1989.

———. *Consumer Expenditure Survey, 1987*. Bulletin 2354. Washington, D.C., 1990.

———. *Employment and Earnings, 1990*. Washington, D.C., 1991.

U.S. Bureau of the Census. *Statistical Abstract, 1900*. Washington, D.C., 1900.

———. *Population, 1900*. Vol. 1. Washington, D.C., 1901.

———. *Statistical Abstract, 1901*. Washington, D.C., 1901.

———. *Statistics of Agriculture, 1900.* Part 1, vol. 5. Washington, D.C., 1902.

———. *Occupations, 1900*. Washington, D.C., 1904.

———. *Supplementary Analysis and Derivative Tables, 1900*. Washington, D.C., 1906.

———. *Manufactures, 1905*. Washington, D.C., 1907–8.

———. *Religious Bodies, 1906*. Washington, D.C., 1910.

———. *Manufactures, 1910*. Washington, D.C., 1913.

———. *Occupations, 1910*. Washington, D.C., 1913.

———. *Population, 1910*. Vol. 1. Washington, D.C., 1913.

———. *Fourteenth Census*. Vol. 10. Washington, D.C., 1923.

————. *Manufactures, 1919.* Vols. 8 and 10. Washington, D.C., 1923.

————. *Hospitals and Dispensaries, 1923.* Washington, D.C., 1925.

————. *Mortality Statistics, 1930.* Washington, D.C., 1934.

————. *Business Census of Hospitals, 1935.* Washington, D.C., 1939.

————. *Occupational Characteristics, 1940.* Washington, D.C., 1943.

————. *Housing Characteristics by Household Composition, 1970.* Washington, D.C., 1973.

————. *Occupational Characteristics, 1970.* Washington, D.C., 1973.

————. *Population, 1970.* Washington, D.C., 1973.

————. *Space Utilization of the Housing Inventory, 1970.* Washington, D.C., 1973.

————. *Historical Statistics of the United States, Colonial Times to 1970.* Vols. 1, 2. Washington, D.C., 1975.

————. *Statistical Abstract, 1978.* Washington, D.C., 1978.

————. *Statistical Abstract, 1979.* Washington, D.C., 1979.

————. *General Housing Characteristics, 1980, U.S. Summary.* Washington, D.C., 1981.

————. *Population, 1980; U.S. Summary PC-80–1-B1.* Washington, D.C., 1983.

————. *Statistical Abstract, 1984.* Washington, D.C., 1984.

————. *Statistical Abstract, 1987.* Washington, D.C., 1987.

————. *Statistical Abstract, 1990.* Washington, D.C., 1990.

————. *American Housing Survey for the United States in 1989.* Washington, D.C., 1991.

————. *Statistical Abstract, 1991.* Washington, D.C., 1991.

U.S. Center for Disease Control. *HIV/AIDS Surveillance* (Dec. 1990).

U.S. Commissioner of Agriculture. *Agricultural Report, 1863.* Washington, D.C., 1863.

U.S. Commissioner of Labor. *Thirteenth Annual Report.* Vol. 2, *Hand and Machine Labor.* Washington, D.C., 1899.

————. *Eighteenth Annual Report.* Washington, D.C., 1903.

U.S. Congress. *Joint Select Committee to Investigate Charities in the District of Columbia.* 55th Cong., 2d sess., 1898. H.R. 776, part 2.

————. Immigration Commission. *Immigrants in Cities.* 66th Cong., 2d sess., 1911. S. Doc. 338.

————. Senate. *Competitive Problems in the Drug Industry.* Hearings before the Subcommittee on Monopoly of the Select Committee on Small Business. 92d Cong., 1st sess., 1967. Part 21.

————. Joint Economic Committee. *Soviet Economy in a Time of Change.* 96th Cong., 1st sess., 1979. Vol. 1.

————. Joint Economic Committee. *Consumption in the U.S.S.R.: An International Comparison.* 97th Cong., 1st sess., 1981.

————. Joint Economic Committee. *U.S.S.R.: Measures of Economic Growth and Development, 1950–80.* 97th Cong., 1st sess., 1981.

————. Committee on Ways and Means. *Background Material.* 99th Cong., 2d sess., March 3, 1986.

U.S. Department of Agriculture. *What the Farm Contributes Directly to the Farmer's Living.* Farmers' Bulletin 635. Washington, D.C., 1914.

————. *Yearbook of Agriculture, 1921.* Washington, D.C., 1922.

————. *The Farmer's Standard of Living.* By E. L. Kirkpatrick. Department Bulletin 1466. Washington, D.C., 1926.

————. *Yearbook of Agriculture, 1926.* Washington, D.C., 1927.

————. *Rural Family Spending and Saving in Wartime.* Miscellaneous Publication 520. Washington, D.C., 1943.

————. *Price Spreads between Farmers and Consumers for Farm Products, 1913–44.* Miscellaneous Publication 576. Washington, D.C., 1947.

————. *Gains in Productivity of Farm Labor.* Technical Bulletin 1020. Washington, D.C., 1950.

————. *Composition of Foods.* Handbook 8. Washington, D.C., 1963.

————. *Food Consumption, Prices, and Expenditures.* Agricultural Economic Report 138. Washington, D.C., 1968.

————. *Food Consumption, Prices, and Expenditures, 1962–1982.* Statistical Bulletin 702. Washington, D.C., 1983.

————. *Agricultural Statistics, 1988.* Washington, D.C., 1988.

————. *Agricultural Statistics, 1990.* Washington, D.C., 1990.

————. *Food Consumption, Prices, and Expenditures, 1968–89.* Statistical Bulletin 825. Washington, D.C., 1991.

U.S. Department of Energy. *Housing Characteristics, 1984.* Washington, D.C., 1986.

————. *Housing Characteristics, 1987.* Washington, D.C., 1989.

U.S. Department of Health and Human Services. Public Health Service. *Physician Contacts by Sociodemographic and Health Characteristics.* Hyattsville, 1987.

————. *Physician Contacts by Sociographic and Health Characteristics, 1982–83.* PHS 87–1589. Washington, D.C., 1987.

————. *Healthy People, 2000.* Washington, D.C., 1991.

————. *HIV/AIDS Surveillance* (Aug. 1991).

U.S. Department of the Treasury. Bureau of Statistics. *Quarterly Report of the Chief of the Bureau of Statistics, Import, Exports . . . 1886.* Washington, D.C., 1887.

U.S. Department of Transportation. *Energy Statistics: Annual Report.* Washington, D.C., 1967.

————. *Energy Statistics: A Supplement to the Summary of National Transportation Statistics.* Washington, D.C., 1976.

U.S. Energy Information Administration. *Consumption Patterns of Household Vehicles, 1983*. Washington, D.C., 1983.

U.S. Geological Survey. *Estimated Use of Water in the United States in 1985*. Circular 1004. Washington, D.C., 1988.

U.S. Industrial Commission. *Hearings*. Washington, D.C., 1900.

U.S. Internal Revenue Service. *Statistics of Income, Source Book, Corporations, 1985*. Washington, D.C., 1985.

———. *Individual Income Tax Returns, 1986*. Washington, D.C., 1989.

U.S. Subsistence Department. *Manual for Army Bakers, 1910*. Washington, D.C., 1910.

U.S. War Department. *Annual Report . . . 1905*. Vol. 2. Washington, D.C., 1905.

———. *Annual Report, 1918*. Vol. 1. Washington, D.C., 1919.

Vanek, Joann. "Keeping Busy: Time Spent in Housework, United States 1920–1970." Dissertation, University of Michigan, 1973.

Van Slyke, Lyman. *Yangtze*. Reading, Mass., 1988.

Veblen, Thorstein. *The Engineers and the Price System*. New York, 1921.

———. *Essays in Our Changing Order*. New York, 1934.

von Weiser, Friedrick. *Social Economics*. 1914; reprinted New York, 1927.

Voslensky, Michael. *Nomenklatura*. Garden City, N.Y., 1984.

Voydanoff, Patricia. *Work and Family*. Palo Alto, Calif., 1984.

Wachtel, Paul. *The Poverty of Affluence*. New York, 1983.

Ward, Barbara. *The Rich Nations and the Poor Nations*. New York, 1962.

Waring, G. E., Jr. In *Journal of Social Science* (Dec. 1879).

Webb, Beatrice, and Sidney Webb. "Labor." In Charles Beard, ed., *Whither Mankind*, pp. 110–41. New York, 1928.

Weber, Adna. *The Growth of Cities*. New York, 1899.

Wechsberg, Joseph. *Red Plush and Black Velvet*. Boston, 1961.

Westoff, Charles, and Norman Ryder. "Family Limitation in the United States." In International Union for the Scientific Study of Population, *International Population Conference, London, 1969*, vol. 2. Liege, 1971.

Whitehead, Alfred North. *Modes of Thought*. New York, 1938.

Wicksteed, Philip. *The Common Sense of Political Economy*. London, 1910.

Women and Communism, Selections from the Writings of Marx, Engels, Lenin, and Stalin. Westport, Conn., 1973.

Wood, Edith Elmer. "Housing." In *Encyclopedia of the Social Sciences*, vol. 7. New York, 1937.

Woodbury, Marion. "Time Required for Housework in a Family of Five with Small Children." *Journal of Home Economics* (May 1918): 226–30.

Zeldin, Theodore. *France 1848–1975*. Oxford, 1977.

Zuzanek, Jiri. *Work and Leisure in the Soviet Union*. New York, 1980.

· I N D E X ·